INSIDE THE CIRCLE

INSIDE THE CIRCLE

Queer Culture and Activism in Northwest China

CASEY JAMES MILLER

RUTGERS UNIVERSITY PRESS
New Brunswick, Camden, and Newark, New Jersey
London and Oxford

Rutgers University Press is a department of Rutgers, The State University of New Jersey, one of the leading public research universities in the nation. By publishing worldwide, it furthers the University's mission of dedication to excellence in teaching, scholarship, research, and clinical care.

Library of Congress Cataloging-in-Publication Data

Names: Miller, Casey James, author.
Title: Inside the circle : queer culture and activism in Northwest China / Casey James Miller.
Description: New Brunswick, New Jersey : Rutgers University Press, [2023] | Includes bibliographical references and index.
Identifiers: LCCN 2022051012 | ISBN 9781978835368 (paperback ; alk. paper) | ISBN 9781978835375 (hardback : alk. paper) | ISBN 9781978835382 (epub) | ISBN 9781978835399 (pdf)
Subjects: LCSH: Homosexuality—China. | Gays—China. | Sexual minorities—China. | Gay rights movement—China.
Classification: LCC HQ76.3.C6 M56 2023 | DDC 306.76/60951—dc23/eng/20221031
LC record available at https://lccn.loc.gov/2022051012

A British Cataloging-in-Publication record for this book is available from the British Library.

References to internet websites (URLs) were accurate at the time of writing. Neither the author nor Rutgers University Press is responsible for URLs that may have expired or changed since the manuscript was prepared.

rutgersuniversitypress.org

CONTENTS

FIGURES AND TABLES

All diagrams and photographs are by the author unless otherwise noted.

FIGURES

TABLES

INSIDE THE CIRCLE

1 · INTRODUCTION
Queer Stories, Chinese Stories

Xiao Yu was a handsome, soft-spoken gay university student I first interviewed in Xi'an, the capital of northwest China's Shaanxi Province (figure 1.1).[1] Xiao Yu discovered that he liked other boys in the third grade when he and a mischievous male classmate would cuddle and kiss while sharing a single blanket during nap time. During middle school, Xiao Yu developed a crush on another male classmate; although Xiao Yu did not dare reveal his true feelings, they quickly became inseparable, spending hours together and chatting about everything, including love. While he never returned Xiao Yu's affections, one night, in the depth of winter, when Xiao Yu had waited for him after high school so that he did not have to walk home alone in the dark, his classmate confided in him, "If you were a girl, I'd pick you." After graduation, his friend joined the military. "I told him to look after himself," Xiao Yu recalled. "When we sent him off to the army, he ran over and hugged me. My tears were about to come out, but I held them in." They kept in touch via letters and the occasional phone call. His friend had recently left the army and was dating women now. "He'll probably get married in the next two years," Xiao Yu said.

Born in 1989 in a semirural municipality some thirty minutes outside of Xi'an, Xiao Yu told me that, like many of the queer people I interviewed, he had wanted to attend university and find a job in China's more prosperous and developed eastern seaboard like his older sister had done.[2] But he ended up staying in the northwest to be closer to his parents. "I had no choice," Xiao Yu explained. "In China, ordinarily speaking, one of the children in the family must stay closer to home. That way, if something happens, at least there will be someone by their side."

Although Xiao Yu had a very good relationship with his parents, no one in his family knew that he was gay, and during family visits relatives would often ask if he had a girlfriend. While he had not yet disclosed his sexuality to his family, Xiao Yu hoped he could tell them one day. "Usually, when I am with my family, I don't let it show," he said. "When I am with other people inside the circle, I can show the true side of my feelings. But when I am with my family, I just act like a child who is all grown up." Like many of my research participants, Xiao Yu used the phrase "the

FIGURE 1.1. Map of northwest China. Map by Michael Siegel.

circle" (*quanzi*) to refer to an imagined community made up of people like him who shared a common queer identity.

I asked Xiao Yu if he planned on ever getting married to a woman. "No," he replied, before hastily contradicting himself, "at least, not until after I am thirty years old. This is a responsibility I have to my family." Unmarried queer people in their twenties come under increasing pressure, especially from parents, to get married and have children. This pressure peaks at the age of thirty, when most people find it impossible to avoid marriage any longer. Xiao Yu felt this responsibility especially keenly because he was his parents' only son. Although his older sister was likely to marry, he explained that "In China, most families regard daughters as marrying out of the family. In this way of thinking, a daughter is part of someone else's family." Xiao Yu dismissed this mindset as "feudalistic," arguing that "young people today don't think this way." Nonetheless, these traditional gendered and filial expectations still weighed heavily on him. "I am getting married for my parents," Xiao Yu told me, even though he was only twenty-two years old at the time.

When I suggested that it might be difficult for him to be married, as he does not like girls, Xiao Yu corrected me, saying, "It's not that I don't like girls. I actually get along with them really well. Sexually, I've never tried it, so I can't render a verdict. But at the very least, I like them. It's a pure kind of affection. Whether my body will be able to like them, I don't know." Although Xiao Yu had several boyfriends since starting university, like many queer men, none of his same-sex relationships seemed to have lasted for very long, and he was still looking for a long-term male sexual and romantic partner. "Fate likes to play jokes on me," he said rather wistfully.

In December 2010, while surfing the web, Xiao Yu discovered Tong'ai, a grass-roots queer men's nongovernmental organization (NGO). Since 1998, Tong'ai had been working to prevent the spread of human immunodeficiency virus (HIV), which causes acquired immunodeficiency syndrome (AIDS), among queer men in northwest China. Xiao Yu became a volunteer in the group, which is where we first met. Like many volunteers, Xiao Yu was motivated to join Tong'ai by the opportunity to meet other gay men and to learn more about himself and the queer community. But he also shared a common desire to make a difference, not just in the health of his peers, but also by working to improve the understanding of homosexuality and to advocate for the rights of queer people in postsocialist China. "When our organization serves this community, it is also gradually influencing the entire society," he explained. "Our first priority is doing [HIV/AIDS] intervention work, creating a civilized and healthy gay community. After this has been done well, our influence will expand, and only then will we be able to carry out the next phase of our work." Xiao Yu's work as a volunteer was also transforming the way he thought about himself. In Xiao Yu's words, "When facing up to things alone, sometimes you are not very willing to think about them. But after I came to Tong'ai and saw so many other people who were like me, it gave me a lot of courage. It has made me feel like I am part of a social force, like there isn't anything I don't dare to think, there isn't anything I don't dare to do."

Based on more than a decade of fieldwork between 2007 and 2019 as well as ongoing conversations with my research participants, *Inside the Circle* offers an intimately personal perspective on queer culture and activism in northwest China. Taking inspiration from the idea of the circle, a term queer Chinese people use to refer to an imagined local, national, or global queer community, this book explores how queer activists in northwest China understand and navigate these overlapping and sometimes conflicting zones of queer and ethnonational belonging. *Inside the Circle* tells the stories of two courageous and dedicated groups of queer activists in the northwestern Chinese city of Xi'an: a queer men's group called Tong'ai and a queer women's NGO named UNITE. These stories offer valuable insights into monumental shifts taking place in contemporary Chinese culture and society while also contributing to broader anthropological conversations about changing understandings of personhood and kinship; the relationship between individual agency and state power; and the spread of increasingly visible and organized forms of queer culture and activism around the world.

Inside the Circle complicates claims that economic and social reforms have led to increasing individualism and selfishness in postsocialist China. Even as they advocate for increased awareness and acceptance of queer people and fight the spread of HIV/AIDS, queer activists in northwest China strive to reconcile their sexual identities with their deeply held beliefs about what it means to be a moral person, including the importance of marrying and having children. The queer

Chinese stories in this book also contribute to the theorization of individual agency and state power. By documenting the development of community-based queer NGOs and activism in northwest China, I challenge the idea that Chinese civil society and queer activism are somehow deficient or inauthentic. Although they often frame their work as collaborating with rather than confronting the state, queer activists in northwest China unwaveringly regard their fight to improve the health and rights of queer people as a social and political struggle. While emphasizing HIV/AIDS education and prevention gives gay men an important source of funding and legitimacy from the state and international donor agencies, the relative invisibility of lesbian activists allows them to focus more explicitly on other cultural and political objectives.

Inside the Circle also intervenes in ongoing debates about the relationship between queerness and normativity. Does being queer necessarily entail being antinormative? How might people in a variety of cultural contexts understand or experience the relationship between queerness and (anti)normativity differently? By exploring the queer Chinese concept of the circle, this book contributes to the development of a more cultural or relativistic (as opposed to acultural or universalistic) queer theory.[3] Rather than describing their choices regarding marriage or their activist strategies as examples of "homonormativity" or "false consciousness," I instead show how queer activists in northwest China take part in local and global expressions of queer culture and activism while also trying to navigate enduring cultural norms and expectations around marriage and reproduction that still inform local understandings of personhood and morality. Embracing non-Western concepts like the circle can help us build a more diverse and inclusive queer theory and may also help queer anthropologists find new ways to transcend old binary oppositions like local and global, East and West, different and similar. In this way, the queer Chinese stories told in this book not only deepen and broaden our understanding of postsocialist Chinese culture and society but also help us to imagine and practice new forms of transnational queer solidarity.

WE'RE HERE, WE'RE QUEER, WE'RE CHINESE

As the first ethnography of queer culture and activism in northwest China, *Inside the Circle* offers a unique perspective on one of the oldest and largest queer cultures in the world. The history of homosexuality in China stretches all the way from the ancient Zhou Dynasty (1046–256 BCE) to the present.[4] And because of its massive population—some 1.4 billion people as of 2019—there are more queer people living in the People's Republic of China (PRC) today than in any other country (United Nations 2019). Despite this, until recently relatively little has been publicly known about queer China. One of the earliest books on the subject was *Their World: A Study of Homosexuality in China*, first published in 1992 by the sociologist Li Yinhe and her partner, the writer Wang Xiaobo.[5] Since then a growing body of research has documented the emergence of urban queer cultures and communities in postsocialist China, in addition to growing lesbian, gay, bisexual, and transgender communities in Hong Kong, Taiwan, and the Chinese diaspora.[6]

Inside the Circle builds on this previous scholarship in several ways. One of these is its focus on queer culture and activism in northwest China, which comprises the provinces of Gansu, Qinghai, and Shaanxi and the autonomous regions of Ningxia and Xinjiang. Almost all previous scholarship on queer China has taken place in large eastern cities like Beijing, Shanghai, and Guangzhou.[7] However, these coastal megacities may not be good stand-ins for the rest of the country, which tends to be relatively less populated and economically prosperous. For example, in 2019 northwest China had approximately one-fifth of the population of eastern China, but only one-tenth of its GDP, resulting in a 44 percent lower per capita GDP (National Bureau of Statistics of China 2020). My queer informants in northwest China often described the region as culturally and socially "backward" and "traditional" compared to an eastern China that they perceived as being relatively more cosmopolitan and progressive.

This is an exciting moment in the study of queer China. Although more research is needed, for the first time we are starting to glimpse the outlines of regional and cultural variations in Chinese urban queer communities.[8] The queer Chinese stories in this book help us to better understand the development of queer cultures and activism in what is an extraordinarily large, diverse, and complex country. For example, while queer people in northwest China may confront many similar familial and social pressures as their peers in other parts of the country, they have developed unique strategies for dealing with them, including an elaborate system of queer kinship described in chapter 3. Also, while queer activists and NGOs in northwest China often have fewer resources and less visibility than their counterparts in places like Beijing and Shanghai, they nevertheless have found creative ways to engage in both local and global expressions of queer culture and activism that are analyzed in chapters 4 and 6.

This book also expands our knowledge of queer China by exploring both queer female and male culture and activism. While most previous studies of queer China have focused on either gay men or lesbian women, only a few have looked at the experiences of both gay men and lesbian women.[9] Although there are significant differences between Chinese gay and lesbian activists in terms of resources, strategies, and priorities, considering queer men and women separately prevents us from forming a more comprehensive understanding of contemporary queer Chinese culture. Studying queer Chinese men and women together helps us better understand their many differences and similarities, including the ways in which gender and sexuality are interrelated in both lesbian and gay cultures; the pressures that both groups face when attempting to reconcile their sexual identities with their duties as daughters and sons; and the obstacles and opportunities they face in organizing and advocating for greater acceptance in a country where queer people are still met with widespread social disapproval and lack basic legal rights.[10]

Finally, *Inside the Circle* contributes to the scholarship on queer China through its focus on grassroots queer AIDS activism. AIDS activism is an important and illuminating lens onto queer Chinese culture and also the changing nature of state power and individual agency in postsocialist China. Although it has brought many challenges and opportunities to queer Chinese activists and communities, very few previous studies of queer China have focused on HIV/AIDS.[11] One common viewpoint I often heard during fieldwork was that HIV/AIDS is "only" a medical issue, and therefore that queer AIDS activism was less interesting or important than activism organized around more explicitly cultural and political themes. However, as queer activists in northwest China are quick to point out, AIDS is a pressing cultural and political problem as well as a medical issue, not only for queer communities in China but all over the world. A focus on the important work being done by AIDS activists helps us to gain a more detailed and complete picture of queer Chinese culture and activism.

THE CIRCLE: TOWARD A CHINESE QUEER THEORY OF PERSONHOOD AND IDENTITY

Inside the Circle explores an idea that was a constant feature of daily life and conversation among my queer research participants in northwest China: "the circle." The circle is a kind of shorthand reference to either a particular or universal imagined queer community or a person's identity as a queer person in reference to their membership within one or more queer communities. In this book, I argue that the circle is more than an idiosyncratic turn of phrase: it is a Chinese queer theory of personhood and identity that not only enriches our understanding of Chinese queer culture and changing notions and practices of kinship within the PRC but also helps us to rethink the relationship between queerness and antinormativity and imagine new forms of global queer solidarity.

Although queer activists in northwest China sometimes used words like gay, "lesbian" (*lala*), "comrade" (*tongzhi*), or "homosexual" (*tongxinglian*) to describe themselves, by far the most popular expression was "people inside the circle" (*quan'er nei de ren*).[12] A circle consists of at least two people who share a common queer identity. A circle can be as small as a few queer friends or a queer family with a half dozen members. Or it can be as large as all the queer people in a Chinese city like Xi'an, a region like northwest China, the PRC, or even the entire globe. Queer circles are not exclusive but overlap and intersect, with a single queer person potentially being inside many circles at once. In this way, even as the people in this book endeavor to find new ways of being both queer and Chinese through their sexual identities and their local queer activism, the concept of the circle also allows them to imagine themselves as members of a broader "imagined community" (B. Anderson 1991), a flexible and scalar "structure of feeling" (Williams 1961) that includes queer people from across the Chinese diaspora and around the world.

The queer concept of the circle recalls Fei Xiaotong's classic formulation of Chinese social organization in his 1948 book *From the Soil: The Foundations of Chinese Society*. Fei argues that, unlike people in the West who resemble individual pieces of straw that combine to create a haystack, people in China relate to one another like the ripples created when stones are thrown into a pond, creating interwoven and overlapping networks or circles of relationships radiating out concentrically from the self (1992, 61–63). According to Fei, whereas the Western understanding of the self is an individualistic one that emphasizes equality and autonomy, the Chinese understanding of the self is an egotistic one in which "everyone stands at the center of the circles produced by his or her own social influence. Everyone's circles are interrelated. One touches different circles at different times and places" (63).

Fei's early distinction between Eastern and Western models of social organization foreshadowed later anthropological discussions contrasting individualist and relational ideas of personhood. McKim Marriott (1976) suggests that traditional Indian notions of personhood are "dividual" in that people and bodies are understood as being made up of substances that are exchanged between themselves and the people, objects, and places that they interact with in their daily lives. Marriott and Ronald Inden contrast Indian "dividual" notions of personhood with the more "individual" personhoods they claim prevail in Europe and North America, in which the self is relatively closed and contained (Lamb 2000, 30–38).[13] What sets Fei's "differential mode of association" apart from other relational models of personhood is its flexible, scalar framework for understanding the relationships between individual and society, which possesses what he describes as a "special quality of elasticity" (1992, 64) in that it can be expanded or contracted to allow people to simultaneously imagine and enact membership in different, potentially contradictory or exclusive social groups. Similarly, as a relational Chinese queer theory of personhood and identity, the circle presents a possible way of dissolving tensions between cultural change and continuity or sameness and difference that animate many current debates within both Chinese and queer anthropology.

The queer stories in this book not only contribute to a deeper understanding of China's complex and changing culture and society but also help us to better appreciate the diverse patterns and expressions of queer culture and activism around the world. I examine how queer activists in northwest China are experiencing, expressing, and transforming their sexual and gender identities as well as other aspects of their private and social lives in the decades following political, economic, and social reforms. I consider the various strategies that queer Chinese activists have developed to reconcile their often conflicting desires for queer identity, community, love, acceptance, and visibility with their sincerely held beliefs about what it means to be good person, including fulfilling their moral and ethical obligations as daughters and sons and as members of the Chinese nation-state. I also show how, through this work, queer activists in northwest China come to see themselves as part of a broader imagined community of queer people around the world.

QUEERING UNDERSTANDINGS OF PERSONHOOD AND KINSHIP IN POSTSOCIALIST CHINA

The history of modern China is one of rapid political, economic, and social change. Following the establishment of the PRC in 1949, the Chinese Communist Party (CCP), under the leadership of Mao Zedong, sought to radically transform every aspect of society. The state collectivized agriculture and industry; controlled the distribution of food, housing, jobs, education, and medical care; and politicized people's daily lives through near constant mass campaigns and class struggle. After Mao died in 1976, China's leaders suddenly switched gears. Under pragmatic new slogans such as "Practice is the only criterion of truth" and "It doesn't matter whether the cat is black or white as long as it catches mice" (Ikels 1996), socialist orthodoxy was shelved in favor of "reform and opening up" (*gaige kaifang*) policies designed to stimulate the economy. The result was several decades of record-breaking economic growth that have lifted millions of people out of poverty and turned China from a relatively poor and egalitarian country to one of the largest and most unequal economies in the world (United Nations 2020, 47).

The queer stories in this book help us better understand the complicated and sometimes contradictory effects of social and economic reforms on gender, sexuality, kinship, and personhood in postsocialist China.[14] Lisa Rofel argues that reforms have created competitive, cosmopolitan "desiring subjects" motivated by the private pursuit of "sexual, material, and affective self-interest" (2007, 3, 17). Whereas the expression of individual desires was once heavily stigmatized, many scholars argue it is becoming increasingly celebrated and even required, reflecting how "the previous socialist sentiment of class consciousness" has been replaced by "a postsocialist sensibility of personal desires" (Kleinman et al. 2011, 4). Although he warns against uncritically applying Western historical models to China, Everett Zhang argues that "no other expression than the phrase 'sexual revolution' is accurate in capturing the enormousness of the changes in sexuality in China over the past decades" (2011, 107).

These changes in love, marriage, and family have often been interpreted as examples of the "privatization" (D. Davis 2014; Ong and L. Zhang 2008) and "individualization" (Yan 2003, 2009, 2011) of Chinese society, in which collectivist notions of personhood and morality have been replaced by the rise of selfish individualism, especially among younger people. Deborah Davis and Sara Friedman (2014, 4) similarly describe an ongoing "deinstitutionalization" of marriage and sexuality in which individual Chinese citizens are experiencing new freedoms in their "pursuit of new possibilities for marital and sexual satisfaction." What these accounts all share is a focus on dramatic cultural change, in which postsocialist reforms have led to broad changes in sexuality and kinship. This begs the question: Is the situation really this straightforward? Have Chinese understandings and practices of personhood and kinship truly been transformed, or are there also examples of cultural continuity to be found?

The stories of queer activists complicate claims of sweeping cultural change in postsocialist China in which economic and social reforms have led to the rise of a selfish individualism that privileges the needs and wants of children over their parents. On the one hand, the emergence of queer cultures, communities, and activism speaks to the enormous changes that are taking place in Chinese society as many people gain more opportunities to express their individual identities and desires. On the other hand, my fieldwork among queer activists in northwest China reveals a much more complicated picture of both social change and continuity. Paradoxically, rather than wholeheartedly embracing cultural change, my research participants struggled to balance their queer sexualities and their deeply felt moral duties to family, including getting married and having children. Far from emblematizing a trend toward the privatization and deinstitutionalization of marriage and family, queer Chinese experiences of personhood, kinship, and sexuality emphasize how individual selfishness and personal desires are only celebrated within the narrow parameters of heterosexual marriage and childbirth.

The desires of queer activists to be understood and accepted by their parents and families, along with their efforts to reconcile their queerness with their moral and ethical obligations as daughters and sons, demonstrate the extent to which "traditional" Chinese notions of personhood, kinship, and sexuality endure despite the many changes that China has experienced in the past century. The queer stories in this book show that many claims in the literature about radical social change may have been overstated. The concept of the circle also speaks to this ongoing tension between social change and continuity: contained in the very language that is used to understand and communicate what it means to be queer in northwest China is a collectivist notion of personhood that sees each individual as being fundamentally composed of their relations with others. Even as they work to embrace and develop their queer identities and communities, fight the spread of HIV among their peers, and advocate for increased awareness and acceptance of queer people in Chinese society, the activists in this book do not wholly embrace individualism but rather seek ways of reconciling their queerness and desires for social change with deeply held beliefs about what it means to be a moral person.

QUEER CHINESE ACTIVISM AND DEBATES
OVER STATE POWER AND INDIVIDUAL AGENCY

The queer stories in this book also inform ongoing debates over the relationship between individual agency and state power in postsocialist China. Many scholars have examined how social and economic reforms have impacted China's public sphere, seeking signs of an incipient transition toward democracy and debating the usefulness of the concept of "civil society" in the Chinese context.[15] Some argue that a so-called "consumer revolution" (D. Davis 2000, 2005) and the retreat of the state from people's everyday lives have reduced the capacity of the state to dominate the public sphere (Wasserstrom and X. Liu 1995). Others dispute such claims, arguing that the glorification of consumption in the postsocialist period has not led to increased personal privacy and individual agency but is yet another mode of coercive state power, which Aihwa Ong and Li Zhang have called "socialism from afar" (2008, 3; cf. Pun 2003). My research among queer activists and NGOs in northwest China suggests that neither of these two opposing narratives is entirely accurate; instead, the picture is more nuanced, with a complicated mixture of new freedoms and continuing political constraints.

By documenting the development of community-based queer activism and NGOs in northwest China, *Inside the Circle* challenges claims that civil society and queer activism in postsocialist China are inauthentic and that economic and social reforms have merely resulted in new configurations of state power that have not led to meaningful increases in individual agency. Although they often collaborate with rather than confront the state, grassroots queer men's NGOs unwaveringly view their fight against HIV/AIDS as a social and political struggle. Indeed, this book reveals how for queer Chinese men, the AIDS epidemic has been a blessing and a curse. Even as HIV/AIDS sickens and kills increasing numbers of queer Chinese men, the epidemic, along with the economic and social reforms that closely coincided with the arrival of HIV in China in 1985 (World Health Organization 1986), has created a space for queer men and their allies to come together to promote the development of local queer communities; improve the physical and emotional health of their peers; and gradually increase the awareness, understanding, and acceptance of queer people.

The paradox of how to advocate for queer people while operating in a political and social environment that is overtly hostile to such efforts is one that queer activists in northwest China face every day. Even as a focus on HIV/AIDS provides a certain degree of political protection and financial resources for Chinese queer men's NGOs, their position remains precarious. Chinese laws and regulations regarding voluntary associations make it virtually impossible for queer NGOs to register with the authorities, meaning that they and their volunteers lack basic protections and operate in a legal gray area. Queer activists must carefully manage their activities and relationships with sympathetic government agencies and officials in order to avoid running afoul of the PRC's state security apparatus, which increasingly regards both domestic and international civil society groups with a high degree of suspicion. Many queer men's NGOs have adapted by avoiding politically sensitive topics like sexuality and human rights and collaborating with the state to provide HIV/AIDS prevention and treatment services, a strategy that many lesbian activists and NGOs find more difficult to adopt. Meanwhile, debates over sexual identity, culture, HIV/AIDS, and the proper course of the Chinese queer movement are taking place among activists, many of whom believe that political change will only take place if state and society gradually come to perceive queer people as healthy and responsible members of society.

WHAT IS SO QUEER ABOUT QUEER ANTHROPOLOGY?

In this book, I argue that the tension between sameness and difference is fundamental to what it means to be queer, including how anthropologists and other scholars define the term and how it is experienced and enacted in the local contexts of everyday queer life and activism. Theoretical tensions between sameness and difference have always animated queer anthropology, a relatively new subfield of cultural anthropology dedicated to the cross-cultural and comparative study of nonnormative expressions of human gender and sexuality around the world (Boellstorff 2007a; Weston 1993). These tensions have fueled questions that have proven difficult to answer, including one posed by Ellen Lewin (2016, 598) regarding "whether [or not] a field of inquiry many choose to label as 'queer anthropology' can adequately represent the full diversity of the populations we study." In other words, how can we respectfully and accurately represent diverse ways of being queer in a complex and increasingly interconnected world without either overemphasizing cultural differences or imposing a teleological vision of queerness that is often based on Western cultural values, theoretical perspectives, and historical experiences? Should queer anthropologists try to discover universal aspects of the queer experience, or should they document the differences between queer cultures around the world? And how can the stories of queer activists in northwest China shed new light on these persistent questions?

The word "queer" in queer anthropology comes from queer theory, a postmodern theoretical perspective that is dominated by Western scholars in fields like English and cultural studies and is associated with "a complex gender politics that transcends differences in bodies, erotic practices, and desires" (Lewin and Leap 2002, 10–11). Some anthropologists like Lewin (2016, 598–599) find fault with "the prescriptive elements of 'queer' as a sensibility and particularly as a discourse of resistance," arguing that "queer perspectives have had the effect of disparaging those whose sense of themselves is less antagonistic to so-called normativity than queer theorists would expect or consider desirable." Lewin's important critique raises the question of whether queerness is compatible with anthropology itself, and, if so, what might be gained (or lost) by queering anthropology. Some scholars define "queer" as a critical theoretical or political orientation that questions and interrogates existing categories, identities, or binaries instead of taking them for granted.[16] Certainly any work of queer anthropology should question cultural categories and binaries. But the same could be said about all kinds of anthropology. What makes this exercise specifically "queer?" What is so queer about queer anthropology?

These questions parallel ongoing ontological debates within the field of queer theory. While David Eng, Judith Halberstam, and José Esteban Muñoz (2005) defend the continued need for queer critiques of normativity in the face of increasing demands by gays and lesbians for "access to the nuclear family and its associated rights, recognitions, and privileges from the state" (10–11), they also call for greater "epistemological humility" (15) within queer studies, recognizing that Western queer theorists occupy places of relative privilege. Similarly, Robyn Wiegman and Elizabeth A. Wilson question the status of antinormativity as the "guiding tenet of queer inquiry" (2015, 3). Arguing that "antinormative stances project stability and immobility onto normativity," thereby reducing "the intricate dynamics of norms to a set of rules and coercions that everyone ought, rightly, to contest" (13), they ask the question, "[W]hat does queer inquiry do when its critical vigor is constituted by something other than an axiomatic opposition to norms?" (20).

Cultural anthropology, with its concern for documenting the experiences of people's daily lives in all their complexity and contradiction, is uniquely positioned to contribute a badly needed dose of epistemological humility to queer studies. As a subfield of cultural anthropology, queer anthropology should respect, even as it critiques and interrogates, forms of difference, decentering Western cultural values, historical experiences, and theoretical perspectives as it seeks to understand what it means to be queer in a variety of cultural locations. I argue that queerness is always a profoundly local phenomenon, as what it means to be nonnormative is necessarily dependent on specific contexts, meanings, traditions, and practices. At the same time, as the concept of the circle emphasizes, queerness is also always a profoundly relational phenomenon; to be queer is to embrace a certain kind of nonnormative identity that is shared with others. Although queerness is always rooted in the local, queer identification can also transcend local, regional, and national boundaries to assume a kind of belonging to an imagined global queer culture. Identifying with the global queer community can be crucially important to queer activists in places like northwest China, most of whom have limited abilities to participate directly in transnational queer culture and are often made to feel as though they are not welcome in their own country.

BUILDING A MORE CULTURALLY RELATIVISTIC QUEER STUDIES

Stories of everyday queer Chinese life and activism also have much to contribute to building a more culturally relativistic queer studies. Following Renato Rosaldo (2000), I understand cultural relativism not as endorsing an outdated definition of culture as relatively static and contained but rather as an incitement for cross-cultural dialogue that asks us to keep an open mind and to decenter our own cultural and historical perspectives. Reflecting on China's position within queer studies, Petrus Liu (2015, 21) challenges "the assumption that renders China as antithetical and exterior to queer theory," characterizing "queer theory as an incomplete project that is constantly transformed by China." However, Hongwei

Bao (2018, 27–28) warns that "In setting up a dichotomy between China and the West, Liu also risks creating an imaginary of a transnational China that is isolated from the global circulation of queer knowledge and practices." By exploring the queer Chinese idea of the circle, this book embraces Liu's call for greater transcultural and theoretical dialogue while heeding Bao's warning against reifying Chinese exceptionalism. The concept of the circle can help us bring seemingly opposite aspects of queer identity and experience—sameness and difference, local and global, East and West—into a productive dialectic in which neither is presumed to be more important than the other. Indeed, the infinitely scalar and overlapping nature of the circle is what makes it a particularly useful theoretical construct to better understand not only what it means to be queer and Chinese, but also what it means to be queer in general.

Inside the Circle also complicates concepts like "homonormativity" and "homonationalism," which Wiegman and Wilson argue have become "regular features of the critical terrain of queer studies" (2015, 8). Lisa Duggan (2002, 179) defines homonormativity as "a politics that does not contest dominant heteronormative assumptions and institutions—such as marriage, and its call for monogamy and reproduction—but upholds and sustains them while promising the possibility of a demobilized gay constituency and a privatized, depoliticized gay culture anchored in domesticity and consumption." That many queer activists in northwest China feel a deep-seated desire or obligation to get married and have children, and that many of them may also yearn for or enjoy increasingly privatized lifestyles of domesticity and consumption, would make them appear deeply homonormative according to Duggan's definition. However, I argue that respecting the perspectives and priorities of queer activists in northwest China and viewing them through the lens of the circle, instead of using concepts like homonormativity that are derived from Western queer theory to evaluate or critique them, helps us to better understand and appreciate the diverse and equally valid ways of being queer in the world today.[17]

Inside the Circle also departs from the recent tendency within cultural and queer anthropology to focus disproportionately on the workings of power, domination, and oppression, which Sherry Ortner (2016) describes as "dark anthropology." In this way, I hope to add nuance to the scholarship on Chinese queer culture and activism. Although I remain sensitive to the effects of power on the lives of queer activists and NGOs in northwest China, rather than criticizing them for "failing" to embrace Western-style identity politics or for collaborating with the state, I instead explore the ways they attempt to reconcile their queer identities and activist goals with their desires to lead morally responsible lives. I show how the concept of the circle, which allows for and even celebrates contradictory and overlapping queer identities and forms of activism, can not only help us better understand Chinese queer culture but also challenge our taken-for-granted assumptions about the relationship between queerness and antinormativity.

RECORDING QUEER CHINESE STORIES:
FIELDWORK AND METHODOLOGY

In March 2007 I started looking for a field site outside of eastern China and cities like Beijing, Shanghai, and Guangzhou. Joan Kaufman, an expert in HIV/AIDS and public health policy in China (2009, 2011, 2012), put me in touch with several grassroots queer men's NGOs around the country. Tianguang, the founder and leader of Tong'ai, a queer men's NGO based in the city of Xi'an, expressed an interest in my project and a willingness to work with me. I was surprised to learn that Tong'ai, founded in 1998, was one of the first grassroots queer NGOs not only in northwest China but in the entire PRC.

Tianguang and the other members of Tong'ai ended up being exceptional hosts, and I quickly fell in love with Xi'an, which is one of China's oldest cities, the capital of several past dynasties, the start of the famed Silk Road, and the gateway to northwest China.[18] Two eight-week research trips in the summers of 2007 and 2008 enabled me to begin developing close working relationships with several core Tong'ai volunteers who later became key interlocutors and close friends. In September 2010 I returned to Xi'an to conduct thirteen months of extended field-work. In order to gain long-term access to the field, I obtained an affiliation with the Xi'an Jiaotong University School of Medicine. Although I was assigned an official Chinese academic advisor who was meant to supervise me and my work, as luck would have it, he turned out to be rather absent and inattentive, leaving me free to conduct my research with very little outside interference.

Because of my extensive preliminary research, I was able to immediately resume fieldwork within Tong'ai and the local queer community. Within three days, I found and rented a small studio apartment directly across the street from the building that housed the Tong'ai office. This allowed me to make the trip between my apartment and the NGO in under ten minutes, greatly facilitating my access to the site. After finishing extended fieldwork in September 2011, to stay abreast of developments within the local queer community, I remained in touch with my research participants using instant messaging software. I also returned to the field for two follow-up visits during the summers of 2017 and 2019 to collect additional information about how recent political changes are affecting queer culture and activism in northwest China.

During fieldwork, I spent most of my time working alongside the thirty or so active staff members and volunteers in Tong'ai. I became a volunteer myself, helping out with daily office tasks and taking part in group activities and community outreach events in local queer meeting places including bars, bathhouses, and cruising areas in public parks, one of which was located a short walk from Tong'ai. I was almost always present at the NGO during its official working hours from two in the afternoon to ten in the evening, Wednesday through Monday, although, like my informants, I often stayed later on weekend nights and came into the office on Tuesdays, our one day off per week. I also attended and documented meetings between Tong'ai and other queer activists and NGOs as well as officials from the local and provincial Chinese Center for Disease Control and Prevention. In addition to conducting fieldwork with Tong'ai, I also spent as much time as I could with the members of UNITE, northwest China's first lesbian NGO, attending their events in local lesbian bars and cafes as well as in private homes. Finally, I was often invited to spend time with my research participants and to accompany them as they went about their daily lives, shopping, eating, and working. These times were some of the happiest and most productive I spent during fieldwork, as they provided me with many opportunities to access what Bronislaw Malinowski describes as the "imponderabilia of actual life" (1984, 24).

Apart from daily participant observation, my other main fieldwork activity consisted of arranging and completing ethnographic interviews and focus groups with a variety of research participants, including gay and lesbian NGO leaders and volunteers, queer community members, and local government officials. Altogether I interviewed fifty-one different people, some of them multiple times over several years, including seventeen current and former members of Tong'ai; nine members of UNITE; four leaders and volunteers from other gay and nongay NGOs in northwest China; two local government officials; two other local gay community members; and seventeen leaders and members of gay and lesbian NGOs from across the PRC.

Almost all of my fieldwork was conducted in Modern Standard Chinese. My research participants occasionally spoke the local Shaanxi dialect, often briefly and in informal or joking situations, which grew easier for me to understand and even take part in over time. Although none of my research participants spoke fluent English, they would sometimes drop an occasional English word into a conversation. In my translations of my informants' words in this book, I place such words in italics to indicate that they were uttered verbatim. During fieldwork I took great pains to record, jot down, or commit to memory the exact words, phrases, and language used by my research participants; in the following chapters I often include specific Chinese words and phrases as I believe, with Malinowski, that such "ethnographic statements," "characteristic narratives," and "typical utterances" constitute the very "spirit" that animates ethnographic understanding (1984, 22, 24).

"HE'S ALSO LIKE THAT": MY POSITIONALITY IN THE FIELD

Like all works of ethnography, this book is partial and limited in several respects. My experiences in the field, including the information I had access to and how I interpreted it, were inevitably shaped by my position as a white, gay, cisgender American man in my twenties and thirties. Although I did not share the same ethnicity, nationality, or native language with my research participants, the fact that I am gay helped to reduce the ethnographic distance between us, affording me access to situations and information that might not have been as readily available had I identified as straight. When meeting me for the first time, people would almost always immediately ask about my sexual orientation; other people who already knew me would quickly tell them not to worry, "He's also [like that] (*Ta ye shi*)." As soon as they found out that I was also "someone from inside the circle," people would almost invariably relax and begin asking me questions about my impressions of Chinese queer culture. Of course, this is not to say that I automatically achieved closeness or familiarity with all my queer research participants, or that experiences of queerness are universal. In fact, it was often during conversations about differences between our queer experiences that I had some of my most enlightening moments in the field.

Although it is possible that my gender prevented me from accessing some information, it usually did not seem to be an impediment during my fieldwork with lesbian informants. Indeed, the members of UNITE quickly claimed me as one of their own, even calling me their "little sister" (*meizi*). It is also likely that my being what Lila Abu-Lughod (1991, 137, 140–141) calls a "halfie," or someone whose "national or cultural identity is mixed" in such a way that "the 'other' that the anthropologist is studying is simultaneously constructed as, at least partially, a self," prevented me from preserving enough "distance" between myself and the subjects of my study and caused me to "slide into subjectivity." Indeed, I do not deny that in many ways I identified with my research participants and their causes. However, in many contexts, especially when everyone present identified as queer, other aspects of my identity became more salient, such as my ethnicity, nationality, and long-term relationship with my Chinese Canadian boyfriend. Upon seeing a picture of my partner, people would initially appear confused and say, "He looks Chinese!" However, more than the ethnicity of my boyfriend, it was the duration of our relationship—our ten-year anniversary took place halfway through my extended fieldwork—that people were most struck by.[19] My relationship frequently served as a useful conversation generator, which I believe helped me to better understand my informants' own expectations and experiences of queer love, romance, and relationships.

One challenge I encountered early on was how to include the experiences of women in my research. Queer anthropology has rightly been critiqued for focusing primarily on gay men and often ignoring or overlooking the experiences of lesbian women (Blackwood 2002; Boellstorff 2007a). The same is true in anthropological studies of queer China, which Elisabeth Engebretsen (2014, 128) writes "has been dominated by a male-gendered perspective." Serendipitously, UNITE was founded just a few months into my extended fieldwork, and I quickly attempted to connect with its leaders and volunteers and to include them in my research whenever possible. Happily, the members of UNITE were extremely welcoming and supportive, inviting me to participate in and observe their events and to spend time with them in their homes and daily lives. However, because of the smaller size of the lesbian NGO, its lack of a dedicated office at the time of my primary fieldwork, and the relative infrequency of its activities compared to Tong'ai, most of the data

I collected pertains to gay men's perspectives, a bias and limitation that is reflected in this ethnography.

Another challenge I faced was deciding what words to use to refer to the sexual orientations or identities of my research participants, both in my own writing and in my translations of conversations I had with people in the field. Queer anthropologists have adopted several creative solutions to this problem. Tom Boellstorff uses italics to remind his readers that words like *gay* and *lesbi* (an Indonesian loanword derived from the English term "lesbian") "have their own history and dynamics: they are not just 'gay' and 'lesbian' with a foreign accent" (2005, 8). Others prefer to use only local terms or to put words like "gay" and "lesbian" inside of scare quotes. While these solutions are innovative, I believe that quarantining words like "gay" or "lesbian" inside of italics or scare quotes may actually do more harm than good by implying that non-Western queer peoples' uses of the terms are somehow different or inauthentic, while also making uses of the words without scare quotes or italicization seem more authentic, culturally consistent, and ahistorical than they really are. However, my use of the words gay and lesbian without italicization or scare quotes in this book should not be taken to imply that these words have a single meaning that can be applied across all social, cultural, and historical contexts.

ORGANIZATION OF THE BOOK

In the following chapters I move from an initial focus on the historical and ethnographic contexts of queer culture and activism in northwest China to a broader examination of the kind of civil society that is taking shape around issues of queer activism and HIV/AIDS prevention and how my informants saw themselves as members of a global queer community. While zooming out from a local to a global perspective, this book also moves forward in time. I trace the emergence of local queer cultures and communities in northwest China alongside state policies of "reform and opening up" and the beginnings of China's HIV/AIDS epidemic in the 1980s and 1990s, exploring the founding of gay and lesbian NGOs in Xi'an in the late 1990s and 2000s and the personal histories of my queer research participants. I examine how these groups and the local queer civil society environment changed from the early 2000s to the late 2010s, including the rise, fall, and revival of Tong'ai over a period of fourteen years. I conclude by looking toward the future, using the concept of the circle to consider what new kinds of transnational queer solidarities are made possible when Chinese queer culture and activism are reconceived as neither fundamentally different from nor lesser than those in the West.

Chapter 2 lays the groundwork for my ethnographic analysis of queer culture and activism in northwest China by examining the historical and cultural contexts for the emergence of gay and lesbian identities, communities, and social movements at the end of the twentieth century, what my research participants colloquially called "the circle." I trace the outlines of the unique "sex/gender system" (Rubin

1975) among queer men and women in northwest China, including the emergence of gay and lesbian cultures and communities; generational differences within the queer community; and structural features of local queer community and culture.

In chapter 3, I complicate claims about the individualization and privatization of sexuality and kinship in Chinese society by examining ideas and practices of love, marriage, and family among queer men in northwest China. I show that, rather than being at the vanguard of a Chinese "sexual revolution," queer men struggle to find ways to reconcile their sexual identities and queer desires with their deeply felt duties and obligations as sons. In chapter 4, I challenge arguments in the literature on Chinese civil society by looking at the growth of queer activism in northwest China. Focusing on two grassroots gay and lesbian NGOs, Tong'ai and UNITE, I show how economic and social reforms are creating opportunities for many queer Chinese people to come together in pursuit of common goals, such as working toward greater social awareness and acceptance of homosexuality and fighting the spread of HIV/AIDS among their peers.

Chapter 5 takes a more critical look at some of the more uncivil aspects of grassroots queer AIDS activism in northwest China, with a particular emphasis on understanding how relations both within Tong'ai and between it and other queer men's NGOs were transformed before, during, and after the arrival of global health initiatives in the late 2000s. In chapter 6, I use the examples of rainbow flags and global gay beauty pageants to intervene in ongoing debates over sameness and difference within queer anthropology. I explore how queer activists in northwest China use rainbow flags and the Mr Gay World beauty pageant to index their membership in an imagined global queer community, as well as how these symbols of global queerness become imbued with new meanings as they are deployed to express and enact uniquely Chinese forms of queer identity and activism. I end the book with a brief conclusion that looks at how the people and organizations described in this ethnography have changed over time and considers how their stories and the concept of the circle can help us better understand what it means to be queer in postsocialist China and beyond.

2 · THE VIEW FROM INSIDE THE CIRCLE

Queer Gender and Sexuality in Northwest China

One spring morning I got a call from Yuanzi, a Tong'ai staff member. "Where are you?" Yuanzi curtly demanded to know. Yuanzi said he was in the nearby Tong'ai office (even though it was Tuesday, our one day off), and ordered me to come right away, saying, "There's something really good I have to tell you." My curiosity piqued, I hurried to the office. When I arrived, Xiao Shan, another Tong'ai staff member, opened the door with a flourish. "The Empress Dowager (*muhou*) has something to discuss with you," he said, gesturing toward Yuanzi, who as usual was sitting regally in front of his laptop computer at a wide table in the large front-office room. Feeling a mixture of excitement and nervousness, I asked Yuanzi what he wanted to tell me. A large grin broke out on his face as he exclaimed, fingers splayed out in front of him for emphasis, "Today we are going to go get our nails done!" Xiao Shan happily added, "Then later tonight we can play mahjong, it'll be so sissy (C)!" As he said this, Xiao Shan mischievously mimed the motion of mixing mahjong tiles with outstretched hands and fingers, showing off his imaginary painted nails.

Several months ago, while we were all sitting around the same table, Xiao Shan had purchased a coupon from one of the many deal-of-the-day websites that had recently become popular in China. The coupon entitled its bearer to a manicure at a new beauty salon along with free sunflower seeds and American-style coffee. When I asked if I could go along, Yuanzi arched his eyebrows and shot me a disbelieving look. "Why not?" I asked, batting my eyelashes and holding up my nails in an exaggeratedly feminine way. We all laughed. Xiao Shan said that yes, I could go, and that I would probably want to have rainbow flags painted on my nails, or sparkles! I asked Yuanzi what he wanted to have painted on his nails. "Orchids," he replied coolly. "Are you sure you don't want chrysanthemums?" I impishly asked, having just learned that, among gay men in northwest China, chrysanthemums

FIGURE 2.1. Xiao Shan shopping for cosmetics in Xi'an. Photo by author.

symbolize the anus, and, therefore, homosexual intimacy and desire. Yuanzi and Xiao Shan's eyes widened in gleeful shock and horror at my remark, and Yuanzi jokingly called me a "witch" (*yaonie*). Acting out his words for us to see, Xiao Shan said that while we were having our nails done, he would sit with one limp hand extended, one leg crossed over the other, his head cocked to one side. He would call Yuanzi "big sister" (*jiejie*), Yuanzi would call me "little sister" (*meimei*), and then the woman doing our nails would throw up all over our hands! We laughed at the thought. Or, Xiao Shan continued, she would get out a knife and stab our hands! We laughed again, although I found this last image somewhat disturbing. Then Yuanzi muttered in disbelief, "I never thought that Mister Ma [*Ma shi*, my nickname in the Shaanxi dialect] would want to get his nails done."

Sadly, by the time we made it to the nail salon it had already closed for the day. Seeing my crestfallen expression, Xiao Shan offered to make it up to me by taking me shopping for cosmetics at a Hong Kong drugstore chain (figure 2.1). After seriously studying my features, Xiao Shan declared that, although the pores on my nose were so big that it "looked like a strawberry," my biggest problem was the huge wrinkles around my eyes. "Look at me," he said. "I am older than you, but I don't have *any* wrinkles." As we walked around the store, Xiao Shan and Yuanzi debated the virtues of various brands and ignored the store employees who told us we were in the women's section. We saw an attractive young man also shopping for cosmetics, and Xiao Shan and Yuanzi's faces became animated with suggestive eyebrow raisings and winks. "200" (*erbai*), Yuanzi whispered, communicating that in his estimation there was a 200 percent chance that the man was gay. As he walked to the cash register, Xiao Shan and Yuanzi swiveled their heads to watch how his butt moved. "How twisty! (*Hao niu a!*)" Xiao Shan exclaimed in a mockingly scandalized way, and Yuanzi nodded, laughing. A large advertisement for men's cosmetics in the store featured a handsome, young-looking Asian man with extremely white, blemish-free skin smiling into the camera. The ad contained the following English text in all caps: "YOUR FRIENDS WON'T ADMIT IT BUT THEY USE IT TOO." I told Xiao Shan what the English said, and he laughed, saying that of course his friends would all admit it because they were all *huo*, a local slang term for gay men.

This lighthearted ethnographic vignette illustrates many features of queer culture in northwest China, including some of the local terms and strategies that people inside the circle use to play with gender and sexuality, express themselves, identify and categorize one another, and create queer kinship networks. In this chapter and the next, I explore the richness and complexity of this distinctive sex/gender system, or what Gayle Rubin calls "the set of arrangements by which a society transforms biological sexuality into products of human activity, and in which these transformed sexual needs are satisfied" (1975, 159).

As China experiences a period of rapid change caused by economic and social reforms that began in the 1970s and 1980s, many people find themselves at once hopeful for and anxious about the future. While urban gay and lesbian community spaces are proliferating, creating new opportunities for the more open expression of same-sex identities and desires, queer people in postsocialist China face a unique set of challenges. These include reconciling their sexualities with conventional familial and social expectations regarding marriage and reproduction that, despite recent social changes, remain firmly in place; striving for greater social awareness and acceptance of homosexuality while trying not to run afoul of enduring government restrictions on the rights of assembly and free speech; and looking for love and intimacy in the face of a burgeoning HIV/AIDS epidemic that is particularly concentrated within urban gay communities.

The careful balancing act that is required of queer activists in northwest China as they navigate the contradictory currents of the postsocialist period makes their lives and experiences an excellent vantage point from which to examine the effects of social and economic reforms. Are emerging queer communities a sign of radical social change, or do they instead represent a continuation of "traditional"[1] Chinese beliefs and practices regarding gender, sexuality, and kinship? Is northwest Chinese queer culture becoming increasingly similar to or different from queer cultures elsewhere, both in China and around the world? To begin answering these questions, this chapter examines what it means to be both queer and Chinese in postsocialist northwest China. Paying particular attention to generational differences between queer activists, I explore the development of a unique queer sex/gender system in northwest China including how my queer informants discovered their sexual orientation and found others like themselves; how sex roles and gender norms are structured inside the circle; and the colorful expressions queer people use to understand and describe themselves and each other. I argue that northwest China's complex and sometimes contradictory queer culture reveals a mixture of both cultural change and continuity, building on other recent research (Evans 2020) that complicates official and scholarly narratives of "rupture" between the socialist and postsocialist eras. The diversity of queer experiences and practices in northwest China also illustrates how what it means to be both queer and Chinese is constantly changing as people continue to find new ways to negotiate their belonging in overlapping local, national, and global queer communities.

THE KIDS ARE ALL RIGHT: GENERATIONAL DIFFERENCES IN THE QUEER COMMUNITY

The complex history of modern China continues to inform the way that people inside the circle understand both themselves and others. One of the key features of the queer sex/gender system in northwest China is the way that the queer community is structured by generation (table 2.1). Instead of a person's age being defined by their current decade of life, such as their thirties or forties, age cohorts are reckoned by the decade of a person's birth, such as people who were born in the 1970s or the 1980s. Members of each age cohort, such as the "post-70s," "post-80s," and "post-90s" generations, are often thought of as sharing a common set of characteristics based on the social, economic, and political dynamics of the decade in which they were born.

Because they were the first generation to reach adulthood after the reform and opening up policies of the late 1970s and 1980s, members of the post-90s generation are viewed by older queers with a combination of both disapproval and envy. People in the post-90s generation are often stereotyped as spoiled, selfish, pleasure-seeking, and extremely "open" (*kaifang*) to new ideas. While the post-80s generation is believed to have similar tendencies, the post-90s generation is often regarded as taking their openness to worrisome extremes. One older queer man who shared such views was Lao Wang, a married working-class gay man who was born in 1965 and volunteered at Tong'ai. During an interview, he recalled how "in the 1980s and 1990s China already had twenty or more years of 'reform and opening up' and people's living standards had gone up a lot. Furthermore, these kids have been spoiled and pampered by their families ever since they were small." Wenqing, a gay man born in 1972 who was also married and from a modest background, shared similar views. One of Tong'ai's oldest volunteers, he operated the group's free telephone hotline. During one of our conversations, he remarked that "People in the post-80s generation have been exposed to a lot of [new] information. They are all very open and are relatively accepting of new trends. For example, if they want to do something, they'll just do it, as long as it makes them happy."

TABLE 2.1   List of Key Research Participants by Year of Birth

Nickname	Year of birth	Age	Sexuality	Relationship status	Occupation
Xiao Wai	1992	19	gay	boyfriend	high school senior
Xiao Feng	1991	20	gay	single	university student
Yangyang	1991	20	gay	boyfriend	university student
Tian'e	1990	21	gay	boyfriend	fashion designer
Xiao Yu	1989	22	bisexual	single	university student
Xiao Kai	1984	27	gay	single	utility company worker
Jiajia	1983	28	lesbian	single	office worker
Xiao Bang	1982	29	lesbian	girlfriend	office worker
Yuanzi	1982	29	gay	boyfriend	queer men's NGO worker
Xiao Shan	1981	30	bisexual	girlfriend	queer men's NGO worker
Paopao	1977	34	gay	single	artist
Wenqing	1972	38	gay	married, with children	salesman
Zhiming	1971	40	gay	married, no children	businessman
Lao Wang	1965	46	gay	married, with children and a boyfriend	unemployed

NOTE: The ages, relationship statuses, and occupations of the people described here correspond to when I first met and spoke with them.

Queer members of the post-90s generation themselves frequently echoed such opinions, expressing a certain degree of ambivalence concerning their location at the forefront of China's postsocialist experiment. Xiao Wai, a precocious high school senior, was born in 1992 and was one of Tong'ai's youngest volunteers. He told me that "The characteristics of people in the post-90s generation are that they are both foolish and fearless and only want to live the good life." He compared this with the post-80s generation, which he described as "solemnly focusing on their future, buying a car, buying a house, and working hard." When I asked what distinguishes those born in the 1960s and 1970s, he only laughed, shook his head, and said, "I don't know! I really have no idea," as if the 1960s and 1970s were such ancient history that they defied his understanding. However, members of previous generations were quick to contrast the openness and selfishness commonly attributed to the post-80s and post-90s generations with the qualities they believed were imparted to them by growing up in China prior to reforms.

During one of our many conversations, Lao Wang wistfully recounted what it was like growing up in urban northwest China as a member of a working-class family in the 1960s and 1970s. Gesturing to the tall, thirty-two-story apartment building we were sitting in, he said, "At that time we seldom saw these kinds of buildings. Xi'an's most famous structure was the Telecommunications

Building near the center of town.[2] Back then that kind of building was so awe-inspiring, so amazing. . . . When I graduated from middle school I had probably never even sat on a sofa, we were that poor." Even though his middle school grades were good and he had been appointed class leader, his family was unable to afford the high school tuition fees and expenses, so instead of continuing his education Lao Wang left Xi'an to find work as an agricultural laborer in the country. Looking back on his life, Lao Wang told me that people of the post-1960s generation "lived through the final stages of the Cultural Revolution, so you could say that they grew up in a very bitter environment."

Wenqing, who grew up in a nearby city in Shaanxi, told me that "the post-1970s generation exists in the space between tradition and modernity. . . . Their thinking is, relatively speaking, a little bit less open; they are slightly more conservative." Zhiming, a married businessman who volunteered at Tong'ai and was born in Xi'an in 1971, described it this way:

> People of the post-70s generation just missed the craziness of the Cultural Revolution. They also just missed the splendor of the reform and opening up period; they were right in the middle. . . . At that time, China was extremely impoverished. After reform, many Chinese people lost their faith; it wasn't like before, when everyone was fervently pursuing socialism. Rather, they set that down and didn't talk about it much anymore.

The result, according to Zhiming, is that "The people in our generation are not quixotic, we don't have idols. Rather, we are very realistic, very pragmatic." Zhiming also attributed some of the differences between his generation and those born after 1980 and 1990 to the one-child policy, saying "Because we made it just before China started its birth control policy [in the 1980s], after us they are all single children. They carry less of a sense of responsibility than we do, because they have been doted on by their parents ever since they were small."

Despite growing up in very different social, economic, and political environments, people from all generations recounted similar stories about when and how they first realized they were queer. Although people discovered their sexualities at a wide range of ages, from elementary school through middle and high school and into university and beyond, almost all my research participants realized they were queer when they unexpectedly began to develop romantic or sexual feelings for someone of the same sex. Many also reported confirming their suspected queer sexualities after being exposed to media depictions of homosexuality, including TV news reports, films, and the Internet.

Xiao Feng, a soft-spoken second-year university student and Tong'ai volunteer from Zhejiang Province who was born in 1991, recalled how "at the end of middle school, when I was about fourteen or fifteen, I still liked girls. But when I started high school, I didn't have any feelings toward girls anymore." He said that when he started to develop feelings for other boys, he did not know what was happening.

"I felt very isolated, very afraid. I wanted to fall in love with girls, but every time I tried, I was defeated. Therefore, I slowly went from struggling [with my sexuality] to ultimately accepting it." Xiao Feng's close friend, Yangyang, a student at the same university who was also from Zhejiang and a Tong'ai volunteer, had a similar story. "I realized [I was gay] in high school, when I was about seventeen or eighteen years old," he told me. "During gym class, when I was with other boys, I would feel aroused. At that time, I had a lot of female friends, and we would sing and play together, but I never experienced that kind of arousal or desire [with them]."

Slightly older, Xiao Kai, a tall, mild-mannered UNITE volunteer and ex-military man from a prefecture-level town southwest of Xi'an, worked for a state-owned utility company and was born in 1984.[3] He described his experiences:

> When I was eight years old in elementary school, I had these kinds of subconscious feelings. I was just starting to be aware of liking other people, and I found that I was different: I liked boys. At that time my heart was full of dread because everyone around me was different; I thought I was the only person in the world like this. I didn't dare tell the people I liked. When I was twelve years old, in the first year of middle school, I saw the word homosexual for the first time on the news. I think the story was about how there was a man who liked other men and wanted to get married.... After I saw that, I was extremely happy, because I wasn't the only person [like this] in the world.

Yuanzi, who was born in a rural district to the northeast of Xi'an in 1982, told me that it was not until he was at university that he first realized he was "this kind of person" (*zheyang de ren*). Like many others of the post-1980s generation, Yuanzi said he discovered his sexuality online, "probably when I discovered Tiangong [a popular website used by gay men in northwest China with personal ads and online chat rooms], and started chatting with everyone, making friends, getting to know people a little bit."

Lao Wang and Zhiming, from the post-60s and post-70s generations, respectively, shared similar stories. "*Aiya*, back then I was in middle school," Lao Wang exclaimed when I asked him when he first knew that he liked men. "I was about thirteen years old; it would have been 1978 or 1979. All the boys liked to mess around with girls and talk about them or whatever, but I wasn't like that. It didn't give me any pleasure. But when I saw a good-looking guy, I really wanted to go and hug him. I wanted to go and kiss him, that kind of feeling." Lao Wang recalled how "sometimes I would have these fantasies, where I would be with him, the boy of my dreams, and we would make love or whatever. I would have these visions." Zhiming did not "acknowledge" (*queren*) that he was gay until he was in university in the early 1990s. "At that time in China, you never saw any *report* or *information* about homosexuality," he said. When I asked him how he felt when he realized he was gay, he told me, "I felt extremely distressed. I felt that it was wrong. How could

I be like this? How could I like boys? How could I be that strange? I didn't know any others, so I thought I was the only one. . . . I tried to avoid it; I just didn't think about it. Afterwards I also had girlfriends, like the rest of my classmates. We all ate together, chatted, played games. I didn't think about how I liked boys."

Several younger queer activists reported discovering their sexuality during playful sexual encounters in elementary and middle school, something that seems to have been a relatively common experience among the post-80s and post-90s generations. Xiao Yu, who was born in 1989, recounted an event that took place in his third year of elementary school:

> During the summer we had an hour of afternoon rest. Our class was small; we all slept in the same classroom. That summer was really hot. . . . [My classmate] put his big blanket down on the floor, and I put my smaller one on top of us. Then we rested together. As I was sleeping, he started to move his hands and feet. I couldn't believe it; I thought it was really odd. Everyone else was asleep. I pushed him away, but he grabbed my hands and put them down there. We started feeling each other down there, and then he kissed me. At that time, I thought a kiss was just a light touch of the mouth, but I didn't know what he was thinking, because he was using his tongue! I thought this was really strange; I wasn't used to it. At first, I kept my mouth tightly closed; I didn't dare open it. Because we had afternoon rest every day, I often slept together with him. After a few times I started to think that actually kissing was a lot of fun!

Such stories of childhood sexual exploration seem to confirm stereotypes of the post-1980s and 1990s generations being extremely "open"; none of my older informants reported similar experiences. However, this does not mean that queer people born in the 1960s and 1970s were not attracted to people of the same sex at a young age, only that they were not able to act on these attractions in the same ways as people from later generations. For people like Lao Wang and others who did not discover their sexuality through early childhood sexual play or experimentation, desire for others of the same sex was restricted to the realm of dream and fantasy, or, as in the case of Zhiming, it was ignored or suppressed. It was not until they contacted other self-identified queer men in later years that such experiences were possible, an act or event that was described by my informants as "joining the circle."

"WE ARE ALL INSIDE THE CIRCLE": STORIES OF FINDING AND JOINING THE QUEER COMMUNITY

The most prevalent way of imagining, discussing, or denoting membership within a group or "community" of queer people in northwest China is the concept of the circle or quanzi.[4] In modern Chinese, the word quanzi not only refers to a literal circle but can also mean a group of people who share a common defining characteristic or interest and is not limited to or expressly associated with being queer. However, among gay men and lesbians in northwest China, quanzi is a marked term that is universally used and understood to index the queer community or a particular subsection of that community (Sun, Farrer, and Choi 2006 and Wei 2015 report similar findings in Shanghai and Chengdu, respectively). A quanzi is also not limited to smaller social networks but can be expanded to include all gay men and lesbians in any city, region, country, or even the entire imagined global queer community.

The term quanzi bears some similarities to the English expression "the tribe," which can be used to refer to other queer people and their allies. However, the meaning of quanzi differs significantly from concepts like "tribe" and "community." Although membership in the circle is not restricted to gay men and lesbians and includes bisexual and transgender people, it is specifically understood to exclude all heterosexual people, no matter their connection or relationship to the queer community (Hu 2011, 51). Also, a person does not automatically join the circle just by being queer; to gain entry, one must first come into contact with other queer people, which can include going to a queer meeting place like a gay bar or an online lesbian discussion forum or having a friendship or sexual relationship with another queer person. Thus, the circle is an inherently relational as opposed to an individual understanding of queerness: a single queer person cannot create a circle by themselves but can only form one by entering into a relationship of some kind with other queers.

Perhaps the most interesting thing about the circle is its seeming flexibility. On the one hand, the idea of the circle is inherently binary. A circle creates a simple border, denotes a single category of inclusion and exclusion. Something or someone is always located either inside or outside of a given circle. On the other hand, a queer person can belong to an almost infinite number of circles contained one within another or overlapping and intersecting in different ways. Just as a circle can be used to circumscribe series of discrete or intersecting queer social networks, a quanzi can also have an ad hoc or transitory quality. For example, gay men and lesbians who get married and lose contact with their other queer friends and acquaintances are often described as having left the circle.

Although there was some disagreement among my informants about whether a quanzi could be formed by only two people (such as the relationship between friends or lovers) or whether it required three or more people, everyone emphasized the scalar nature of the circle. As Zhiming simply put it, "A circle means a group (qun) of people." A small coterie of friends can be a quanzi, as can a larger group of people, such as members of a gay or lesbian NGO, people who frequent a given gay or lesbian commercial establishment such as a bar or bathhouse, or a group of friends who belong to the same text messaging group. The quanzi is also not limited to China or to Chinese people. As Xiao Feng told me, "As long as you are gay, no matter what country you come from, what province, what region, we are all inside the circle. You are from the U.S., I am from China, but we are both considered inside the circle." In this way, the circle resembles Benedict Anderson's (1991) description of nations as "imagined communities," except in this case people are united not by a single language, culture, or mass media, but rather by sharing a similar nonnormative sexual orientation or gender identity. The circle is also not limited to the present, but can expand to include an imagined global community or nation that includes all queer people everywhere, past, present, and future.[5]

The stories queer men in northwest China told me about how and when they "came into contact with" (*jiechu dao*) or "joined" (*jiaru*) the circle are as diverse as those of how they first realized they were gay. Many gay men, especially those of younger generations, reported joining the circle by stumbling upon or searching for gay websites, discussion forums, chat rooms, or text messaging groups. Paopao, a painter, photographer, and Tong'ai volunteer who was born in a prefectural Shaanxi town in 1977, described how he did not join the circle until he was twenty-seven years old, after he had graduated from art school and started working at an advertising agency:

> Every person there had their own computer, so I could go online. That was the thing that made me most satisfied about that job and is why I persevered there for two years. It was around 2004; Asia already had a lot of [gay] websites. I went to a gay discussion forum where you could post messages. There I met a doctor who had started his own clinic. Afterwards we started chatting on QQ [a popular instant messaging platform in China].

In contrast, Xiao Wai, who was born after 1990, joined the circle when he was only seventeen. With an air of nonchalance, he recounted how he "first searched for a few websites, looked around for a bit; that's about how I entered the circle. Then I searched for some QQ groups and added a few, chatted with some people." When I asked him if seventeen was considered a young age to come into contact with the circle, he shook his head, saying "These days it doesn't count as early. . . . I've met people who are thirteen or fourteen who have joined the circle."

Gay men from older generations often described becoming aware of the circle through "chance" (*ouran*) events or encounters. The following is Zhiming's story of how he stumbled upon the circle during a business trip to the eastern city of Tianjin:

> It was the end of 1998, around October. The autumn sky was high, and the air was crisp and refreshing. One afternoon at around three or four o'clock I was taking a walk in a park along the river. This park was a *gay* place (gay *dian*), but I didn't know it then. At that time in China the Internet was still very rare; people weren't used to computers. So, as I was walking in the park, I went to use the restroom, and someone harassed me. He was really scary. It was 1998, and I was only twenty-seven, so I was probably fairly attractive. As I was using the toilet, someone behind me felt my butt! It really scared me!

Zhiming smiled and laughed at the memory before continuing:

Right away I knew that something wasn't right. I was really frightened, so I just left. But as I was walking home, I thought—because I had known all along that I was *gay*, but I kept it suppressed. But as I grew older, that part of my heart grew stronger. I wanted to find other people, people that I could truly communicate with. . . . So, after a couple of days, I went back to the park. This time I didn't go inside the restroom, I just sat outside on a bench, pretending to read the newspaper. Then I ran into him; you could say he was the first person inside the circle I ever met. He greeted me, saying, "What time is it?" I told him what time it was. Then he asked me, "Do you have a light?" I said that I did, gave him my lighter, and he smoked a cigarette. Then he asked me, "Where're you from?" Just like that, we started chatting. Then he said, "Do you know what kind of place this is?" I said that I didn't know. He said, "This is a meeting place for homosexuals!"

Zhiming, who ended up taking the man he met in the park back to his hotel room, contended that his affair in Tianjin technically did not count as him entering the circle, because a relationship between two people was not enough to form a quanzi. Therefore, Zhiming argued, he did not really become a member of the circle until a year later when he returned from Tianjin to Xi'an and gradually made contacts within the gay community there. Similarly, even though Lao Wang met his first boyfriend in 1985 when he was twenty years old, he maintained that the circle did not yet exist in Xi'an at that time. "Back then, I guess you should say there wasn't one," Lao Wang told me. "I only knew that there was this kind of a circle in 2007. That's when I finally found out that Xi'an had so many [gay men]!" he said, laughing.

Other informants dated the existence of the circle in Xi'an to the late 1980s. According to Lang, the manager of the Tiangong website, at that time the circle mainly consisted of people meeting in parks and public restrooms. Before the existence of the Internet or commercial gay spaces like bars or bathhouses, he told me, "Things were extremely chaotic (*luan*). [People] were running wild." He said that around the center of town some people started cross-dressing and going out on the streets, slowly forming a "small circle."[6]

Wenqing described first encountering Xi'an's quanzi in the early 1990s when he was twenty-two years old:

This was very early. I was with this friend, and I probably liked people of the same sex a little bit, but I didn't understand the circle too much. He probably understood the circle [more than me]. One time he told me he would take me to a place. He said there were a lot of friends there, and I slowly came into contact [with the circle]. After contacting them I found out [more] about the circle; when I was chatting with them, I found out what places in Xi'an were meeting spots, what places had more gays, and I slowly began to understand.

Wenqing recalled how the circle had changed in the years since 1994, saying how back then "I think it was more intimate. Only a small group of people knew about the quanzi, it wasn't like it is today, very open."

By the time I began fieldwork in the late 2000s, a thriving queer community had developed in Xi'an consisting of websites and online discussion forums like Tiangong; an assortment of private gay and lesbian enterprises including bars and bathhouses; and social groups devoted to recreational pursuits ranging from swimming and badminton to board games and hiking. The city was also home to an expanding queer civil society made up of a growing number of grassroots gay and lesbian NGOs working on a range of issues related to queer culture and public health.[7] However, although the local queer community had grown and changed significantly, people still complained about it being as disorderly or chaotic as it had been in the beginning, in the late 1980s and early 1990s. Then, as now, the circle was the defining symbol of queer identity, community, and belonging in northwest China. As people gradually became aware of their own queer desires and realized that there were more people like them not only in China but around the world, the concept of the circle, as a flexible and relational model of queer identity and community, helped them see themselves as not isolated or alone but as members of larger imagined local, national, and global queer communities.

BEYOND THE BINARY: SEX ROLES AND GENDER NORMS INSIDE THE CIRCLE

Apart from the circle, one of the most fundamental structures of the queer sex/gender system in northwest China is another seemingly binary apparatus of "1s" (ones, yi) and "0s" (zeros, ling), "tomboys" (T) and "wives" (P), as well as a host of other sexual and gendered dualities (table 2.2). This constellation of queer antonyms shapes how many people inside the circle perceive their own genders and sexualities. However, even within this elaborate system of opposing terms, people find ways to move beyond the binary, carving out new terrain between 1 and 0 or T and P, such as "0.5" (ling dian'er wu) and "savage Ps and femme Ts" (ye P niang T).

In many respects, the 1/0 binary resembles the idea of "tops" and "bottoms," in which the 1 or "top" is the penetrating partner and the 0 or "bottom" is the penetrated partner; 0.5, then, corresponds to "versatile" men who can perform both sexual roles. Xiao Shan, a devout Buddhist and Tong'ai staff member who was born in 1981 in a rural village located in the mountains outside of Xi'an, succinctly explained the relationship between 1, 0, and 0.5 during one of our many interviews, saying, "The 1 is the person who penetrates, and also he can't accept being penetrated. The 0 is the person who is penetrated by others and is also unable to penetrate others. 0.5 is someone who can penetrate others and be penetrated by others." As Zhiming laughingly explained to me, "1 resembles a stick (gunzi), so it represents the penis, and 0 resembles the asshole."[8] Although 1s and 0s were used to describe only sexual roles when they were first adopted in the 1990s, their significance has since widened

TABLE 2.2   List of Queer Sex and Gender Terms in Northwest China

1	one, *yi*	o	zero, *ling*
tomboy	*T*	wife	*P*
man	*nanxing*	woman	*nüxing*
active	*zhudong*	passive	*beidong*
penetrating	*charu fang*	penetrated	*bei charu fang*
offensive	*gong*	defensive	*shou*
attacking	*gong*	receiving	*shou*
husband	*laogong*	wife	*laopo*
butch	*meng*	femme	*niang*
male	*gong*	female	*mu*
manly	*MAN*	sissy	*C*
"pure top"	*chun yi*	"big-old bottom"	*da mu ling*

to include a range of interlocking and reinforcing stereotypes and assumptions about a person's gender and sexuality based on whether they are the penetrating or penetrated partner during sex.

One potentially unique aspect of the queer Chinese sex/gender system is how 1s and os are understood as separate genders. My queer informants in northwest China often described 1s as the "man" or the "husband" and os as the "woman" or the "wife" in a same-sex relationship. "o is equivalent to the woman; 1 is equivalent to the man," Xiao Wai explained. "o is the penetrated, 1 is the penetrator. It's that kind of relationship." Writing about queer culture in the northeast Chinese city of Dalian, Tiantian Zheng (2015, 77) argues that gender differences between queer men who identify as 1s or os are so large that they no longer share "a sexual identity based on a common sexual orientation." While they may have understood 1s and os as inhabiting different genders to some degree, I did not find a similar sentiment among queer men in northwest China. Rather, nearly all my informants were quick to point out that gender and sexual differences among queer men should not be exaggerated. When I asked Xiao Feng to describe the 1/o system, he replied, "It's not really a system, it's just that among gays some are more prone to do the male role or the female role, 'female role' being in quotation marks." These conflicting findings point to possible differences between regional queer Chinese cultures.

A similar binary sex/gender system also exists among queer women in northwest China, although instead of differentiating between 1s and os, many members of the *lala* or lesbian community identify as Ts or Ps. Jiajia, a lesbian woman who was born in Xi'an in 1983 and cofounded UNITE, northwest China's first queer women's NGO, described how "Among lesbians, Ts belong to the more masculine category; gay men would call them tops, and Ps would be bottoms." According to Lucetta Kam, the T/P distinction originated in Taiwan, "Where *T* is classified as the masculine role and *P* (or *Po*) is the feminine role" (2013, 26 n. 4; c.f. Engebretsen

2009, 6 n. 7). Xiao Bang, another lesbian UNITE cofounder, who was born in Xi'an in 1982, told me she thought "T comes from the English word *tomboy*, that is a masculine woman. I read in an article that in Taiwan the meaning of P is 'wife' (*po*), that is, the wife of a T." Xiao Bang told me that she identified as a T, saying "Ever since I was little, I have been more like a boy."

According to my lesbian informants, the T/P distinction also involves both sexual and gendered differences, with T women often described as taking on a more active, "masculine" (*gong* 公) sexual role and P women behaving in a more feminine, "receptive" (*shou* 受) manner. Xiao Bang described the average T as someone who "acts out a more male role" that is characterized by "making money, taking care of the family, and undertaking more physical labor." Likewise, Jiajia described the stereotypical P as being more willing to cook and clean. However, the seemingly rigid binary between T and P is also more flexible than it initially appears. Queer women in northwest China also have several terms to describe lala who identify neither as T nor P, analogous to the "0.5" designation among queer men. One term is *bufen*, which literally means "to make no distinction." Kam writes that in Shanghai bufen "refers to *lalas* with an androgynous gender presentation or *lalas* who refuse to label themselves as either *T* or *P*. *Bufen* usually claims to have a more fluid desire that is not limited toward either *T* or *P*" (2013, 70 n. 13; c.f. Engebretsen 2009, 8). Another term used by queer women in northwest China is *H*, which symbolizes the middle ground between T and P due to the shape of the letter H, where two vertical lines are joined by another, smaller horizontal line.

These findings suggest that, while significant gender differences do exist between 1s and 0s or Ts and Ps, the binary nature of the queer Chinese sex/gender system should not be overstated. Queer men in northwest China often struggle to define exactly what they mean by "masculine" (*yanggang*). When I asked Xiao Feng, he replied, "It's MAN,[9] but its exact characteristics are hard to determine. Just like if you asked me how many bites of food I ate today, I wouldn't know how to respond." For Xiao Wai, being masculine meant being *zheng*, a word with a variety of meanings including serious, upright, positive, and straight. Many queer men define masculinity by describing stereotypical differences between men and women in Chinese culture. Yuanzi stated that "In China people have always regarded men as taking a more active role and women as taking a more passive role, in terms of sex, but also in terms of society." To illustrate his point, he quoted a Chinese idiom: "Men are respected, women are obedient" (*nanzun-nübei*). Other gay men define queer masculinity in terms of sexual roles and preferences. Zhiming compared 1s and 0s to *gong* (攻) and *shou* (守 or 受), saying, "*Gong* is like 1, that is to say, it represents a kind of assertiveness. Gong means 'to attack' (*gongzhan*), 'to capture' (*gongxian*), like going to war, so it represents strength." Shou, on the other hand, can mean "defend" (守) or "receive" (受).[10]

Interestingly, queer men in northwest China seem to have a much easier time describing the various qualities they associate with being feminine. Almost all my male informants believed that whether a man was a 1 or a 0 could be easily determined by observing their external appearances, including how they talked, walked, and comported themselves in daily life. "os have many characteristics," Xiao Feng said. "In general, their mannerisms are more feminine; for example, they stick out their little finger, or the way they move seems very 'soft' (*rou*). Also, their tone of voice or the way they talk is very effeminate. When they walk, they probably sway back and forth. But you can't say that this is true 100 percent of the time." Xiao Wai described how, "On the outside, many os behave in a more sissy (*C*) way, a bit more 'girly' (*niang*).[11] Also, os ordinarily need a person to hold them, take care of them, whereas 1s usually don't like that; they like to hold others, give others the feeling of being taken care of." Similarly, Xiao Shan argued that "os, for example, are usually very effeminate in their actions or the way they dress. They definitely want to be the one who is protected, and when they are penetrated, they will feel very satisfied. Regarding their bodies," he continued, "when it comes time to penetrate others, they will probably have a bit of a physical problem. But it's hard to say. Some people are really effeminate (*mu*), but they are pure tops (*chun yi*)."[12]

Among queer men in northwest China, the relationship between 1 and o is not only understood as one of difference but also one of value, with 1s and their associated masculine traits being regarded more positively and os and their imputed feminine characteristics often being the target of teasing, jokes, and sometimes even scorn and rejection by other queer men. While exaggerated or campy femininity is often playful and humorous, it also seems to point to a strong undertone of misogyny and a bias against effeminacy among many of my queer male informants in northwest China. Xiao Feng told me "I don't think C is good, it's not like being a man. There aren't a lot of people in our circle who like guys who are C." The personals section of the Tiangong website frequently contained posts with phrases like "old, ugly, or effeminate need not reply" (*lao chou mu wu rao*) or "no femmes or sissies" (*bu niang bu C*). During Tong'ai events, queer men would seldom admit that they were os in front of others. Interestingly, a similar dynamic does not seem to exist among queer women in northwest China, in that Ps are not assigned a lower social status than Ts or vice versa. Although some lala complained that Xi'an was a "T land" (*T yu*) because it contained too many Ts and told me they did not like women who were too MAN, Ts in general are not a disfavored category among queer women in the way that os often are among queer men.

A variety of tests can be used to determine whether a queer man is a 1 or a o. During fieldwork, I was often the unwitting subject of such investigations. One day, as I was walking in Xi'an with a group of gay men, one of my companions told me I had something stuck to the bottom of my shoe. I raised my right shoe up above my left knee to see what I had managed to step in but was surprised to find nothing there. This elicited hoots and howls of laughter among my informants that were intensified by my confused expression. One man explained that it was a test, and that I had done the "correct" thing; if instead I had lifted up my foot behind me, looking over my shoulder to see what was there, this would have indicated that I was C. I asked if there were other such tests, and the same man told me that my fingernails were all dirty. I gamely held my hands away from me at arm's length, palms facing outward, fingers splayed open, to investigate my nails. The man shook his head and jokingly said that I had responded in the C way—the "correct" or masculine response would have been to make two claws by curling my fingers inward, palms facing me. Yuanzi later described a similar test: "When holding a glass of water, some men will raise up their little finger, what we call 'orchid fingers' [*lanhuazhi*, a pose in Beijing opera that stresses an actor's femininity]. This is extremely effeminate; this means the person is definitely a o." Lao Wang similarly claimed you could tell if a gay man was a 1 or a o by offering him a mirror. "The 1 probably wouldn't care," he explained. "But the o would probably pay attention to the mirror, see how he looks, if his hair was messed up or if his face was dirty or whatever."

When I asked how people knew whether they themselves were a 1 or a o, some told me that they found out through similar experiments. Xiao Feng described how his friend Yangyang tested him: "I laid down on my bed, and he pressed himself down on top of me to see whether I was more prone to being passive or active. We have a saying," he continued. "'When you don't know if you are a o or a 1, you can tell from how you are in bed.' If you're passive, you're usually a o; if you're active, you're usually a 1." Others argued that whether a person is a 1 or a o depends on both innate dispositions and formative sexual experiences. Lao Wang rather sheepishly described how his identity as a 1 was confirmed when he attempted to bottom for another 1 whom he had a crush on. "After I did it," he said, "I really didn't have any of that comfortable feeling, only that extremely painful feeling." Xiao Wai said he always knew that he was a o. "Ever since I was little, I needed someone to lean on," he told me. "When having sex with my first boyfriend, he asked me whether or not I wanted to 'top' (*gong*) him, and I discovered that I couldn't, I couldn't do it at all, not even a little bit. So I knew that I was a o."

Despite the extensive and seemingly binary system of 1s and os and Ts and Ps, the queer sex/gender system in northwest China actually contains a wide spectrum of possible genders and sexualities. Many people were quick to point out that not all 1s are stereotypically masculine nor all os stereotypically feminine. Even the "versatile" role of o.5 is not fixed; as Yangyang explained me, a person can also identify as being a o.3 or a o.6: "If the number is bigger than o.5 you lean toward being the man; if the number is lesser than o.5 you lean toward being the woman." A common saying among queer men in northwest China, "sissy 1s and butch os" (*C yi meng ling*), turns the dominant sexual and gender binary inside the circle on its head. As Zhiming explained, "'C yi' means [a top who is] relatively feminine; even though he looks really effeminate in terms of his sexual role he actually is a top. And 'meng ling' means even though he looks strong, he is actually a bottom."

A similar saying, "savage Ps and femme Ts" (*ye P niang T*), exists among queer women in northwest China. Jiajia explained that the expression describes a situation in which Ts are relatively more "effeminate" (*niang*) and Ps are relatively more "savage" or "uncivilized" (*yeman'er*). "This can also be the case" among queer women, Jiajia argued, laughing. "For example, some people say that I am very effeminate; I look like a T, but when I interact with other people, I can be relatively effeminate." Jiajia argued the extent to which a queer person differentiates between T and P depends on their age. "Younger lala place a lot more emphasis on separating *T* and *P*," she said. However, she claimed, as many lala get older, they gradually rethink their position on differentiating between T and P. "If they have decided that they really are going to walk down this road, not get married or whatever, then they gradually start to rethink how two people get along together," she said. "They will consider whether two women who are together necessarily need to copy [straight people]. . . . Then they will gradually stop differentiating between T and P." Xiao Bang similarly told me that the more she understood lala culture, the less she thought of herself as a T, saying "I don't think that we should attach that kind of heterosexual model, that kind of male privilege model onto two women. I think that it isn't fair to the T." Some queer men like Zhiming also thought that people should not differentiate between 1s and 0s. "I think that it isn't so absolute," he said. "If two people extremely love one another, alternating between bottom and top really well, isn't this better? There is no need to make those kinds of distinctions."

Despite many queer activists in northwest China either complicating or completely rejecting the 1/0 or T/P binaries, their existence, and the significance of how they structured dominant and pervasive understandings of both gender and sexuality inside the circle, illustrates how the development of queer cultures in postsocialist China is not an example of historical "rupture" but rather demonstrates both cultural change and continuity around gender and sexual norms. Ideas of queer male masculinity based on regressive and exaggerated notions of gender differences between men and women and a pervasive undercurrent of misogyny among queer men in northwest China further demonstrate how being queer does not always entail being antinormative; rather, queer cultures can be complex and contradictory, challenging gender and sexual norms in some areas while reinforcing them in others.

COMRADES, GOODS, AND "THAT SORT OF PERSON": QUEER IDENTITY TERMS IN NORTHWEST CHINA

Wenqing Kang writes that at the turn of the twentieth century Chinese cultures possessed "a huge vocabulary describing male same-sex relations, and men engaged in such relations" (2009, 19). This rich vocabulary included many words derived from China's long history of same-sex sexuality, such as *duanxiupi* ("the obsession with the cut sleeve"), *fentaozhihao* ("the love of sharing a peach"), and *Longyangjun* (the name of an emperor's famous male lover). Others were slang terms, colorful euphemisms, or words borrowed from foreign languages like *nanchong* ("male favorite"), *nanse* ("male beauty"), *nanfeng* ("southern mode" or "male mode"), *xianggong* (a term used to refer to young male sex workers or Beijing opera actors who played female roles), *renyao* ("freak," "fairy," or "human prodigy"), *jijian* ("buggery" or "sodomy"), *zouhanlu* ("to take the land route"), *houtinghua* ("flowers of the rear garden"), *jiangnan zuonü* ("to use a man as a woman"), and *tongxing lian'ai* ("same-sex love" or "homosexuality") (19).

Although these words are no longer commonly used, there are still numerous expressions that denote queer identity and desire in contemporary northwest China. Several continue to be euphemisms, such as the phrase "people inside the circle" (*quan'er nei de ren*). The word *tongxinglian* or "homosexuality," which was popularized during the Republican Period, is still used by many queer people today, despite its often more negative, medicalized connotations, in addition to the term *tongzhi* ("comrade") and *huo*, a slang term meaning "goods" that seems to be unique to northwest China.[13] However, the borrowed terms *gay* and *lala* are most prevalent. Despite attempts by some cosmopolitan queer activists in Beijing to popularize the term *ku'er* ("queer") in mainland China (Bao 2018, 85–87; Rofel 2007, 103), this word is largely unused in the northwest.[14] What are the different meanings associated with these terms? Who uses them more often, why, and in what contexts? Answering these questions can help us develop a more detailed and contextualized understanding of the queer sex/gender system in northwest China.

The compound word *tongzhi* is comprised of two ideographs, *tong* ("same") and *zhi* ("goal," "spirit," or "orientation"). Sun Yat-sen, a Chinese revolutionary who helped overthrow the Qing Dynasty, famously used *tongzhi* to translate a Russian word meaning "comrades," or people who share the same revolutionary spirit and goals (H. Fang and Heng 1983, 496; A. Wong and Q. Zhang 2001, 263). However, Hongwei Bao (2018, 69) argues that the modern meaning of *tongzhi* is informed by much earlier works in classical Chinese dating back to the fourth century BCE, when it referred to "people with the same ethics and ideals." Before the 1949 Communist Revolution, *tongzhi* was widely used by both Republican and Communist cadres to express camaraderie and fellowship as well as egalitarian and revolutionary ideals (70). During the Maoist period, *tongzhi* was promoted by the state as a universal term of address to replace older titles and honorifics like "boss" (*laoban*), "sir" (*xiansheng*), and "madam" (*taitai*) that were regarded as bourgeois and feudalistic (Bao 2018, 71; Scotton and W. Zhu 1983, 479). Not only did *tongzhi* have no hierarchical, gender, or class connotations, but it was also seen as infusing ordinary speech with revolutionary fervor (Chou 2000, 1–2). *Tongzhi* gradually became a generic term of address or even an intimate greeting among friends or lovers, eventually becoming almost synonymous with "person" (H. Fang and Heng 1983, 496). However, after the death of Mao in 1976, *tongzhi* quickly declined in usage because of its old-fashioned communist connotations (Bao 2018, 72; A. Wong and Q. Zhang 2001, 264).

In 1989, during Hong Kong's first Lesbian and Gay Film Festival, two queer activists appropriated the term *tongzhi* to index a culturally specific and positive representation of Chinese same-sex eroticism and politics (Bao 2018, 73; Chou 2000, 2; A. Wong and Q. Zhang 2001, 264). Whereas Western gay and lesbian activists' appropriation of the word queer confronts the mainstream by repossessing a pejorative term, the use of tongzhi emphasizes a resistance strategy that is more focused on social harmony than on confrontation with dominant cultural and social sexual norms. According to Chou Wah-shan (2000, 2–3), tongzhi quickly became the most common word used by queer people and organizations in Hong Kong and Taiwan to describe themselves. The term later began to be adopted by queer activists and groups in mainland China, although with less visibility and more caution (X. He 2002). Tongzhi has also been taken up by the news and popular media in Hong Kong and Taiwan and, more recently, by independent and state-controlled media outlets in the PRC (A. Wong 2002).

Despite the historical and political significances of the term tongzhi, most queer activists in northwest China prefer to use gay or lala to refer to their own identities and sexualities. Contrary to previous claims in the literature, I did not find that men who self-identified as gay tended to be from younger generations "who came of age after socialism had been dismantled in China" (Rofel 2007, 87) or "after China was incorporated into the global capitalist system" (Wei 2007, 584–585). And unlike what other researchers have reported in Beijing (Zhou 2022, 288) and Shanghai (Bao 2018, 61), the use of the term gay among queer men in northwest China is not restricted to or indicative of younger, cosmopolitan, or middle-class identities. Instead, equal numbers of men from all generations and class backgrounds prefer the term gay for a variety of reasons. Although a handful of my queer male informants reported that they identified as tongxinglian, and this word was sometimes used interchangeably with tongzhi and gay, most of my informants expressed negative attitudes toward this term, which is consistent with what scholars have reported about other parts of China. At least one queer man (a member of the post-90s generation) preferred not to use tongxinglian, tongzhi, or gay to refer to his sexuality, preferring instead the more euphemistic expression "people inside the circle."

Many queer activists in northwest China who prefer tongzhi are unaware of its rich semiotic history. Tian'e, a gay fashion designer and Tong'ai volunteer who was born in 1990, told me that he preferred tongzhi not only because he felt that it lacked the discriminatory connotation of tongxinglian, but also because it was relatively "ambiguous" (hanhu) and most people outside the circle had not heard of it. Tian'e said that he also sometimes used the word gay, "but not too often. [This is] because during high school my teacher said that the English word 'gay' meant young people who misbehave and are promiscuous." Similarly, Wenqing told me that "I don't say I am tongxinglian, because in China when people hear the word tongxinglian they probably feel some antipathy. But if you say tongzhi, some people, especially older people, won't understand what it means, and younger people will recognize it but won't think about it too much." This linguistic ambiguity is a common reason why many people prefer tongzhi.[15] Wenqing said he very rarely used the word gay, but that "Inside the circle, when everyone is together in a group, chatting or playing games or things like that, [they] call each other *gay*. . . . It's like it has become colloquialized."

Queer men who prefer tongzhi often emphasize its meaning of sharing a common identity or sense of purpose. Tian'e described how for him "tongzhi means 'sharing one will and one road' (*zhitong-daohe*). Everyone is the same. Tongzhi includes people who are like me, who have the same sexual orientation, including lala, transsexuals, and transgender people. Tongzhi aren't only Chinese," he added. "I think that foreigners can also be tongzhi." Like the circle, the word tongzhi has become a way to express and imagine a universal queer identity and community not only in China but around the world. Yuanzi, who preferred tongzhi, also stressed its original meaning of "sharing a common objective." But he expressed a more nuanced and ambivalent attitude toward the term, saying, "Before, in the Maoist period, when men and women would address each other [as tongzhi] we all shared a common objective. At that time, it meant that we needed to liberate all of China, to make more people move toward happiness, move toward a better life. That's what tongzhi means." However, Yuanzi felt like tongzhi no longer held the same meaning for queer people in China today. "We gays really don't share a common objective," he argued. "Sex is probably the only common objective that we all share."

Queer men from the post-1990s generation often do not like to use the word tongzhi precisely because it still carries its earlier revolutionary meanings. Yangyang explained that "in general I use *gay*. I don't use tongzhi because the meaning of this word still hasn't completely changed over. Before, in the time of Mao, this word was used to address leaders and cadres and whatever." As with tongzhi, some queer men prefer using gay because they think that fewer people outside the circle understand what it means. Paopao said that "if there is someone nearby who doesn't know what *gay* means, then he probably doesn't understand us, or he is new. In public places most people don't know." However, other queer men prefer gay because they feel that its meaning is more well understood than tongzhi. Xiao Wai told me that he did not use tongzhi very often was because "some people, especially some older people, don't understand what tongzhi means. . . . More people understand *gay*, because, for example, a lot of literature now talks about *gay* topics." These findings underscore how even among queer activists in northwest China people from different generations and backgrounds can differ in their attitudes toward and understandings of terms like tongzhi and gay.

Many queer men prefer the term gay because it is easier to say or because they like its original meaning in English of being happy. As Yuanzi explained, "English words only have one syllable, 'gay,' or only one letter, 'G.' So people probably think it is simpler." Xiao Yu, who identified as bisexual (*shuangxinglian*), told me that "I've never used this word [gay], but if I had to choose, I would want to use *gay*, not tongzhi, because *gay* also means 'happy.'" Lao Wang said that he "doesn't understand English that much" and mainly uses gay more often because "I just see everyone else talking like this and go along with the mainstream." Xiao Kai reasoned that fewer people in northwest China used the term tongzhi compared to queer people in more cosmopolitan eastern China. "When I went to Beijing and Changsha, I discovered that more young people there use tongzhi," he told me. "I think that Xi'an is still a bit culturally backward. In more prosperous cities like Beijing, people like to use newer, more fashionable words to express themselves." Xiao Kai's remarks show how China's rich vocabulary used to describe male same-sex sexualities continues to grow and evolve over time, including how words like ku'er and tongzhi are interpreted by queer men in northwest China as indexing a certain sophisticated and cosmopolitan queer identity associated with eastern cities like Beijing and Shanghai while words like gay or euphemisms like "people inside the circle" are assigned more local or backward connotations associated with regions like northwest China.

Among queer female activists, the most common identity term is not tongxinglian or tongzhi but rather the word lala. According to Elisabeth Engebretsen, "Lala was introduced to mainland China from Taiwan through feminist and LGBTQ networking via the Internet in the late 1990s" (2009, 4 n. 2). Although Kam writes that "Lala has become a collective identity for women with same-sex desires and other non-normative gender and sexual identifications" (2013, 1), Engebretsen argues that "The word is better conceptualized as a collective umbrella term that incorporates same-sex sexual subjectivity but is not necessarily primarily defined by it" (2009, 4 n. 2). According to both the literature and my own informants in northwest China, the Chinese term lala is derived from *lazi*, a transliteration of *les*, which is itself an abbreviation of the English word "lesbian" that first originated in Taiwan. Kam argues that lala is used among lesbian women alongside other words including *les*, tongzhi, and *nütong* (a female-specific version of tongzhi). In Shanghai, Kam reports that lala and les are often used in more informal situations, whereas tongzhi "is used in more formal and political occasions where community solidarity is emphasized" (2013, 1 n. 1). However, queer female activists in northwest China use the word lala almost exclusively, rarely using other terms to refer to themselves or other queer women. "Tongzhi is more often used to describe men, gays," Jiajia explained during an interview. "Women generally call themselves lala."

So far, this discussion has focused primarily on global and national words and terms used in China to denote queer identities. However, there are also many local terms based on regional dialects and local histories that are used to connote homosexuality in China. Examples that have been discussed in the literature include "crystal" (*boli*), a local slang term for gays that is associated with Taiwan (Sang 2003, 335) but is also used in mainland China; "rabbit" (*tuzi*) in Beijing and northern China; "addiction" or "ass devil" (*pijing*) in Shanghai and southern China (Kang 2009, 37; Wei 2007, 574); "pancake" (*bingzi*) or "button" (*kouzi*) in Wuhan; and "wandering men" (*piaopiao*) in the southwest Chinese city of Chengdu (Wei 2007, 574). One regional queer identity term that has not been extensively discussed in the literature is *huo* 货, a word used inside the circle in northwest China to refer to men who are sexually and romantically attracted to other men.

The origins and significance of the term huo 货 are complex and derive from the interaction between the Shaanxi dialect and standard Chinese. The character huo has two principal sets of meanings: "currency" or "money" (*huobi*) and "goods," "merchandise," or "commodities" (*huopin*). Huo also has a third meaning when it is used to refer to people instead of things; in this case huo takes on an insulting or belittling meaning like "garbage" (*huose*) or "idiot" (*chunhuo*). Zhiming was quite interested in and knowledgeable about the etymological history of huo. He described how, in the past, instead of huo 货, queer men in northwest China used two other words, also pronounced huo 伙 and 祸, each with its own meanings. Huo 伙 is an abbreviation of the word *jiahuo*, which in standard Chinese is a colloquial expression that means "fellow" or "guy" but which carries a more negative connotation in the Shaanxi dialect, such as "rascal" or "scoundrel." Huo 祸 means "misfortune" or "disaster" (*huohai*). "If you say that someone is a huohai," Zhiming explained, "that means they are a disaster, they are no good. It's an insult, a way to yell at someone." According to Zhiming, gay men in and around Xi'an first started to use huo to refer to one another because they needed to develop a "coded language." "For example," Zhiming said, "if the two of us were talking about another person who was also gay, you would need to find another word, you couldn't say, 'He is like us, a *gay*!' That would probably draw people's suspicions, displeasure, or attacks. So they appropriated this word, [huo]." Zhiming speculated that over time, huo 伙 and 祸 were gradually replaced by huo 货, perhaps because more people were familiar with huo 货.

Recalling Wei Wei's (2007) description of the term piaopiao in Chengdu, in northwest China the queer meaning of huo (hereafter 货, unless otherwise indicated) is only understood by queer men and is not used as a derogatory term by the general population. Huo is often used in a joking, teasing, or mockingly scandalous way; referring to oneself or to another person as a huo usually triggers some snickering or wry smiles. As such, it is a playful term of queer identification that carries a distinctly local flavor and significance; because the word is only used in northwest China, when used in conversation it indexes the fact that everyone present is a local. Huo therefore contrasts with words like tongzhi and gay, which are generally understood to include all people who are attracted to others of the same sex. Although I was not able to determine exactly when the word huo 祸 started to be written as huo 货, it is intriguing to speculate that this transition may have had something to do with China's opening up and reform, in particular the development of a market economy dominated by the production and exchange of various "goods." Huo bears some similarities to the Western gay slang term "trade," which refers to a casual sexual partner who is often married, working-class, and exhibits stereotypically "masculine" features and mannerisms, and who may or may not identify as being gay but has sex with other men, possibly for money (see

Baker 2002; Humphreys 1975). However, when I heard the term spoken in north-west China, it was never used to denote a sex-for-money exchange.[16]

Apart from words like tongzhi, gay, and huo, many queer activists in northwest China use more euphemistic expressions like "people inside the circle" to refer to themselves and others. Expressions like these are useful precisely because of their degree of imprecision. Unlike saying "gay" or "homosexual," which particularly in public places or mixed settings can attract unwanted attention, simply asking whether someone is "inside the circle" is a relatively safe and discreet figure of speech that will be understood by those the speaker wishes to be understood by and is likely not to register with others. In this way, the language of the circle itself acts as a safe, anonymizing queer space. As Xiao Feng explained, "In China, to directly reveal your identity can cause a lot of pressure.... Therefore, I wouldn't use extremely taboo words to indicate that I was gay or whatever. But inside the circle, everyone is the same kind of person, so you don't need to be so secretive." When even "inside the circle" is not anonymous or general enough, other euphemistic phrases like "that sort of person" (*zheyang de ren*) or even simply "that" (*neige*) are often used to refer to other queer people. As with "inside the circle," these phrases are common in queer-only environments and contexts but can also be convenient to use in public places where a more direct discussion of homosexuality would be indiscrete. While walking down the street, or while eating in a restaurant, my male informants would frequently debate whether guys who caught their eye were "that sort of person," asking each other "Do you think he is or isn't . . . that?"

"WITCHES" AND "DISHES" AND "BEARS," OH MY! OTHER SLANG TERMS INSIDE THE CIRCLE

In addition to tongzhi, gay, and huo, people inside the circle often use a variety of other, more informal and idiomatic terms to describe and categorize one another. Two examples of such terms that are extremely common among queer men in northwest China are the synonyms *yaonü* or *yaonie*, loosely translated as "witch," that can communicate a mixture of both playful and reproachful meanings. The root word of yaonü and yaonie is *yao*, which means "evil spirit," "demon," "wicked," "bewitching," or "seductive." The character yao 妖 consists of a female radical 女 and a phonetic radical 夭 (the latter guides pronunciation); consequently, compound words containing *yao* often connote femaleness. For example, *yaojing* can mean both "evil spirit" or "demon" and "seductress" or "siren." Yaonie also carries the connotation of sin, or a person or event associated with evil or misfortune. Therefore, labeling someone as a yaonü or yaonie means describing them as evil, sinful, lecherous, or like a seductive or bewitching female monster, spirit, or demon.

Unlike the Western archetypal image of an ugly, warty old woman riding a broomstick and wearing a black pointy hat, yaonü and yaonie are portrayed in Chinese popular culture as young, beautiful, coquettish, and mischievous characters in period drama TV series like *Schemes of a Beauty* that many of my queer male informants in northwest China watch and that serve as fertile sources for colloquial gay kinship terms and expressions.[17] Because the feminine beauty and vampish mannerisms of such characters as well as their dangerous hypersexuality all resonate with attributes of gay men who are considered C or "femme" (*niang*), yaonü and yaonie were quickly adapted by queer men in northwest China as joking and reproachful epithets for one another.

According to Judith Zeitlin, the word *yao* and related terms and expressions have a long history of association in China with male same-sex sexuality, androgyny, and gender changes or reversals. The term *renyao* was used in philosophical and historical writings as early as the third century BCE to refer to human freaks or monsters as well as to describe female or male impersonators who were regarded as omens of political unrest and instability caused by an excess of *yin*, negative feminine energy that in Daoist philosophy is regarded as the opposite of *yang*, positive masculine energy. "For example," Zeitlin writes, "a commentary to the *Book of Changes* states: 'When a woman metamorphoses into a man, this means that *yin* is thriving and a base person is on the throne; when a man metamorphoses into a woman, this mean that *yin* has prevailed over *yang*, and it is responsible for the fall [of the dynasty]'" (Kang 2009, 33). Kang writes that in the early 1900s "the prevalent understanding of renyao was one of men and women who appeared as the opposite gender, representing a potential threat to society and a bad omen for the country" (34). Examples included intersex people, cross-dressers, actors who impersonated female characters in Peking opera, and "any men who behaved and dressed in a feminine fashion and had sex with other men" (34). These historical meanings likely inform contemporary understandings of yaonü and yaonie among queer men in northwest China, where, in addition to being a way to jokingly put on exaggerated displays of seductive femininity, they are also used to deliver mild expressions of rebuke or chastisement.

One afternoon at the Tong'ai office when Yuanzi was in a particularly cynical mood, he kept calling the younger volunteers yaonü who were always "throwing themselves at one guy or another" (*pu lai pu qu*). The volunteers all laughed and brushed off his remarks. But under the humor I detected a vein of seriousness. For the past several days, Yuanzi had been openly worrying about the potentially negative health effects of sexual promiscuity among young gay volunteers and lamenting his inability to "subdue" (*shoufu*) them.[18] Others also feared that there were too many yaonie inside the circle. Xiao Shan often fretted about there being an "excess of yin" among queer men in Xi'an and the effects that long-term exposure to this imbalance might have on his own masculinity. One day Xiao Shan suddenly emerged from the bathroom at the Tong'ai office, where he had been gazing at himself in the mirror. With a perturbed expression, he melodramatically wailed, "*Aiya*, I don't know how this is happening; I am getting more and more C! I didn't use to be this C, I used to be really masculine. . . . These days there is too much yin energy in this circle. . . . It's contagious. . . . The longer you stay the more C you get." Such exaggerated mimicking of femininity, the linking of femininity and yin energy to sexual promiscuity, and understandings of femininity as contagious are further examples of the undercurrent of misogyny that is often present among queer men in northwest China.[19]

A common way for queer men in northwest China to describe other men they are sexually attracted to is to refer to them as a "dish" (*cai*). This usage of "dish" resembles the word "type" in English, as in "he is my type," except in northwest China this is expressed by saying "he is my dish" (*ta shi wo de cai*) or "he is the kind of dish I like to eat" (*ta shi wo xihuan chi de cai*). The act of looking for cute guys to hook up with is frequently referred to by queer men as "looking for a little dish" (*zhao caicai*).[20] This bears an interesting resemblance to Polari, an argot spoken in some urban queer communities in the United Kingdom from the beginning of the twentieth century to the 1970s, in which food metaphors were used to indicate sexual attraction and the word "dish" denoted a particularly attractive man or the anus (Baker 2002, 172). Despite some differences in the meanings and usage of the word "dish" in these two queer subcultures, it is nonetheless striking to see how two very different societies at different times came up with such similar slang terms.

Queer men in northwest China also use a unique animal-based, nonbinary classificatory system to categorize each another as either monkeys (*houzi*), baboons (*feifei*), or bears (*xiong*), based upon their physical appearance and body type as well as the type of men they find attractive. As Yuanzi laughingly explained it to me, "This group of people is very thin; they give people the impression that they are just like monkeys, because monkeys are thin. This group of people is really fat and chubby, like bears, like grizzly bears. This group of people looks really strong and robust, just like a baboon, really muscular. So, they are baboons."[21]

According to my queer male informants, this system of classifying gay men into three animal-based categories became popular in northwest China around 2005. In addition to describing the way people look, the monkey/baboon/bear triad is also used to describe the kind of body type that people find most attractive. Although many of my informants espoused the idea that "opposites attract," reflected in sayings such as "bear-monkey love" (*xiong hou lian*), there also existed instances of "monkey-monkey love" (*hou hou lian*) and "bear-bear love" (*xiong xiong lian*).[22] Similar to the phenomenon of 0.5, the monkey-baboon-bear classificatory grid is not absolute; people who blur the lines between categories are described as "meaty monkeys" (*rou hou*) and "skinny bears" (*shou xiong*). I also heard one instance of a relatively large and hairy man being described as a "hairy bear" (*maomao xiong*), which somewhat resembles how in North American gay culture different animals such as bears, cubs, and otters are used to refer to different archetypes of queer men. Queer slang terms like witches, dishes, monkeys, baboons, and bears are sources of much mirth and merriment inside the circle and shed further light on northwest China's unique and complex queer sex/gender system.

NORTHWEST CHINA'S CONTRADICTORY AND CHANGING QUEER CULTURE

By listening to the stories of four generations of queer activists in northwest China, including how they discovered their sexualities and created queer social networks, the various sexual and gendered binaries they deploy to shape queer culture and identity, and the language they use to describe and express themselves and their relationships, we can start to develop a deeper and more nuanced appreciation of what it means to be queer in postsocialist China. Throughout this discussion, I have sought to emphasize the complexity, richness, and often contradictory nature of queer culture in northwest China. Rather than asking "What does it mean to be gay in China?" (Kong 2011, 146), this chapter instead explores how, even within one region of China at one relatively brief point in time, there exists a multitude of different ways of being gay and lesbian, and what it means to be queer and Chinese is in a constant state of flux.

The stories in this chapter depict a dynamic and changing local gay and lesbian culture in northwest China. This queer sex/gender system is neither a complete continuation nor a total rupture with traditional Chinese attitudes toward gender and sexuality, many of which remain highly influential in the present. Similarly, current beliefs and practices around queerness in China are neither entirely similar nor different from those elsewhere, but instead represent complex legacies of traditional Chinese cultural attitudes toward and understandings of gender and sexuality as well as localized interpretations and translations of Western or transnational queer practices. The result is a unique local sex/gender system that combines elements of both the past and present and of local, national, and global queer cultures.

The next chapter will continue this investigation into northwest China's unique sex/gender system by examining how queer men look for love, intimacy, affection, and a sense of familial belonging in the face of enduring social gender and sexual norms and expectations, including getting married and having children. It will consider the effect that these pressures have on the intimate romantic lives of queer men and their experiences and understandings of love, as well as the various strategies men from different generations adopt to deal with "the marriage problem" and "coming out" to their families. It will also explore the ways that queer men seek to create alternative familial spaces and relationships through the development of elaborate, humorous, and heartfelt queer kinship networks.

3 · "FALLING LEAVES RETURN TO THEIR ROOTS"

Queer Love, Kinship, and Personhood

Originally a Western holiday, Valentine's Day has become increasingly popular in postsocialist China, where it is called *Qingren Jie* or "The Lovers' Festival." One Valentine's Day I sat with six queer Chinese men inside a private room in a crowded teahouse near the Xi'an city center. The thin door and walls of our room temporarily created a small, fragile space inside which we could let our guard down and indulge in the sometimes effeminate mannerisms and playful patois of those inside the circle. We spread ourselves out on a couch and several chairs that were clustered around two tables, one covered in mahjong tiles and another with small white plates of savory snacks like seasoned sunflower seeds and salty dried green beans, compliments of the establishment. A waitress periodically blustered in and out to refill our teapot with fresh hot water; each time she entered, our casual chatter was interrupted as we froze and waited for the embarrassed server to leave, closing the door behind her and restoring our modest partition against the outside world.

Our conversation quickly turned to love, family, and the "marriage problem" (*jiehun wenti*), a phrase that queer men in northwest China use to describe the pressures they invariably experience from their parents and the wider society during their mid-to-late twenties to get married and have children. I revealed that it was my ten-year anniversary and said how much I missed my boyfriend, who was waiting for me back in the States. When Xiao Hei, a middle-aged gay AIDS activist from Xinjiang, asked me if I was surprised by how "tolerant" (*baorong*) Chinese society was of homosexuality, Zhengzheng, a gay businessman from Xi'an in his early thirties, objected, arguing that society placed too much "pressure" (*yali*) on gay men. Zhengzheng's brows furrowed as he described how even in rare cases when your parents did not pressure you to get married, you must nevertheless put pressure on yourself, because Chinese people always put their parents' needs first. Although he spoke in general terms, Zhengzheng's anguished expression suggested that he was speaking from personal experience.

Zhengzheng argued that there are two main reasons why gay men in China must get married. The first is what he called "the economic problem" (*jingji wenti*): When you are old, who will support you? Not many people can save enough money to support themselves when they are elderly, he contended. The second reason, he continued, is that when you are old, have no children, and your parents have already passed away, won't you be lonely? Left unspoken was an understanding that relationships between queer men are unable to last a lifetime. "Love is a matter between two people; marriage is a matter between society, between family," Zhengzheng concluded, suggesting a worldview in which queer love is narrower, more individualistic and transient, whereas heterosexual marriage's social significance gives it a longer shelf life. Zhengzheng remarked on how it is difficult for two gay men to stay together for very long. After a long moment of silence while we all sipped our tea, Zhengzheng suddenly said, "Being in love is just like brewing tea: the more times you add water to the same cup, the weaker the flavor; the longer you are together with someone, the weaker your love."

The door suddenly opened again, and Lao Wang, a forty-six-year-old gay Tong'ai volunteer, entered the room along with Xiao Shan, a Tong'ai staff member in his early thirties. Lao Wang, who had recently started dating Xiao Hei, carried a bouquet of red roses wrapped in blue tissue paper and accented with white baby's-breath blossoms. The flowers had recently been misted with water, and the dark green leaves of the roses glistened with dew, looking as young and fresh as the love between Lao Wang and Xiao Hei. As Xiao Hei delightedly accepted his gift, I noticed that the bouquet contained only eleven roses. When I asked Lao Wang why, he quoted two Chinese idioms, *yisheng-yishi* ("one life, one world") and *yixin-yiyi* ("one heart, one wish"), to explain how the number eleven signifies feelings of eternal love and unending devotion. Considering this unabashed display of queer romance, I could not help but ask the group if Zhengzheng's earlier analogy between being in love and brewing tea was not a bit pessimistic. With an even expression, Xiao Hei replied that Zhengzheng was not being pessimistic but simply realistic: in northwest China no one's parents would approve of their son being in a relationship with another man. Seeing my dismayed expression, Xiao Shan laughed and said, "Casey is so innocent, he's more innocent than all of you, even if he is from the U.S."

⌒

This chapter examines notions and practices of love, kinship, and personhood among four generations of queer male activists in northwest China. As the preceding ethnographic vignette illustrates, even in an era of rapid social change in which queer people are increasingly participating in global rituals of romantic love like giving one's boyfriend a bouquet of roses on Valentine's Day, many queer men in northwest China nevertheless continue to experience same-sex love and relationships as inherently short-lived. While the existence of queer people is sometimes offered as an example of a postsocialist turn toward individualism and the privatization of marriage and family, this chapter explores how and why some queer men in northwest China struggle to reconcile their queer identities with their deeply felt moral obligations to parents and family, often articulating apparently anachronistic desires that harken back to previous socialist or traditional values of self-sacrifice and filial piety. What are we to make of these seemingly contradictory queer experiences of love and kinship? What might they reveal not only about what it means to be queer in a city like Xi'an today, but also about the limits and extent of changing ideas of family and personhood in Chinese culture and society more broadly? What, if anything, is specifically queer about moments and tensions like these?

Since the 1990s, anthropologists and sociologists have documented the spread of romantic love and companionate marriage around the world (Cole and Thomas 2009; Giddens 1992; Jankowiak and Fischer 1992; Padilla et al. 2007). Such changes in notions and experiences of love and intimacy are often linked to social and economic processes associated with globalization and modernity, including the development of increasingly individualized personhoods and the spread of market capitalism and commodity consumption (Wardlow and Hirsch 2006). A similar shift is occurring in postsocialist China as ideals of romantic love and free marriage that were valorized during the 1919 May Fourth Movement are again being promoted by the state. Many scholars argue that notions of personhood and sexuality are changing as China becomes more privatized and individualistic (D. Davis 2014; Ong and L. Zhang 2008; Yan 2009). Arthur Kleinman et al. (2011) suggest that selfish individualism is increasingly celebrated in China as "the previous socialist sentiment of class consciousness" is replaced by "a postsocialist sensibility of personal desires" (4). Deborah Davis and Sara Friedman similarly describe an ongoing "deinstitutionalization" of marriage and sexuality in which Chinese citizens are experiencing "new possibilities for marital and sexual satisfaction" (2014, 4). Citing increasing rates of premarital and extramarital sex, a resurgence of prostitution and pornography, and the increasing visibility of homosexuality (Farrer 2002, 2014; Farrer and Sun 2003; Sun, Farrer, and Choi 2006), some scholars even argue that China is undergoing a "sexual revolution" (D. Davis 2014; E. Zhang 2011).

By the 2000s and 2010s, there seemed to be a scholarly consensus that the personal interests and private desires of children in postsocialist China now take precedence over the needs and expectations of parents and ancestors. The work of Yunxiang Yan, who argues that "desires and personal freedom have become so important in everyday negotiation and contestation among family members that an individual would be unlikely to sacrifice his or her interests simply for the sake of reproducing the family" (2003, 6–7), is perhaps most associated with this thesis. In his sweeping and authoritative body of research on the privatization and individualization of kinship and personhood in reform-era China, Yan describes a "changing moral landscape" (2011, 36) marked by a "shift of moral emphasis from family responsibilities and self-sacrifice to individual rights and self-realization" (46), which he argues amounts to a "challenge to the conventional way of doing person-hood" in Chinese society (2017, 10–11; see also Kleinman et al. 2011, 11; E. Zhang 2011, 124).[1]

Yet in recent years many scholars including Yan have begun to articulate more nuanced understandings of changing notions and practices of personhood and kinship in postsocialist China. Rather than being simply abandoned, Yan now argues that filial piety has been redefined as a kind of "descending familism" in which parents no longer expect "unconditional obedience and submission" from their children but instead work to build relationships of "intergenerational inti-macy" in which the focus of both parents and children has shifted "from ancestors to grandchildren" (2016, 246). More recently, Yan and others have described this shift as a kind of "neo-familism" that "emphasizes family solidarity and intergen-erational dependency as well as the ethical value of self-sacrifice" (Yan and Wei 2021, 454). Rose Keimig (2021) similarly reports a renegotiation of filial piety among Chinese parents in elder care homes that emphasizes harmony, balance, and benev-olence between generations, rather than hierarchy, reciprocity, and obligation.

In this chapter, I build on this work by exploring understandings and prac-tices of love, kinship, and personhood among queer men in northwest China. The experiences and choices of queer men complicate previous arguments about the privatization and individualization of kinship and personhood in postsocialist China. Preserving the newfound intimacy between parents and queer children often requires the latter to sacrifice any hope of long-term same-sex love or the open expression of individual queer personhoods. Unable or unwilling to "come out" (chugui) to their parents, the vast majority of queer men in northwest China are already married or plan on marrying and having children in order to uphold tradi-tional notions of filial piety. I argue that, like many people outside the circle, queer Chinese men experience romantic intimacy as existing along a processual contin-uum, with passionate or sexual love at one end of the spectrum and its denoue-ment, familial or affectionate love, at the other. However, due to a lack of support and recognition of queer relationships, many queer men in northwest China regard same-sex love as essentially impermanent, unable to last longer than a few months or years. Even as many queer men in northwest China are fashioning new, alternative forms of intimacy and queer kinship by engaging in "contract marriages" (xinghun) with lesbian women or by developing elaborate "gay fami-lies" (tongzhi jiazu) with one another, these forms of fictive kinship are also seen by queer men as fleeting and even frivolous, not as replacements or substitutes for the biological family or lineage, which are permanent and indispensable.

Because of their sensitivity to traditional family values, the lives and experi-ences of queer activists are an excellent barometer of changing attitudes toward kinship and personhood in postsocialist China. As Sarah Lamb observes in her research on single women in India, "those who depart from the conventional path of marriage are also situated outside of a familiar social identity, and from that position they speak penetratingly about their society's social-cultural norms"

(2017, 64). Indeed, queer experiences of love, kinship, and personhood reveal how, while many heterosexual children in postsocialist China may be able to pursue their individual happiness and still be regarded by themselves and their parents as filial, things are much more complicated for queer children, who often have to choose between embracing their own queer desires and identities or sacrificing them in order to retain intimate and filial relationships with parents. Queer sons in northwest China almost invariably choose the latter. Thus, rather than being wholly redefined or renegotiated, filial piety continues to require obedience and submission to parents to the extent that queer children are still expected to remain in the closet, get married, and have children of their own. Rather than serving as examples of increasing individualism, queer men instead demonstrate the enduring importance of relational personhoods in postsocialist China.

Despite a growing body of ethnographic research on queer cultures and communities in the PRC, queer practices and experiences of love and kinship remain relatively understudied given their potential to inform scholarly understandings of changing families and personhoods in the postsocialist period. Because northwest China can be more socially conservative, queer culture in the region serves as a useful foil for queer cultures in the northeast and southeast, which are often more progressive and internationalized. For example, scholars report that in Taiwan (Brainer 2019), Shanghai, and Guangzhou (Yan and Wei 2021) so-called "rainbow parents" have become increasingly supportive of their queer children, sometimes even coming out themselves and publicly advocating for gay rights. This is not the case in northwest China, where the vast majority of my queer informants are not able to be out to their parents, and those who were out often discovered that their parents still expected them to get married and have children. These differences show how queer Chinese cultures can vary dramatically from one region to another and add further nuance to changing understandings of love, kinship, and personhood in postsocialist China. These experiences also inform ongoing debates in queer studies over the relationship between queerness and normativity. By respectfully considering the seemingly normative priorities and perspectives of queer men in northwest China around marriage and family rather than dismissing them as examples of homonormativity, I demonstrate how queer anthropology can act as a corrective for a queer theory that often simply equates queerness with antinormativity.

FAMILY, COMING OUT, AND THE MARRIAGE PROBLEM

By their mid-to-late twenties, queer people in northwest China experience increasing pressure from parents, family members, friends, and even coworkers to get married and have children. Known inside the circle as the "marriage problem," this pressure usually peaks at the age of thirty and affected almost all my informants, regardless of their gender or class backgrounds. While Travis Kong (2011, 160) suggests this pressure is perhaps felt especially acutely by queer men as they have traditionally been responsible for "continuing the family line" (*chuanzong-jiedai*), other scholars point out that queer Chinese women also experience a pressure that is no less acute and may in many cases be even more restrictive of their personal desires and autonomy.[2] Because the data I collected on queer experiences of love, kinship, and personhood in northwest China mainly came from my male-identified research participants, in this chapter I focus on their experiences.

The marriage problem is closely linked to traditional understandings of gender, kinship, and personhood, which are in turn related to norms and expectations of filial piety (*xiao*), the Confucian ideal that children are obligated to support, revere, and obey their parents; continue the family line; and avoid creating family conflicts (Ikels 2004). Because of China's former one-child policy, a birth planning program implemented from 1979–2021, many younger queer Chinese people have no siblings, which only increases the social pressures they face. Kong observes that marriage and childbirth not only act as sources of "moral privilege and access to social and material power" but are also a "precondition for becoming a successful citizen" (2011, 159). Similarly, Lisa Rofel argues that traditional notions of filial piety continue to inform contemporary understandings of what it means to be a morally responsible adult, as family remains "the metonym for belonging, not simply to the nation-state but to Chinese culture writ large" (2007, 100).

Queer men in northwest China frequently emphasize the profound importance of family in their lives as well as the deep feelings of love, duty, and obligation they feel toward their parents. Xiao Feng, who was born in 1991, told me, "Family is very important. Our families give us support and assistance, economically, spiritually, and psychologically. Our parents dote on us, forgive us, make us feel like the family is a harbor of love." Xiao Shan, who was born in 1981, shared this understanding of the family as a place of protection against the outside world. "The Chinese [character for] family (*jia* 家) has the roof of a house," he told me. "The meaning of this is that it will protect you, keep you from harm, keep you from the cold, the heat, the wind, the rain. . . . Inside [a family] everyone has a feeling of security." These feelings are particularly strong among younger queer men who were born in the 1980s and 1990s, whose accounts of warm familial affection and intimacy are usually absent among older generations of queer men who were born or grew up during the Cultural Revolution.

For many queer men, the feelings of love and security they associate with their families of origin come with a profound sense of debt and responsibility to parents. Yangyang, a gay university student in Xi'an who was born in 1992, said, "I think that family is indispensable. It wasn't easy for your parents to give birth to you, and it also wasn't easy for them to raise you. I feel that repaying your parents is as it should be." For Xiao Wai, another gay student who was also born in 1992, having a good relationship with family is very important. "China has an old expression, 'falling leaves return to their roots' (*luoye-guigen*)," he told me. "Family is the one thing Chinese people care about the most." Other expressions I often heard queer men in northwest China recite include "out of a hundred virtues, being filial comes first" (*bai shan xiao wei xian*) and "there are three ways of being a bad son: the most serious is to have no heir" (*bu xiao you san, wu hou wei da*). The ubiquity of such sayings underscores how traditional ideas of family and filial piety remain central to understandings of personhood and morality among younger queer men even in the postsocialist period.

As they approach their thirties, many queer men in northwest China find that parental pressure to get married becomes increasingly acute and more difficult to evade. In some cases, this unyielding pressure eventually causes queer men to rethink their opposition to marriage. Yuanzi, who was about to turn thirty, shared that his feelings regarding marriage had changed as he grew older. "I thought that a person should be relatively free, go out, go to other places, travel to other cities," he said. "I wanted to live my own life like that. . . . But now, those of us in this crowd who are twenty-seven or twenty-eight are just starting to face the marriage problem." When I asked him what changed his mind, he described the pressures from family that men his age face: "Everyone constantly thinks that you ought to get married. Especially your parents and relatives. If you don't get married, everyone nags you." Laughing ruefully as he described several ill-fated attempts his mother had made to set him up with various women, Yuanzi said, "It's mostly because of this that I feel like, forget it, I might as well get married. . . . Because, after all, your parents are your parents, there's nothing we can do. It's impossible for us to fight with them, fight over a few little things until everyone is unhappy." Yuanzi's sentiment, which is widely shared among queer men his age in northwest China, underscores how queer children often sacrifice their own desires and happiness in order to preserve relationships of intimacy and filial piety with parents.

Early on in my fieldwork, I did not understand when my queer informants told me that they had no choice but to get married. Why couldn't they just refuse to marry, I wondered? Wouldn't parents eventually be forced to accept this decision? My informants dismissed such suggestions as dangerously naïve. As Yuanzi explained, if you don't get married your parents "will be very upset. They will worry that you are not happy. They will worry that if you don't get married now, if you don't have a son, if you don't have medical or old-age insurance, what will you do when you get old? You will be very lonely." Experiences like this reveal how a shift in understandings of filial piety from making parents happy to making children happy can often be more complicated for queer children to navigate. Instead of prioritizing their own happiness and desires, most of my queer informants in northwest China choose to marry and have children in order to prevent parents from worrying about them.

In rare cases when queer sons refuse to get married, parents often "force" (*qiangpo*) them to marry by becoming depressed, refusing to eat, or even threatening to hurt or kill themselves. One Tong'ai volunteer recounted how, when he had told his parents that he was not going to get married, his mother grabbed a kitchen knife and threatened to stab herself unless he changed his mind. Stories like these, which are relatively common, demonstrate the lengths to which some

Chinese parents will go to enforce traditional familial and gendered expectations on their queer children.

Even when queer sons do manage to come out to their parents, this usually does not resolve the marriage problem. Parents often find it easier to accept their sons' homosexuality than to accept that he will never marry or have children. This point was driven home to me one spring evening when I was having dinner with two queer men before a Tong'ai activity. As we ate our wonton soup at the side of the road in the cool night air, one of my companions, a young man called Xiao Niu, recounted how he discovered his mother knew that he was gay during a recent argument at their home. His mother had said to him, "You're just afraid that I know!" "What is it that I am afraid you know?" he demanded. "You are afraid that I know you are *gay!*" she replied. After a long silence, Xiao Niu's mother poured them both a drink. "Now that you know, aren't you sad?" Xiao Niu asked his mother, to which she replied, "What's the use of being sad?" Xiao Niu smiled wryly as he finished telling the story. Then his face slowly slid into a frown, and he sighed, "But I still have to get married." Stories like these indicate the enduring power of traditional beliefs regarding family, filial piety, and marriage among queer men in postsocialist northwest China.

Understandings and practices of coming out in northwest China also attest to the continued importance of parents and family among queer men. Most of my queer informants define coming out as being open about their homosexuality to their immediate social networks, including friends, coworkers, and family members. Unlike many queer people in the West, who see coming out as a neces- sary step toward self-acceptance and an important political strategy to combat homophobia (Boellstorff 2005, 17; Weston 1991, 44–47), my queer informants in northwest China describe coming out as a highly personal tactic in managing their relationships with people outside the circle. Younger queer men in particular often stress the negative effects that coming out might have on their families, especially the pain and worry that such news might cause parents.

Most discussions of coming out focus on whether, when, and how to tell one's parents, as if other aspects of coming out are of secondary importance. As Xiao Kai, who was born in 1984, said, "In China the standard for coming out is telling your parents, because the concepts of family and marriage are really strong. After you tell your parents, the pressure should go down a lot. I haven't directly told my parents. I've indirectly told them through my behavior and other things that I like boys." Xiao Kai's coming out strategy resembles that of many queer men in north- west China and involves a lot of preparation as well as the hope that carefully dropped hints or objects like gay movies or magazines will raise the subject indi- rectly, rather than forcing a confrontation. Shuzhen Huang and Daniel C. Brouwer (2018) theorize that such tactics allow "coming home" to or "coming with" the family, as opposed to coming out, as the latter runs the risk of endangering rela- tionships between parents and queer children, and the former prioritizes finding ways to accommodate queer desire and identity while maintaining strong family relationships. Indeed, while some of my younger queer male informants were out to a few close friends or classmates, almost none had directly discussed their sexualities with family members, especially their parents.[3]

A lack of legal protections and widespread workplace discrimination also make it difficult for many queer people in northwest China to come out. Especially in state-owned enterprises, great care must be taken to prevent accidental or unwanted disclosure of one's queer identity. "State-owned enterprise culture is extremely traditional. Once men reach a certain position, they must get married," said Xiao Kai, who worked for a state-owned utility company. "There is no way that I can let my workplace know about my identity, or else I would probably lose my job." The danger of workplace discrimination is also very real for queer employees of private companies. Xiao Shan lost his job at a travel agency when coworkers found materials on his computer related to his queer activism at Tong'ai. The experience gave him a rather nuanced view of the closet, which he did not see in terms of a strict in/out dichotomy. "After you open that closet door and come out, I think you can go back inside when you run into danger," he told me. "You don't need to lock the closet door after you leave it." Xiao Shan's perspective underscores that strategic decisions about how and whether to come out of the closet should not be viewed only in negative or repressive terms. Instead, as Steven Seidman et al. argue, "Closet practices might also be seen as productive, as they not only avoid the risks of unintended exposure, but also create a protected social space that permits individuals to fashion gay selves and to navigate paths between the straight and gay worlds" (Kong 2011, 107).[4]

When they cannot delay getting married any longer, queer men in northwest China have two options: entering into a "fraudulent marriage" (*pianhun*) with a heterosexual woman or negotiating a "contract marriage" (*xinghun*) with a lesbian woman. Marrying a heterosexual woman affords some queer men the chance to have biological children and thus to alleviate another form of parental pressure that ensues immediately after marriage: the production of grandchildren. Many married men attempt to maintain a hidden queer sexual and social life, a choice they often rationalize by referring to traditional Chinese attitudes toward marriage that downplay conjugal love and intimacy and emphasize the importance of finding a "suitable" (*heshi*) partner. However, new ideologies of romantic love and companionate marriage in postsocialist China have made this strategy more difficult for queer men and also more painful for their heterosexual wives, many of whom likely expect a companionate marriage and instead find themselves trapped inside a loveless union (Chou 2000, 103; J. Zhu 2018, 1079).[5]

Queer men in northwest China justify their decisions to marry and have children in a variety of ways. Many declare that "love is not the same thing as marriage" and argue that, due to feelings of guilt, queer men "treat their wives even better" than straight men. That queer men "have no way out" (*mei banfa*) is a constant refrain in their conversations about marriage, which tend to focus more on their own feelings of frustration and guilt than on how mixed-orientation marriages might affect others.[6] Although it may be tempting to interpret this discourse as a symptom of selfish individualism, during my fieldwork I gradually came to understand how, for many queer men in northwest China, getting married and having children is not seen as a voluntary, selfish act but rather as a moral imperative of filial piety and relational personhood. Queer men are acutely aware of how mixed-orientation marriages can negatively affect not only themselves but also their wives and children, especially when they end in divorce.

Older married queer men who have children frequently find that instead of alleviating social pressures, marriage only brings with it a whole new set of problems. According to Wenqing, who was born in 1972, despite the tremendous pressure he faced from family and friends to get married, the pressures he felt after marriage were even greater. "When you haven't yet married the pressure is very small," he told me. "But after you get married you must be responsible to your family. Furthermore, if you have children, you also need to be responsible to them. As for your wife, you must be responsible to her, too. . . . Caring for her, preserving harmony in the family—this all requires responsibility." After Wenqing finished speaking, a sorrowful expression came over his face. "It would have been better if I didn't get married," he said. Wenqing's repeated use of the word "responsibility" (*zeren*) emphasizes how, far from embracing a privatized, selfish individualism, queer men in northwest China continue to keenly feel their obligations to parents and family, demonstrating the durability of relational personhoods in the postsocialist period.

Many older queer men express regret about getting married. Lao Wang, who was born in 1965, got married when he was twenty-six years old. "Back then it wasn't a matter of wanting to get married or not," he said, "because we were born right at the end of the Cultural Revolution when China was still closed off." For Lao Wang, marriage was "a way to prove to other people that you are a normal person, that you aren't different or whatever. It's also a way to conceal yourself. But if I were young now," Lao Wang continued, "I definitely wouldn't choose to get married." "Why?" I asked. "It's really very exhausting," he replied. "For example, your wife; at minimum it is extremely unfair to your wife." With an anguished expression, Lao Wang told me how he had recently quit his construction job to become a full-time caregiver to his wife, who was suffering from kidney disease. Although this work was exhausting, Lao Wang thought it was a way for him to make amends to his wife: "I felt like after all these years, I had really wronged her," he explained. "She wants me to be by her side, to prepare meals for her, to do whatever for her. It gives her a lot of joy, makes her feel a kind of satisfaction, that I am faithful to her." Stories like this reveal how, far from being simple acts of selfish individualism, marrying and having children only increase queer men's familial duties. Such accounts also underscore how queer men in northwest China continue to experience marriage and fatherhood as fundamental moral obligations that require them to sacrifice their own private desires in order to fulfill their duties to parents and family.

Given older queer men's negative experiences of marriage and fatherhood, I was surprised by how many younger queer men in northwest China actively desire to get married and have children. While some declare that they will not get married and criticize older married queer men for doing so, most queer men from the post-90s generation plan on getting married, although they intend to delay this for as long as possible. Even in the postsocialist period, many parents' understandings of homosexuality and expectations regarding marriage and childbirth have not changed significantly. As Xiao Feng explained, "Because my parents are very traditional, they can't accept the fact of homosexuality. Therefore, in the future I will have no choice but to get married." Like many younger queer men in northwest China, although Xiao Feng felt he had no choice in the matter, he also found some aspects of marriage appealing. "People probably want to get married because of China's tradition of 'holding grandchildren' (*bao sunzi*)," he said. "I have also been influenced by tradition; I want to get married and have a son, to be accountable to my parents." Xiao Feng's remarks, which are not uncommon among younger queer men in northwest China, illustrate the enduring appeal of an idealized model of old age as "[living] a happy family life surrounded by sons and grandsons (*tianlun zhile, ersun raoxi*)" (H. Zhang 2009, 215).

Many younger queer men in northwest China express desires to marry and have children that they do not attribute solely to parental or social pressures. For them, marriage offers the promise of a life-long, stable, committed relationship that many feel is impossible to find inside the circle.[7] "I really want to [get married]," Xiao Shan told me. "I really wish that I could attain a little piece of real— I don't know if you could call it love—what I mean is having someone who really cares about me, who really loves me, and spending the rest of our lives together, like two clasped hands. When she is in difficulty or is sick, I can take care of her, and she can also take care of me. This is much better than two people being alone." The fear of ending up alone and abandoned in old age, without anyone to love or care for, is something younger queer men often mention during discussions of the marriage problem. Such fears were very real for Yuanzi, who earned a meager ¥1,500 ($220) a month working at Tong'ai and had no retirement savings. "What will we do when we get old?" he asked me rhetorically. "We don't have old-age insurance. We're not in business or making a lot of money that we can hoard for ourselves. If we don't have any of that, once we get old, we will be truly miserable." Anxiety about old-age care is not limited to queer men but reflects wider social unease about how to care for the elderly in a postsocialist period characterized by rising economic inequality, a rapidly aging population, skyrocketing medical costs, and declining rates of family care (Keimig 2021; H. Zhang 2009). However, queer people may feel such anxieties more acutely as they contemplate a future without children.

For many queer men in northwest China, fears about the possible consequences of not getting married and having children extend beyond old age into the afterlife. Paopao, a devout Buddhist, told me he feared that "If you don't find a girl, get married, and have children, in your next life you will be reborn as a cow or a horse. [Only] if you have children will you be reborn as a person."

FIGURE 3.1. Yuanzi and his older brother cleaning their ancestral tomb. Photo by author.

Such beliefs are fairly common among my queer informants, many of whom are Buddhist. One year, Yuanzi invited me to accompany him, his mother, and his older brother as they visited and cleaned their ancestors' graves during the Tomb Sweeping Festival (*Qingming Jie*). Buildings and people grew sparser as we left behind the dusty outskirts of Xi'an in a rented minivan. We finally arrived at the tomb of Yuanzi's paternal great-grandparents, a large, circular mound of yellow earth in the middle of a waving green field of wheat that was covered with weeds and marked by a tall black tombstone. I helped Yuanzi pull weeds while his older brother shored up the mound with a shovel, then watched as they burned colorful paper offerings to their ancestors (figure 3.1). We drove back to the city in silence, Yuanzi staring pensively out the window. Finally, he turned to me and said, "Who doesn't hope that one day, when they are dead, their children and grandchildren will come and sweep their graves, like we did today?" Such sentiments complicate claims about the privatization and individualization of postsocialist China by demonstrating the enduring importance of traditional views and practices of filial piety and relational personhood, even or especially among queer men.

"EASY COME, EASY GO": PASSION, INTIMACY, AND THE IMPERMANENCE OF QUEER LOVE

One manifestation of the tension many queer men in northwest China feel between their individual sexual desires and their filial obligations to parents is the contradictory ways that they experience same-sex love. During my fieldwork, almost all of my queer male informants expressed a desire to "fall in love" (*tanlian'ai*) and have a long-term romantic and sexual relationship with another man. However, most of them were single, and almost none were in long-term relationships. Those who had boyfriends seemed smitten and expressed tender hopes that they would be able to stay together indefinitely. At the same time, there seemed to exist an almost universally held belief that, unlike straight relationships supported by the heteronormative institutions of marriage and family, queer male relationships were unable to endure beyond a period of a few months to a few years. How to make sense of this seeming paradox? Why do queer men spend so much time and effort looking for love when their outlook on the long-term future of queer relationships is so bleak? And what might this reveal about changing kinship practices and personhoods in postsocialist China?

Queer men in northwest China of all ages and class backgrounds frequently discuss the frustrations they face when looking for love. Many queer men report having relationships with other men, but none that last very long. "I still haven't fallen in love," Xiao Feng admitted when I asked if he had a boyfriend. "I want to fall in love with someone, but this type of thing can't be forced." Like many of his peers, Xiao Feng argued that true love depends on "fate" (*yuanfen*), a Buddhist concept that views interpersonal relationships as determined by the events of previous lifetimes rather than as acts of individual free will. However, instead of fate, it seems that for many queer men in northwest China, the main factor standing in the way of long-term gay relationships is the lack of support for such relationships from parents and society. With a wistful smile, Xiao Yu described the difficulties he faced in finding love. "After starting university, I've been with a few people, had a few boyfriends," he said. "They were all easy come, easy go (*haojuhaosan*). Sometimes I feel like a lonely star; no matter where I wander, I will always end up alone." Xiao Yu explained how "it's as if the feelings that my body has [for men] are doomed to have a time limit. This time limit can be very short, like two weeks. Or it can be longer, like a few months or even a couple of years." When I asked why this was, he replied, "You have to consider the realities and practicalities of life, factors like family, feelings of social recognition, and the like."

At the time of my fieldwork, most younger queer men in northwest China looked for partners on websites or by using text messaging, social networking, or dating applications. Xiao Kai recounted meeting his first and only boyfriend online while he was serving in the army: "Every day we would stay in touch through phone and text message," he recalled. "I was afraid that other people would find out, so I could only call him secretly after everyone else had gone to sleep." After maintaining his secret long-distance relationship for six months, Xiao Kai finally met his boyfriend in person. "The first time we met I was extremely excited," he said." Despite these initial feelings of excitement, no doubt heightened by the covert and restricted nature of their relationship, like the romantic connections of most queer men in northwest China, Xiao Kai's relationship did not last for very long. He was once again single when I interviewed him.

Although most of my queer male research participants were single or dating, several were in committed romantic relationships. Tian'e was dating Xiao Long, a gay university student his own age. They met while volunteering at Tong'ai and started "hanging out" (*wan*, a term that literally means "play" but that also carries romantic or sexual overtones). When I interviewed Tian'e, he and Xiao Long had been dating for three months. Although Tian'e maintained his own apartment, Xiao Long was required to live in student housing on his university campus. Tian'e therefore spent most nights sleeping in Xiao Long's crowded dormitory room that he shared with five other roommates, several of whom were also queer and did not seem to mind this arrangement. Even though Tian'e was not a student, because there were so many people coming and going he was able to live in the dormitory without attracting attention from school officials.

Tian'e's story is rather unusual as most of the queer men I interviewed were not fortunate enough to be able to live with their boyfriends, instead living with their parents or families. But even though his situation seemed ideal, Tian'e was pessimistic about the future of his relationship. Tian'e described how Xiao Long did not want his straight friends knowing about their relationship because he feared they would not be supportive. "This makes me really uncomfortable," Tian'e said. "I think that we should say [we are a couple], but society doesn't permit it, because it's not the same as normal relations between husband and wife." Tian'e summed up the obstacles queer men faced in their pursuit of long-term relationships:

> Two men don't have a legal or social framework to preserve their marriage. So, it's very hard to stay together. In ordinary male-female marriage, they also don't necessarily have to be in love with each other. Some marriages in China are arranged marriages; that's the only reason why they are together, but they will be together for life. That's because there is a legal and social framework. That social framework includes the pressure that parents and friends give them to not get divorced. Parents will say, "[She or he] is so filial, you can't get divorced." Friends will also say, "[She or he] is so good to you, you can't divorce." It's only this pressure that keeps them together.

Tian'e's remarks illustrate how most of my queer male informants in northwest China experience queer love and romance; it is not that queer men are uniquely unable to stay together or that they do not want to, but rather because of a lack of social and familial support that their relationships are unable to stand the test of time.

These data from northwest China parallel other ethnographic accounts of queer female and male love and relationships across China. In the northeast, Li Yinhe and Wang Xiaobo (1992) report that relationships between queer men in Beijing are relatively short-lived, lasting from a few months to a few years. Elisabeth Engebretsen documents how same-sex love and relationships among lesbian women in Beijing are also often regarded as having "no future" (2009, 7). Writing about the southwestern Chinese city of Chengdu, Wei Wei argues that "the pursuit of a committed gay relationship was not encouraged in the gay world, given all the social consequences both parties had to bear from their stigmatized relationship" (2007, 578). Kong reports similar findings among queer men in Hong Kong, where people from both older and younger generations describe gay love as "always short-term, fleeting and transient" (2011, 103). This striking uniformity suggests that social and familial pressures are causing queer people across postsocialist China to experience same-sex love as inherently short-lived, complicating claims of sexual revolution and increasingly privatized or individualized practices of kinship and personhood. Rather than experiencing increasing freedoms to pursue individualistic and "selfish" desires, queer people from around China continue to sacrifice long-term queer romance and individual happiness in order to fulfill their filial duties and preserve harmonious relationships with parents and families.

Social and family pressures, especially those around marriage and reproduction, are no doubt among the largest obstacles facing queer Chinese people and their relationships. However, another explanation for why many queer people in northwest China think of their romantic relationships as inherently short-lived can be found in how they experience love itself. In discussion after discussion with male queer activists from a range of ages and class backgrounds, I was repeatedly told that relationships between queer men cannot last because of how initially strong feelings of "passionate" or "sexual love" (*jiqing*) are quickly "watered down" (*danhua*) and transformed into feelings of "familial love" (*qinqing*). Straight relationships, I was often told, are just as susceptible to a precipitous loss of romantic and sexual passion, but are able to last because of the social support afforded by heteronormative institutions and expectations of family, marriage, and parenthood.

Queer men in northwest China use several expressions to explain how sexual passion inevitably transforms into familial intimacy. According to Tian'e, "There is a phrase that expresses this really well: 'love doesn't last a lifetime (*meiyou yibeizi de aiqing*).' After a while, love begins to lack feeling. It starts to turn into familial love." Lao Wang quoted the saying "absence makes the heart grow fonder" (*jiu bie sheng xin hun*) to illustrate the relationship between sexual passion and familial love: "After [being with someone for] a long time, it's just as if all you ate every day was *mantou* [a kind of plain, steamed white bun]. You would eat it until it didn't taste like anything anymore, and then you would think of a way to eat something else, to switch to something new." I asked him how long this transformation usually took. "Ordinarily not very many [men] are able to stay together for more than half a year," he replied. "After a short time, they will start looking a bit for other people. After he no longer has any desire for his [partner's] body, he will look for others, for someone new, for a kind of discovery." Remarks like these illustrate how queer men in northwest China embody the heteronormative pressures and expectations of family and society by experiencing same-sex love as inherently impermanent.

The idea that love involves an inevitable transition from sexual passion to famil-ial intimacy is not unique to queer men in northwest China. In a sampling of eth-nographic material from 166 societies, William Jankowiak and Edward Fischer (1992) find that in almost all of them people differentiate between what they call passionate and companionate love. In her ethnography of the Ju/'hoansi, for example, Marjorie Shostak reports that women describe their feelings for husbands and lovers as being "necessarily different. One is rich, warm, and secure. The other is passionate and exciting, although often fleeting and undependable" (2000, 239). In his study of love in the northern Chinese city of Hohhot, Jankowiak writes that heterosexual couples experience love as occurring in two distinct stages: the "attraction phase," which is characterized by "passionate" or "romantic" love, and the "attachment phase," which is marked by "the growth of a more peaceful, com-fortable, and fulfilling kind of love" (1993, 192; see also Pimentel 2000). Among young heterosexual men and women in Shanghai, James Farrer reports that, although premarital sex and breakups are becoming increasingly common, straight couples still regard the transition from passionate to more intimate forms of love as an important step toward "deeper emotional ties," "increasing commitment," and the goal of marriage (2014, 68).

These findings differ from understandings and experiences of love among queer men in northwest China, who widely regard the shift from passion to inti-macy as heralding the end of a romantic relationship rather than as a progression toward increased stability and commitment. "Chinese society hasn't legalized same-sex marriage," Tian'e lamented. "Two men don't have a legal or social frame-work to preserve their marriage, so it's very hard to stay together." Lao Wang also believed that the situation would be different if queer men could get married, arguing that "If [gay relationships] were also protected by law, things would be a bit better." Many of my informants argued that if queer relationships were given the same recognition and support from society and family as heterosexual unions, they too might be able to survive the inevitable transition from attraction to attachment.

In addition to an inevitable decline in passionate love and a lack of social and familial support, queer men in northwest China also blame the spread of con-sumerism, new media, and communication technologies like the Internet for the short-term nature of same-sex love. While many queer people see these changes as positive developments that allow them to connect more easily with one another, others feel they are having a deleterious effect on the quality of queer relationships. Xiao Kai, sounding older than his twenty-seven years, described how difficult it was for queer men to find each other before the existence of the Internet and of gay bars and bathhouses. "At that time, gay romantic life was very good, because communication wasn't very convenient and society's opposition to homosexuality was also very strong," he said. "In that situation it was very difficult to find a boyfriend; it was even more difficult to find someone with whom you 'shared one will and one road' (zhitong-daohe), so gay men really treasured that kind of feeling." However, he argued that "After 2000, along with the emergence of bathhouses, bars, nightclubs, brothels, places driven by money, as well as the spread of the Internet, feelings between gay men have become indifferent." Xiao Kai continued:

> The development of the Internet gave gays more chances to make boyfriends, and this ought to be a good thing. But, on the contrary, in the past few years the romantic life of gay men in China has become more and more unstable. . . . Right now, young people don't take pride in monogamy; instead, they think that if you don't have a lot of partners, it's because there is no market for you, that you are very poor.

Here Xiao Kai explicitly attributes a decrease in the longevity of queer love and relationships to market reforms and the spread of consumerism in postsocialist China. Instead of helping queer couples find love and stay together, new media technologies and queer consumption venues are encouraging queer people to cycle through relationships more quickly to demonstrate their value on the sexual marketplace. This argument adds further nuance and complexity to claims of a sexual revolution in postsocialist China by showing that increasing consumerism and new opportunities for queer men to seek each other out and develop relationships are paradoxically making it more difficult, not easier, for them to find long-lasting love.

Complaints that young people in China are becoming increasingly shallow and materialistic when looking for love are not limited to those inside the circle. One of the most popular Chinese TV programs while I was in the field was *If You Are the One* (*Feicheng Wurao*), a game show in which a series of male contestants tries to get a date with one of twenty-four single women by surviving several rounds of questioning. Part of the show's popularity comes from its frank and open discussion of romantic and material concerns among young people, something that had never been seen before on Chinese TV. A Beijing model named Ma Nuo gained instant notoriety after she told an unemployed male contestant on the show, who did not own a car and invited her to take a ride on his bicycle, that she "would rather cry in [the back of] a BMW." A male contestant, Liu Yunchao, achieved similar infamy after he bragged about having several sports cars and ¥6,000,000 ($878,000) in the bank (Lin 2010); he was later voted off the show. The runaway success of the show and the public critiques of rising materialism in China that this provoked led the Chinese government to force the show to make several changes, including featuring older contestants and "eliminating remarks that could have negative social impacts" (E. Wong 2011).

A lighthearted queer version of *If You Are the One* called *If You Are Gay* (*Feitong Wurao*) is frequently played at queer men's NGOs like Tong'ai. One night in the Tong'ai office, the thirty or so men playing the game were taking it more seriously than usual. A handsome young man who looked to be in his early twenties asked a contestant, a slightly older man in his mid-thirties, "Does the housing complex where you live require a parking fee?" Everyone laughed and yelled in admiration of how skillfully he had asked the question; what he really wanted to know was "Do you own a car?" ("*Ni you meiyou baoma?*" literally: "Do you own a BMW?"). The contestant, looking slightly embarrassed, replied that no, he lived in company housing that did not charge a fee for parking. The questioner, undeterred, then asked, "How many [credit] cards do you have?" Everyone laughed again, and a few men complimented how "direct" (*zhijie*) the questioner was being. Such scenes support arguments about the complex effects of increasing materialism on queer relationships. As Xiao Kai put it, "Chinese gays right now are very hypocritical. They want to find their true love, but when they are faced with it, they are unable to overcome objective problems such as economic issues, buying a house, sex life, marriage, etc."

If love between two men is met with so many problems and was seen as inherently short-lived, then why do so many queer men still pursue romantic relationships? At the time of our interview, Xiao Wai had a new boyfriend whom he had been with for almost half a month. When I asked him why he wanted to have a boyfriend, he said simply, "At least when you are tired you have someone you can lean on. When you want to go out you have someone to go with you, you don't always have to be alone." Xiao Wai's remarks illustrate how, despite all the obstacles facing them, queer men in northwest China still believe in love.

The picture that emerges from this ethnographic exploration of love between queer men in northwest China is not one in which people are selfishly and individualistically pursuing their own private sexual desires irrespective of the expectations of their families of origin and society. On the contrary, the way queer men in China widely regard same-sex love as intrinsically impermanent demonstrates the extent to which they internalize and embody traditional norms and expectations about the importance of filial piety, marriage, and reproduction, as well as how the increasing consumerism and materialism of postsocialist Chinese society are further complicating their search for "Mr. Right."

CONTRACT MARRIAGES AND GAY FAMILIES: QUEER KINSHIP IN NORTHWEST CHINA

On one crisp October afternoon, I accompanied Yuanzi to a public park in Xi'an to attend an event for gay men and lesbian women who were interested in arranging contract marriages with each other. When we arrived at the entrance of the park, Lang, the manager of a Xi'an website for gay men who had organized the event, asked us to write our names, phone numbers, occupations, and ages on a sign-in sheet. Of the twenty-two people participating in the event that day, only two were women. After searching for a suitably secluded spot inside the park, far away from pedestrians and families who were out celebrating China's National Day holiday, we finally formed a large circle in a grassy area hidden behind a stone wall. Following a round of self-introductions, Lang asked the two women what type of man they were looking for. One of the women revealed that they were actually a lesbian couple who had been together for eight years and that her partner "wants me to find a guy who suits me." We discussed the advantages and disadvantages of different arrangements, such as living together or maintaining separate apartments, whether to have children, and how to deal with family visits and holidays. Most people seemed to think that marrying for a few years, having a child, and then divorcing was most desirable, but one gay man argued that this would not work because after you divorced your family would just put pressure you to remarry. Lang concluded the event by saying that the issue of contract marriages was a serious and "multilayered" problem that everyone needed to consider carefully.

Even as most queer men in northwest China are married or plan on one day marrying and having children, they are also experimenting with a variety of queer kinship practices, including negotiating contract marriages with lesbian women and constructing elaborate gay families with one another. These novel forms of queer kinship are compelling examples of changing notions of family in postsocialist China. However, rather than indexing the privatization of marriage or the rise of selfish individualism, these queer kinship practices further underscore the ongoing importance of traditional understandings and practices of family and of relational personhoods. Rather than allowing them to pursue their individual desires by opting out of heteronormative marriage and childbearing arrangements, contract marriages enable queer children to maintain intimate and filial relationships with their parents by presenting a façade of heterosexual marriage and remaining in the closet. And rather than serving as a substitute for the biological family or lineage, gay families instead provide at best a partial and temporary respite from the pressures and demands of what Adrienne Rich (1980) calls "compulsory heterosexuality."

The queer kinship practice of contract marriage or *xinghun* has become increasingly common across postsocialist China in recent decades (Engebretsen 2009, 2014; S. Huang 2018). Xinghun is an abbreviation of *xingshi hunyin*, which literally means "in the shape of a marriage" or "pro-forma marriage" (S. Y. Wang 2019, 13). Although Lucetta Kam (2013) reports that the phrase "cooperative marriage" (*hezuo hunyin*) is common in Shanghai, I did not encounter this term in northwest China. Tiantian Zheng (2015), who has done fieldwork among queer men in northeast China, translates xinghun as "fake marriage," which indexes a more negative or critical stance toward the practice that is sometimes but not always present among my queer informants in northwest China. Stephanie Wang (2019, 14–16) argues that contract marriages often connote positive identities and meanings including cosmopolitan, middle-class queer identities and solidarity between gay men and lesbian women.

In Xi'an, contract marriages are regarded by many queer men as a more ethical and hopefully more convenient solution to the marriage problem than mixed-orientation marriages. As Yuanzi explained:

There are some gay men who feel that, if I go and find a normal girl to marry, a straight girl, first, it will hurt others. But second, it will also hurt ourselves. We would all have to live our lives under a lot of repression. So, everyone thought of a solution, that is, for gays to look for lesbians. . . . Together they can also form something like a family, where everyone lives together. This is what is called a xinghun, taking the idea of marriage and turning it into a kind of appearance.

Yuanzi's account of contract marriages is largely positive in that it frames them primarily as a means of allowing queer men to avoid causing harm to "normal" women while satisfying their filial duties and their parents' desires by entering into an ersatz marriage arrangement. However, other queer men in northwest China are more critical of contract marriages, mainly because they involve the unfilial act of dishonesty to one's parents. Xiao Shan argued that "xingshi means something that is fake," and that people in a contract marriage "are just putting on a show. . . . They are just trying to deceive their parents."

Although they give some queer children a temporary respite from parental pressure, contract marriages sidestep rather than solve the marriage problem. And while they may be motivated at least in part by avoiding causing harm to heterosexual women, contract marriages are often more advantageous to queer men than queer women. In her analysis of contract marriages in Beijing, Engebretsen demonstrates that even as they are an important coping strategy for some queer people and can relieve some of the pressure to conform to traditional gender norms and expectations, contract marriages ultimately serve to "reaffirm the dominance of the heteronormative [patriarchal] family as society's basic moral and social unit" (2017, 86). Indeed, Engebretsen argues, "lesbians have the most to lose in *xinghun* arrangements, and usually do, compared with gay men, for whom personal independence and access to resources are much less curtailed" (92).

Although they were a frequent topic of discussion while I was in the field, successful contract marriages were relatively uncommon among my research participants. Contract marriages required the successful negotiation of many irksome details including the precise living arrangements of the queer couple(s) involved, the allocation of property rights, and how to deal with family visits and holidays. Despite these difficulties, many of my queer male informants were actively looking for lesbian marriage partners. Paopao, who was already thirty-four, had recently met a twenty-eight-year-old lesbian and introduced her to his sister and parents. When I asked him why he wanted a contract marriage, he replied, "Because I'm afraid of coming out, afraid of telling my parents. If I find a lesbian and get married it will appease my parents, coworkers, and friends. Even though I'll feel like I am deceiving them, I'll be a bit more comfortable. I won't need to suffer as much." Although Paopao's willingness to deceive his parents in order to relieve the pressure he faced from his family can be interpreted as an example of selfish individualism, the fact that he and many other queer men in northwest China feel obliged to engineer such complicated and difficult solutions to the marriage problem in order to appease their parents also demonstrates the continuing importance of filial piety and relational personhoods among queer men in the postsocialist period.

Many queer men in northwest China understand that contract marriages are only a temporary solution to social and parental pressures. According to Paopao, "After a contract marriage, if you don't want kids you have to tell your parents that your wife can't have children, and this is even more trouble." Yuanzi agreed, arguing that although "the benefits of contract marriage are that it can probably help to ease the family pressure from both sides to get married," this relief was fleeting because "One, two, or three years later your parents will definitely start nagging you, 'Oh, how have you two gone two, three years and still no children?'" For Yuanzi, such worries turned out to be prophetic. After many years of futile searching, in 2012 Yuanzi finally arranged a contract marriage with a lesbian woman he met online. They had a traditional wedding, including posing for wedding photos and inviting friends and family to a wedding banquet, and even lived in an apartment as a couple for a time. However, tensions soon emerged between them, and by 2017 Yuanzi had moved out of the apartment, which his wife was then sharing with her lesbian partner. Meanwhile, Yuanzi had moved back in with his mother and was facing renewed pressure from his biological family to have a child.

While contract marriages were somewhat rare during my fieldwork in northwest China, one common queer kinship practice that emerged around 2008 and has not been reported to exist outside of northwest China is the phenomenon of "gay families" (tongzhi jiazu).[8] By 2010, almost all my queer male informants belonged to one or more gay families, and some, like Xiao Shan, had become gay "mothers" (mama) and were actively recruiting gay "daughters" (nü'er) or "sons" (erzi) to join their expanding queer households.

Queer men in northwest China often compare gay families with heterosexual or biological families. When I asked him to explain what a gay family was, Yuanzi said, "If a group of people thinks that their relationships (guanxi) are very good, they can form a small organization that is analogous to a family. The idea behind this family isn't sexual; it's just the relationship between a parent and a son or a daughter, or the relationship between brothers and sisters." Indeed, as in a biological family, sexual relationships between queer family members are so taboo that people jokingly remark any such infractions would result in the incestuous couple being "struck by lightning" (da leipi). Like biological families, gay families also provide queer men with love and support, including food, a place to stay, or loans of money when needed. Just as a queer mother is obligated to provide for her queer daughters and sons, so are her queer children obligated to respect and obey her, a queer facsimile of traditional practices of filial piety.

Gay families in northwest China are not limited to a few queer nuclear family members but tend to grow over time and can become quite large, amounting to a kind of queer lineage. This is one reason why the word jiazu is used to describe this queer kinship practice instead of words like jia or jiating. As Yuanzi explained:

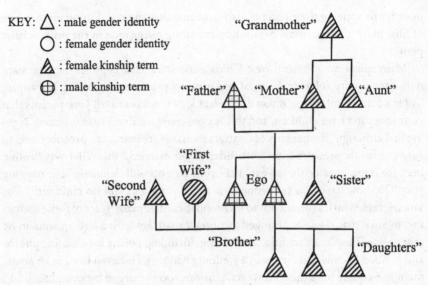

FIGURE 3.2. Gay kinship diagram. Diagram by author.

Inside the circle, we don't use the word "family" (*jia*) because it is too small. In [heterosexual] society, jia is just parents, sons, and daughters. Inside the circle, we use a word with a much larger scope, which is jiazu.... For example, Xiao Shan today might acknowledge (*ren*) a new daughter, Xiao Xi, and tomorrow he might acknowledge another new daughter, Xiao Wai. The day after he might acknowledge a new son, Xiao Gua, and like that his gay family will slowly become bigger and bigger. So, we use a larger concept, something with a larger scope. That's jiazu.

Fictive kinship practices and language among queer men in northwest China are not new; people have been using female kinship terms like mother and "older sister" *jie* to refer to one another for decades. However, by 2008 the practice of creating gay families was becoming increasingly structured and formalized in Xi'an. In 2010, some queer men even began describing gay families as a kind of queer "kinship system" (*qinshu zhidu*) based on "hierarchical relationships of seniority" (*lunzi-paibei*). To become a gay parent, someone who has an established reputation inside the Xi'an queer community will recruit gay children by "establishing a relationship" (*ren*) with or "pulling" (*la*) in people from their queer social networks.

Like David Schneider's (1980) analysis of American kinship, I found that kinship practices among queer men in northwest China can vary widely from group to group. Although most gay families use only female kinship terms, some use male kinship terms or a combination of both female and male terms (figure 3.2). When a gay family member uses male kinship terms like "father" (*baba*) or "son" (*erzi*), this usually indicates that he takes an "active" (*zhudong*) role during sex, while the use of female kinship terms like mother or daughter can often imply a "passive" (*beidong*) sexual role. Although queer women in northwest China also use playful fictive kinship terms like "little sister" (*meizi*), to my knowledge they do not address each other using masculine terms. A gay child can form their own gay family by taking on gay daughters or sons, who would refer to the head of the gay extended family or lineage as grandmother or grandfather, and their gay parent's sisters and brothers as aunts or uncles. Boyfriends are often also considered gay family members; a gay daughter might call their queer uncle's boyfriend "aunt" (*jiuma*, mother's younger brother's wife), or a gay son might call their queer brother's boyfriend "sister-in-law" (*er sao*, older brother's second wife, second in this example because the older brother is in a heterosexual marriage to a biological woman, his first wife). Because gay families often have overlapping memberships, any two queer people in Xi'an might be related to each other in different ways as gay cousins, nieces, or daughters-in-law.[9]

Gay families in northwest China exist along a spectrum ranging from more structured or, in the words of my informants, "real" (*zhende*) jiazu that span several generations and employ a formal system of female kinship terms to smaller and more informal or "relaxed" (*songsan*) groupings of friends that tend to mix female and male kinship terminology. At the time of my fieldwork, some of the larger and more influential gay families had even given themselves names, including "The Family of Broad Beneficence" (*Guangze Jiazu*) and "The Seven Fairies Family" (*Qi Xiannü Jiazu*), which took its name from a legend concerning seven celestial maidens who descend from heaven to Earth in search of love. In this way, gay families in northwest China resemble the queer "houses" of North American ball culture documented in the film *Paris is Burning* (Livingston 2005), which feature similar relationships between queer mothers and daughters.[10]

In many ways, gay families in northwest China also resemble the gay and lesbian families of choice that Kath Weston (1991) describes in San Francisco in the 1980s. Like their North American queer counterparts, gay families in northwest China tend to naturalize biological understandings of relatedness, even as they emphasize the act of creation as opposed to the biological necessity of biogenetic kinship; they also exhibit fluid and overlapping boundaries and are marked by exchanges of emotional and material support. However, unlike North American gay and lesbian families of choice, gay families in northwest China emphasize cross-generational kinship relationships like mother and daughter rather than tending to refer to one another as brothers and sisters, regardless of age.[11] Also, whereas Weston reports a "relative absence of institutionalization or rituals associated with emergent gay families" in San Francisco (113), joining a gay family in northwest China requires the verbal acknowledgment of both gay parent and child, and the creation and maintenance of fictive queer kinship bonds is often formally marked by the periodic exchange of gifts or food between gay family members, usually when such bonds are first formed and at least annually thereafter when gay families come together during the Lunar New Year, a time when biologi-cal families also traditionally gather.

Gay families in northwest China demonstrate a strikingly less individualistic notion of personhood compared to North American gay and lesbian families of choice. Very few members of the Chinese gay families that I knew had come out to their biological parents or families, unlike in the United States, where Weston argues queer kinship developed "only after coming out to blood relatives emerged as a historical possibility" (110–111). And whereas many of Weston's North Ameri-can queer informants saw gay families of choice as "substitutes" for biological families, especially when coming out to their families of origin resulted in rejec-tion and exclusion, the same is not true of gay family members in northwest China, who typically did not see themselves as "critiquing" or "challenging" (22) hegemonic notions and practices of kinship.

Despite the increasing ubiquity and formality of gay families in northwest China, most queer men there seem to regard them as unserious, simply a "whimsi-cal" (huixiexing) way of describing relationships between close friends. Indeed, the use of queer kinship terminology within the circle is frequently accompanied by extreme amusement and jocularity, and calling someone "older sister" can often be a lighthearted form of teasing or expressing affection. Gay families can certainly be playful and humorous, which is reflected in their frequent use of joking kinship terms inspired by popular TV series like Schemes of a Beauty, a historical drama set in the Han Dynasty (206 BCE–220 CE) that was extremely popular among queer men in the early 2010s. These nicknames or joking kinship terms can be used alongside more formal kinship terms such as mother and daughter and are a constant source of hilarity and creativity inside the circle. One group of Tong'ai volunteers even formed an informal gay family modeled after an imperial harem, with titles such as "empress dowager" (muhou), "imperial consort" (guifei), and "imperial concubine" (meiniang).

Such joking kinship terms were found in many of Xi'an's gay families during the 2000s and 2010s. In Zhiming's gay family, in addition to being called brother or uncle, he was also given the nickname "supreme imperial concubine" (taifei). As Zhiming described the meaning of his nickname, "Taifei was the most lofty and supreme position. She also had a lot of power; only if the emperor died could she become the supreme imperial concubine. She was also very pretty; if she was the wife of the emperor she must have been very pretty! So taifei means not only pretty but also powerful. That's why they call me taifei." At first Zhiming told me these playful gay kinship terms "didn't have any special significance." But then he grew more serious and said, "Actually, I'll tell you what the meaning is. Ordinarily in our work and in our lives, especially in China, we are really fake. You must con-ceal your identity. There is a lot of pressure. But when you are in the circle, every-one likes to goof off, relax a bit." The use of these joking gay kinship terms further underscores how, for many people inside the circle, gay families serve as a retreat or escape from the sexual and gendered pressures faced in everyday life, where they can let their guard down and be themselves in the company of close friends.

Indeed, for many queer men in northwest China, gay families have a much deeper and more profound significance. Xiao Feng argued that only "in this kind of family can your true self emerge. That is, [only] in this family can you live your life as a gay man." Many queer men told me that being part of a family inside the circle gives them a sense of purpose and belonging that they lack in other aspects of their lives. As Yuanzi said:

> In the beginning, there weren't gay families, there wasn't this concept of a lot of people coming together. In this environment, we thought that one person was just one person, lonely or not. There was a very lost kind of feeling inside the circle. But after we had jiazu, everyone felt like, "Whoa, there are so many relatives standing by my side." . . . That is to say, I have a sense of belonging or a feeling of family.

Xiao Shan expressed a similar sentiment, saying "I think that gay families are very meaningful. If everyone went along without these types of connections we would be lacking in solidarity; if we didn't have these kinds of relationships and forms of address, we would be lacking in care and support for one another." For many queer men, belonging to a gay family can be liberating. "Among straight people, things must be reckoned in terms of age and gender," Xiao Shan said. "But in the *gay* circle, you can ignore age and gender; you don't need all that. . . . I really think that it is freer, because if you are like a younger sister or are a o I can call you 'younger sister.' This shows the independence of gays; I don't need to be constrained by society."

Despite how important they are for many queer men in northwest China, like same-sex love, gay families are often also seen as essentially impermanent. Yuanzi described to me how "a gay family changes as time goes by; as the kind of passion that it begins with, the kind of contact or feeling between people becomes weak or watered down, the family will slowly disperse. Every gay family is like that." This had already happened to Yuanzi's own gay family. "Before," Yuanzi recalled, "every New Year our gay family would sit around the same table and share a meal together, but not anymore." In this way, gay families in northwest China bear a striking resemblance to the uterine families described by Margery Wolf (1972, 32–41) in rural Taiwan. Like gay families, uterine families are not eternal but instead are recreated in every generation. Gay and uterine families are also alike in that they both exist outside of and go unrecognized by male-dominated and heteronormative structures and ideologies of kinship and lineage, even though it could be argued that both gay and uterine families are ultimately necessary for the survival of the patriline itself.

Queer kinship practices in northwest China like contract marriages and gay families demonstrate both cultural change and continuity, including how processes of privatization and individualization are unfolding alongside the continued importance of traditional values of filial piety and relational personhood. Contract marriages and gay families also demonstrate the complex relationship that exists between queerness and (anti)normativity in postsocialist China. In the words of Hongwei Bao (2018, 161), such forms of kinship "encourage us to conceptualize new possibilities of connectivities, relationalities and socialities that queerness may entail." Instead of openly rejecting heterosexual marriage or entering into a mixed-orientation marriage with a heterosexual woman, many queer men in northwest China are attempting to reconcile their queer identities with their relational personhoods and filial duties by arranging contract marriages with lesbian women. And even as contract marriages and gay families, like queer love and relationships, are experienced as temporary and often mirror or even sustain heteronormative and patriarchal structures and institutions, they nonetheless provide important alternative familial spaces in which queer people are able to express themselves more openly and briefly seek refuge from the heteronormative expectations and demands of their biological families and society.

RETHINKING QUEERNESS AND (ANTI)NORMATIVITY

This chapter examines experiences of love, kinship, and personhood among four generations of queer men in contemporary northwest China. It explores the joys and challenges that queer men find in their relationships with boyfriends, biological family members, and friends; the passion and pain they endure as they search for love, only to have it slip away from them; and their fears of facing the future and old age alone. It analyzes how queer men debate and strategize about when and how to tell their parents about their sexualities while maintaining and prioritizing continued relationships of intergenerational intimacy and harmony, as well as how they struggle with increasing pressure from family and society to get married and have children. And it describes the playful and sometimes profound connections queer men form through alternative marriage practices and elaborate gay families, as well as how they understand these experimental forms of queer kinship, like same-sex love, to be fleeting and impermanent compared to the biological family and lineage, which are still idealized as eternal and everlasting. Such investigations deepen our knowledge of queer Chinese culture and add further complexity to our understandings of privatization and individualization in postsocialist China.

The growing visibility of queer communities, alongside the alleged privatization and individualization of personhood, marriage, and family, has often been portrayed as another example of how the pursuit of private desires has triumphed over traditional and socialist values and practices of filial duty and collective self-sacrifice. However, the experiences and choices of queer men in northwest China complicate the argument that the retreat of the socialist state and the advent of social and economic reforms have "created a social vacuum of moral values" (Yan 2003, 16) in which consumerism and individualism mean that people are no longer willing to sacrifice their own hopes and desires for what they believe to be the benefit of their parents and families. The experiences of queer Chinese men also reveal how China's so-called "sexual revolution" is not as emancipatory as one might think. As Adam Phillips argues, "If sex is the way out of the family, falling in love is the route back, the one-way ticket that is always a return" (1994, 39). Even as sex may seem like an escape from the family, a selfish indulgence, or an expression of private desires, to the extent that individual sexual passions are transmuted into the stable bonds of heterosexual matrimony and biological reproduction, ultimately the family prevails.

Exploring queer experiences of love, kinship, and personhood also helps us to better understand the complex and ongoing tensions and negotiations between the past and the present, personal desires and filial duties, and individualization and collectivism that are taking place across Chinese society. Far from serving as the avatars of a Chinese "sexual revolution" or "the forerunners of a 'desiring China'" (Bao 2018, 81), many queer men in northwest China instead make the seemingly anachronistic choice to marry and have children in order to uphold enduring collectivist notions of filial piety and relational personhood. Even as they yearn for long-lasting queer love and intimacy, due to heteronormative social pressures and expectations, queer men experience queerness, including same-sex love and relationships, as intrinsically impermanent. Rather than coming out or constructing alternative families of choice, queer men are instead fashioning new forms of queer kinship that are not understood as replacements or substitutes for the biological family, but rather as temporary refuges that help them to resist, survive, and ultimately maintain an ongoing system of compulsory heterosexuality.

Queer experiences of love, kinship, and personhood in northwest China also demonstrate the need to develop more nuanced and culturally relative understandings of the relationship between queerness and antinormativity. At a moment when Chinese state and society seem to be celebrating the expression of individual interests as a harbinger of postsocialist modernity, queer people are nevertheless expected to sacrifice their own "selfish" desires in order to uphold both traditional values of filial piety and the heteronormative demands of marriage and childbirth. However, the "no future" of queer love and desire in China is not, as in Lee Edelman's (2004) formulation, a consequence of turning away from the heterosexual family and biological reproduction. On the contrary, many queer men in northwest China eventually turn away from their own transitory queer desires and identities in order to pursue what they see as the more enduring bonds of heterosexual marriage and family.

Taking a more culturally relative approach to understanding the relationship between queerness and antinormativity allows us to understand that this does not make queer men in northwest China any less authentically queer. Rather, the struggles of queer men to navigate the liminal space between traditional family values and collectivist notions of personhood, on the one hand, and their individual and private queer identities and desires, on the other, encapsulate not only the contradictions of postsocialist Chinese society but also what is perhaps a universal and timeless aspect of the queer condition: the ongoing tension and negotiation between past and present, personal desires and familial duties, normativity and antinormativity.

4 · "LIVING IN THE GRAY ZONE"
Queer Activism and Civil Society

One chilly November evening I was sipping hot green tea in the Tong'ai office with Tianguang, the group's founder and director. Tianguang was telling me the story of Edgar Snow, an American journalist who, during the Chinese Civil War (1927–1949), was allowed to visit the revolutionary headquarters of the Chinese Communist Party (CCP) in the nearby city of Yan'an. There, Snow was given extraordinary access to Mao Zedong, the leader of the CCP who would go on to win the war and rule the People's Republic of China (PRC). Snow wrote a book about his experiences called *Red Star Over China* (1938) that positively portrayed Chinese socialism. Tianguang argued that by describing Mao and the CCP as idealistic reformers rather than violent revolutionaries, Snow helped shift U.S. support away from the Chinese Nationalist Party. By the time the United States discovered the truth about the CCP it was too late, and Mao had already gained control of China.

Tianguang said he was telling me this story because he hoped that I would introduce Chinese queer activism to the outside world just as Edgar Snow had acquainted Americans with Mao and the CCP. "Give American gays an authentic and detailed introduction to us and to other Chinese gay community-based organizations," Tianguang urged. "Make them understand the work we are doing, what we are seeking, what our goals are. Just like Snow introduced America to Mao Zedong, the CCP, and the so-called 'liberated areas,' you can introduce us to Western countries, to Western societies, make them understand us better." Continuing his analogy between queer Chinese NGOs and the early CCP, Tianguang argued:

The situation of gay community-based organizations today is a lot like that of the CCP in Yan'an: they both faced a lot of difficulties, primarily policy challenges. [Gay] community-based organizations right now are not legally recognized by the government, just like how back then the Nationalists didn't recognize the CCP as a real, legal party. We also have no source of income; not only does the government not recognize us, but they don't give us any support or resources for our work. . . .

We don't know what lies ahead for us, because we don't know what kinds of policies the government will have or how they will treat groups like ours in the future.

⟿

This ethnographic snapshot introduces some of the key themes that I explore in chapters 4 and 5 of this book, as I pivot from an analysis of queer gender and sexuality to an investigation of grassroots NGOs, HIV/AIDS, and queer activism in northwest China. Tianguang's striking comparison between queer NGOs and the early CCP demonstrates how, even in an era of sweeping economic and social reforms, the legacy and latent power of the socialist state is never far from people's minds. As Hongwei Bao (2018, 190) argues, "the socialist past lays a foundation and provides inspiration for contemporary Chinese gay identity and queer politics." Indeed, for many if not most queer activists in northwest China, the 1949 communist revolution is more relevant to their present struggles than the 1969 Stonewall riots. Although the partial withdrawal of the postsocialist state has opened up new spaces and opportunities for queer people and social organizations to enter China's expanding public sphere, queer activists and NGOs still occupy a precarious position in a legal "gray zone" at the margins of state and society.

In this chapter I consider whether and how concepts like civil society and the public sphere can be used to interpret the impacts of social and economic reforms on queer activism in postsocialist China. I describe the emergence of a nationwide social movement of grassroots queer NGOs alongside the gradual retreat of the postsocialist state and China's growing HIV/AIDS crisis. In the spirit of Edgar Snow, I tell the stories of two community-based queer NGOs in northwest China: Tong'ai, an older queer men's group that focused on HIV/AIDS prevention and treatment, and UNITE, a newer queer women's organization with a more overtly cultural and political agenda. Focusing first on Tong'ai, I explore the identities and spaces created by queer community activism, including why some queer activists decide to become volunteers, what kinds of activities they engage in, and how they see their work fitting into the wider social and political changes taking place in postsocialist China. Turning to UNITE, I examine its organization and strategy as well as differences between queer men's and women's activism in northwest China.

Studying queer activism in northwest China not only helps us better understand what it means to be queer and Chinese in the postsocialist period, but also reveals the effects of social and economic reforms on Chinese society more broadly. While they are never completely free of state power and control, grassroots queer NGOs like Tong'ai and UNITE are able to take advantage of the greater opportunities for civil society organizing created by reforms and the AIDS crisis to pursue their own agendas, either by working with the state or by going it alone. The result is a growing and complex queer movement in the PRC that challenges conventional understandings of both civil society and queer activism. By exploiting their perceived status as gatekeepers of underground and at-risk urban communities of MSM or "men who have sex with men" in order to gain legitimacy and resources from the state, or by taking advantage of a long-standing official disregard for queer female sexuality in order to fly under the radar, queer NGOs in northwest China are able to survive and in some cases even thrive despite continued state antipathy toward both queerness and civil society. The perseverance of queer NGOs and volunteers and the sacrifices they make to carry out their work in support of their communities not only demonstrate the existence of a robust queer civil society in postsocialist China, but also complicate arguments that social and economic reforms have led to an increase in privatization and selfish individualism.

WHAT'S IN A NAME? CIVIL SOCIETY IN POSTSOCIALIST CHINA

The term "civil society" is today used to describe a theoretical space between family and state in which civic organizations serve as checks on state power (Hann 1996; Weller 2005). However, the idea of an inherent opposition between state and civil society is a relatively recent assumption in Western political philosophy. Raymond Williams dates this assumption to the seventeenth century, when "a fundamental conflict came to be expressed in what was eventually a distinction between society and *state*: the former an association of free men ... [and] the latter an organization of power" (1983, 293). Jürgen Habermas argues that a civil society, what he calls "the basically privatized but publicly relevant sphere of commodity exchange and social labor," emerged in eighteenth-century Europe as an expansion of long-distance trade, which was created by a network of horizontal economic ties between private citizens that challenged vertical relationships of dependence between state and subject (1989, 27). In tandem with a flourishing and increasingly critical press, a liberal public sphere gradually formed as the new bourgeois class began to demand a greater say in how the state regulated civil society (36).

Marxist scholars theorize civil society not as a fundamentally antagonistic relationship between a state and its citizens but rather as struggles over power between economic and social classes. Karl Marx (1978b, 187) argues that civil society does not mediate between the individual citizen and the state, but rather enables the domination of one social class over another through control of the means of production and state coercion. Antonio Gramsci refines Marx's ideas by developing the idea of hegemony, or "intellectual and moral leadership" (Kurtz 1996, 106), to explain how dominant classes maintain power primarily through obtaining the consent of the dominated. Like Marx, Gramsci understands state and civil society not as "two bounded universes, always and forever separate, but rather a knot of tangled power relations" (103).

Despite their lack of consensus on the meaning of civil society, Western scholars have often rather uncritically applied the concept to non-Western countries like the PRC. Robert Weller writes that "the events of 1989 in China and Eastern

Europe caused a minor stampede of Western China scholars looking to identify the 'sprouts' of civil society in Chinese tradition, or to blame the failure of the student movement on the lack of such traditions" (1999, 15). While some have critiqued such efforts as revealing a rush to apply Western models of modernization to "developing" countries (Dean 1997, 173), others have pointed out that in China state and society are often seen as pragmatically and morally entwined rather than mutually exclusive and opposed (Flower and Leonard 1996).

After the postsocialist reforms that began in the late 1970s, the number of social organizations in the PRC grew exponentially. Today NGOs provide services that were once performed by the state and address the social problems caused by rapid economic growth, including "rising unemployment, growing inequality, an aging population, at-risk children, gender and labor rights issues, and health and environmental problems" (Shieh and Schwartz 2009, 4). As the number of social organizations has steadily grown, the state has tried to control and limit their activities. Regulations issued in October 1989 required all NGOs to register with the Ministry of Civil Affairs. In 1998, new regulations required all registered social organizations to be supervised by a separate government agency. Despite these regulations, the number of officially registered NGOs increased from 167,506 in 1993 (B. He 1993, 122) to more than 400,000 by 2010, with an estimated additional 3,000,000 unregistered social organizations (S. Wilson 2012, 551).

Relationships between Chinese social organizations and the state range from direct government supervision and control to more indirect forms of supervision and surveillance. On one end of this spectrum are so-called "government-organized NGOs," or GONGOs, that are controlled by the state and serve as "transmission belts" (Frolic 1997, 57) for state policies and priorities. In the middle of the spectrum lie groups that are formally registered with the state through the Ministry of Civil Affairs or the Ministry of Commerce. At the far end of the spectrum exist a variety of quasi-legal, unregistered, "bottom-up" social service organizations (S. Wilson 2012, 553), including most queer NGOs. However, even unregistered NGOs must work closely with government agencies and avoid sensitive political activities, or they risk state interference and repression (Shieh and Schwartz 2009, 6–10; Weller 1999, 126–127).

A host of neologisms has been coined to describe state-society relations in postsocialist China, including "state-led civil society" (Frolic 1997), "alternate civilities" (Weller 1999), and "semi-civil society" or "nascent civil society" (B. He 1993). However, as Yunqiu Zhang argues, "To assert that civil society does not apply to China is to work from an ideal type of Western civil society" and "to argue that Chinese are so peculiar in their social behavior that there is no way for them to form something like civil society" (1997, 146). Even in many Western countries, civil society organizations often work closely with the state and receive state funding (S. Wilson 2012, 552). Recalling Gramsci's conception of state and civil society as an intricately interconnected network of power relations involved in the production and projection of hegemony, Timothy Brook and Michael Frolic argue that "state and society are densely interactive realms everywhere, as much in the West as in China. Civil society might be better thought of, therefore, as a formation that exists by virtue of state-society interaction, not as something between, separate from, or autonomous from either" (1997, 12).

In this chapter, I examine the types of power relations that are being maintained, resisted, and transformed by queer activists and NGOs in northwest China. What kinds of political cultures are taking shape within queer NGOs? How do they interact with each other and the state? On the one hand, by cooperating with the government to deliver HIV/AIDS education and prevention services to MSM that the state cannot reach on its own, queer men's groups like Tong'ai often work with the state rather than opposing it. On the other hand, queer NGOs like Tong'ai and UNITE also demonstrate how civil society groups in postsocialist China are taking advantage of the "zones of autonomy" (S. Wilson 2012, 563) created by social and economic reforms to create spaces in which the kinds of counterhegemonic identities, practices, and discourses that James C. Scott (1990) calls "hidden transcripts" can emerge outside of the full view and control of the Chinese government.

REFORMS, HIV/AIDS, AND THE BEGINNINGS OF CHINESE QUEER ACTIVISM

China's AIDS epidemic started in the early 1980s as the state gradually ended decades of economic and cultural isolation. The epidemic proceeded through three distinct phases, with HIV first spreading among intravenous drug users in southwestern Yunnan Province. The second phase involved unsafe paid plasma donation practices in rural villages in Henan and its six neighboring provinces, Anhui, Hebei, Hubei, Hunan, Shanxi, and Shaanxi (Kaufman, Kleinman, and Saich 2006, 3). By 2007, sexual transmission was responsible for over half of the estimated 50,000 new HIV infections in mainland China each year, 44.7 percent occurring during heterosexual contact and 12.2 percent between MSM (L. Wang et al. 2009, 417). Joan Kaufman argues that the sexualization of AIDS was created by "changing sexual behaviors and norms, massive internal migration . . . and an emerging epidemic among hard-to-reach gay men" (2009, 157). By the mid-2000s, estimates of HIV prevalence among urban MSM had increased dramatically in many Chinese cities: from 0.4 to 5.8 percent in Beijing (Ma et al. 2007); from 0.64 to 9.1 percent in Chengdu; and from 10.4 to 12.5 percent in Chongqing (Feng et al. 2009). This rapid increase caused some experts to describe the growing HIV epidemic among urban MSM as "a ticking time bomb" (F. Wong et al. 2009).

The spread of HIV in countries around the world has often initially been blamed on external forces or internal minority groups. In the early days of the North American AIDS epidemic, the medical establishment and the media claimed that AIDS had spread to the United States via Haiti; later, domestic groups including Haitian immigrants, gay men, and heroin addicts were blamed (Farmer 1992,

210–212). In the PRC, the first reaction of the state and medical profession was to label HIV/AIDS a "Western disease" and to scapegoat ethnic minorities, sex workers, and MSM for its spread (Gil 1992; Hyde 2007). Kaufman writes that "the illicit behaviors associated with the epidemic by the Chinese public were highly stigmatized—homosexuality, illegal drug use, and prostitution—all considered vices of the West and social problems that had been wiped out by socialist China after 1949" (2012, 226).

Although the epidemic reinforced negative stereotypes about MSM in China, including long-standing associations between homosexuality, sickness, and deviance, the HIV/AIDS crisis also afforded queer men a unique opportunity to mobilize. In 1997, Zhang Beichuan, a physician who was a leader in China's early response to the spread of HIV among MSM, began publishing the *Friends Exchange* magazine under the auspices of Qingdao University Medical College.[1] Joan Kaufman describes how "The magazine, about homosexuality, dealt with psychological support needs, AIDS prevention education, and international events. Each copy passed through many hands and was one of the few sources of information for this hidden population in China" (2011, 166). The publication and circulation of *Friends Exchange* supported the formation of many of China's first queer community-based NGOs, including Tong'ai in northwest China.

In response to government inaction and indifference to the spread of HIV among MSM, by the late 1990s queer activists around China began organizing to fight HIV/AIDS. By 2005, there were more than ten grassroots gay NGOs in the PRC (B. Zhang and Kaufman 2005, 125); by 2008, activists had organized dozens of gay NGOs with more than six thousand volunteers in over thirty-five cities, where they provided toll-free telephone hotlines, HIV/AIDS education and outreach events, online social networking and peer education, and other forms of queer community-building and support (State Council AIDS Working Committee Office and UN Theme Group on AIDS 2008, 14). Beginning in 2003, increasing international pressure and the limitations of a domestic public health system that had been weakened by economic reforms compelled the Chinese Center for Disease Control and Prevention (China CDC) to begin cooperating with unregistered gay civil society groups to implement voluntary HIV/AIDS testing and counseling campaigns in "hard to reach" queer urban communities (Kaufman 2009, 157–160). One of those groups was Tong'ai, the first queer NGO in northwest China and one of the earliest queer NGOs in the PRC.

FROM TIANANMEN TO AIDS: THE BEGINNINGS OF TONG'AI

Tianguang, the founder and leader of Tong'ai, traveled a circuitous path on his way to becoming a queer AIDS activist. Born in 1961 in Hebei Province, experiencing both the Cultural Revolution and the subsequent social and economic reforms left him, like many in his generation, deeply disillusioned with state socialism and the CCP. After participating in the nationwide democracy protests in 1989, Tianguang was sentenced to three years in jail in northwest China. Two years after his release, as he was browsing a bookstore in Xi'an, Tianguang came across a copy of *Same-Sex Love* by Zhang Beichuan (1994), one of the first books on homosexuality published in the PRC. Tianguang wrote to "Teacher Zhang," as Zhang Beichuan is affectionately called inside the circle, and the two became friends. In 1998, when Zhang began publishing *Friends Exchange*, Tianguang volunteered to help distribute the magazine in northwest China. This was the beginning of what would become Tong'ai, although Tianguang did not realize it at the time. "The idea of Tong'ai didn't exist yet," he told me. "Back then there were no bars or bathhouses, only parks, those kinds of open-air places. At that time, I also got a few friends, including some gay friends, and we would all go to these places and distribute *Friends Exchange* and what [information] we knew about HIV/AIDS."

In 2002, Tianguang attended a national HIV/AIDS training conference in Nanjing that was organized by Zhang Beichuan and the China STD/AIDS Association, a GONGO affiliated with the Ministry of Health. "It wasn't until 2002 that I really realized the true threat that HIV/AIDS posed to this community," Tianguang said. After returning from Nanjing, Tianguang decided to start an NGO dedicated to HIV/AIDS prevention among MSM. He named the new organization the "Gay AIDS Working Group" (*Tongzhi Aizibing Gongzuo Zuzhi*), usually abbreviated as *Tong'ai*, "*tong*" meaning "same" or "together" and the first syllable in the words "gay" (*tongzhi*) and "homosexual" (*tongxinglian*), and "*ai*" meaning "love" as well as being a homonym with the first character in the word AIDS (*aizibing*). Tianguang explained he picked the name Tong'ai because of its linguistic ambiguity:

Tong'ai can be interpreted as "Gay AIDS Working Group." But it can also be interpreted as "With Love Working Group" or "Community AIDS Working Group." When we are talking with nongay people, we can explain ourselves without being too specific. . . . On the one hand, it gives the people who participate in this work some protection. On the other hand, in terms of politics, it gives us an explanation; we don't have to worry that the government will find our name too sensitive.

Financial support for the new group came in the form of a ¥5,000 ($600) monthly subsidy from Barry and Martin's Trust, a British charity that, working in conjunction with Zhang Beichuan, began supporting HIV/AIDS activism in China in 1996. This funding, although modest, allowed the group to rent an office space and start a gay telephone "hotline" (*rexian*) that offered information about sexually transmitted diseases including AIDS and emotional, psychological, and legal support to queer men across northwest China. The first Tong'ai office was a dilapidated one-room shack Tianguang rented from a family friend. After complaints from the neighbors about strange men coming and going at all hours, the group was forced to move into a spare room in a friend's home. "It was a very small room," Tianguang recalled, "just big enough to fit a desk and a telephone so that we could operate the hotline."

In addition to staffing the hotline, which operated for two hours on Monday, Wednesday, Friday, and Sunday nights, Tong'ai's first volunteers also conducted community outreach at gay cruising areas in public parks and in the growing number of underground gay bars and bathhouses in Xi'an. In 2005, Tong'ai participated in its first HIV/AIDS prevention project when the Chinese Academy of Medical Sciences gave the group ¥20,000 ($2,400) to administer 250 HIV tests to MSM. Tong'ai later received additional HIV testing and prevention projects from various Chinese government agencies, including the Ministry of Health, the Ministry of Science and Technology, and the Academy of Medical Sciences.

In 2007, Tong'ai moved into a two-bedroom apartment on the sixth floor of an aging eight-story residential walk-up that was converted into a cramped yet cozy office. It was there that I first began volunteering at Tong'ai later that same year. In 2008, Tong'ai began participating in large-scale HIV projects supported by global health initiatives including the Bill and Melinda Gates Foundation and the Global Fund to Fight AIDS, Tuberculosis, and Malaria, which were implemented in partnership with GONGOs like the Chinese Association of STD and AIDS Prevention and Control and the China CDC. In April 2009, Tong'ai was able to move to a much larger office space in a newly constructed eighteen-story high-rise building with two elevators, on-site parking, rooftop gardens, and a shopping center. In August 2010, Tianguang hired three volunteers to work as full-time staff members. By then, the bulk of Tong'ai's funding came from HIV/AIDS testing and treatment projects.[2]

DEVELOPING THE HEART AND SERVING THE COMMUNITY: BECOMING A QUEER VOLUNTEER

Like other grassroots queer NGOs across China, Tong'ai was made up of volunteers who willingly donated their time and energies to fulfill the group's mission of fighting HIV/AIDS, developing the local queer community, and working toward greater awareness and acceptance of homosexuality in Chinese society. While volunteering was a way to make queer friends, it often required hard work, long hours, and personal risk with very little or no financial compensation. The turnover rate among Tong'ai volunteers was very high, making it difficult for the organization to cultivate and maintain a skilled and reliable workforce. The number of active volunteers waxed and waned over the years; in the group's heyday in 2008 there were eighty-six registered volunteers, including some thirty "core" (hexin) volunteers of all ages and class backgrounds. By 2010, there were more than one hundred registered volunteers, but the number of core volunteers had dropped to less than a dozen, mostly queer university students.

Tong'ai volunteers discovered the group in a variety of ways, including by word of mouth; Internet searches; Tong'ai outreach activities in gay bars, bathhouses, and parks; the hotline; and *Friends Exchange* magazine. Zhiming was one of Tong'ai's earliest volunteers. Recalling what the group was like before 2002, he said, "At that time, Tong'ai hadn't yet become a fixed organization. It was just Teacher Tian [an honorific title referring to Tianguang] doing some volunteer work. He would go out and distribute copies of *Friends Exchange* that Teacher Zhang sent over from Qingdao. My friend and I would help distribute them, but back then no one said, 'You are a Tong'ai volunteer.'" Wenqing, another long-serving Tong'ai volunteer, found the group through *Friends Exchange*. "There were people distributing it on the street, in front of the post office," he recalled. "It was December 1, World AIDS Day. That's how I saw this magazine. They had a telephone number for the gay hotline, so I gave them a call." Wenqing started volunteering for the Tong'ai hotline, eventually becoming its manager.

People's motivations for volunteering were as diverse as the volunteers themselves. Da You, a gay man who was born in 1960 and worked as a motorcycle deliveryman before becoming the manager of the largest gay bathhouse in Xi'an, was another early volunteer who joined Tong'ai after attending a community outreach activity. "Because I am a bit older, I became in charge of community outreach," he said. When I asked him why he wanted to volunteer, Da You replied, "The more I understood about HIV, the more scared I got. Why was it scary? Because all around me friends were constantly getting it. . . . We must do this kind of work, teach everyone how to protect themselves. If we don't, everyone would be even more afraid, and the infection rate would be even higher." Like Da You, many Tong'ai volunteers were motivated by a sense of duty and urgency to fight the spread of diseases like HIV/AIDS in their community. Zhiming reported a similar reason for becoming a volunteer. "After 2005, too many diseases had appeared," he said. "For example, HIV/AIDS and STDs like syphilis and genital warts. Some people that I knew had even died from AIDS. This drove me to do something for the people in this community. That is why I joined."

Others started volunteering out of curiosity or saw an opportunity to find queer friends and lovers. Paopao, who was also a Tong'ai volunteer, told me, "I didn't understand Tong'ai's background and what kind of organization they were, [only] that they took care of the gay community. I thought that was great! I could interact with people, make a lot of new friends, find a boyfriend. So, I went." Like most of Tong'ai's younger volunteers who had joined in recent years, Yangyang discovered the group while chatting on his phone with Yuanzi, one of Tong'ai's three paid staff members. "He said that he was working here, and I was really interested," Yangyang said. When I asked him why, he replied, "I think that Tong'ai is a very warm family. Everyone can tell their stories, make some new friends, and learn some new knowledge." Many younger volunteers described Tong'ai as a kind of extended "queer family" (*tongzhi zhi jia*). Xiao Yu, a Tong'ai volunteer who was born in 1989, told me, "Even though we were all strangers, there was still a feeling of relatedness. It's probably because we are all the same kind of people; in our subconscious, we all feel a kind of closeness."

Still others volunteered because of their religious beliefs. Yuanzi, who is a devout Buddhist, was introduced to Tong'ai by one of its oldest volunteers who later became a full-time staff member, Xiao Shan, whom he met at a Buddhist retreat. "He said that there was this kind of an organization that was doing work for a special community. I said, 'All right, that's good.' Because I felt that if we all had faith, if we could do some devotional, compassionate deeds for people, that it would be something very meaningful," Yuanzi recalled. For the group's many Buddhist volunteers, reducing suffering through the prevention and treatment of HIV/AIDS and other STDs was a way of practicing their faith. In 2010, again at Xiao Shan's encouragement, Yuanzi started working at Tong'ai full time.

The Chinese word for "volunteer" (*zhiyuanzhe*) contains two characters, *zhi*, which can be interpreted as "developing the heart" and means "will, aspiration, or ambition"; and *yuan*, which can mean "hope" or "desire" as well as being "willing" or "consenting" to do something (Harbaugh 1998, 12, 96). Xiao Feng thought of volunteers as "those people who devote themselves to others but who don't seek compensation. They should be good people." Others, including Xiao Wai, told me, "I think that 'volunteer' is just a name. As long as you are willing to serve everybody, to do something, it doesn't matter what you call it." Yuanzi similarly argued that what makes someone a volunteer is not filling out a form or receiving a title, but whether they are willing and able to be of service to the community. "I think that word [volunteer] is like a hat," Yuanzi said. "You wear it on your head; it looks good, and it sounds good, too. But in the end, how many people can actually get something done? That's why I don't advocate the word 'volunteer.' As long as there are brothers and sisters who are willing to help each other out, as long as you have that kind of heart . . . that is enough." Despite their differing motivations for engaging in grassroots queer HIV/AIDS activism, what all Tong'ai volunteers shared was a desire in their hearts to become involved, serve others, and make a positive difference in their local queer community. That so many queer men of all ages and class backgrounds felt called to become volunteers, despite a lack of financial compensation and the personal risks it entailed, not only demonstrates the existence of a vibrant queer civil society but also complicates depictions of increasing incivility and selfish individualism in postsocialist China.

WORK AND PLAY: DAILY LIFE IN A QUEER NGO

Most of the work in Tong'ai consisted of organizing a variety of almost daily community outreach activities in the local queer community. The Chinese word for "activity" (*huodong*) is composed of two characters, *huo*, meaning "to live" and depicting the sound of rushing water, and *dong*, meaning "to act" or "to move" (Harbaugh 1998, 192, 228). If volunteers were the body and soul of Tong'ai, then activities were its lifeblood, the way the group became a space for local queer cultural and political organization.

Tong'ai activities can be separated into four main categories, depending on whether they took place inside or outside of the office and whether they were conceived of as "work" (*gongzuo*) or "play" (*wan*). Work activities that took place inside the office included meetings between group members and outside visitors; answering the hotline; educational presentations on sexual health; voluntary counseling and testing (VCT) and treatment for HIV/AIDS and other STDs;[3] and daily office and administrative tasks such as cleaning, keeping track of project expenses and receipts, preparing project reports, organizing activities, and performing online "publicity" (*xuanchuan*) through Internet discussion forums and group texts. Before 2010, Tong'ai activities mainly took place at night and during the weekend, and only Tianguang and a handful of core volunteers had keys to the office. After several full-time staff members were hired in August 2010, work hours were set from 2 P.M. to 10 P.M., with Tuesdays off. However, in practice, Tong'ai staff and volunteers were often called upon to work outside these hours, coming in early for impromptu meetings or working late, especially on the weekends or when the group was completing HIV testing and prevention projects.

The line between work and play could be blurry, and even when work did get done it was usually accompanied by a great deal of socializing. Many activities held in the group office were primarily for fun, including movie screenings and card, mahjong, and dating games. Even during these more lighthearted activities, categories of work and play often overlapped; playing games frequently coincided with individual VCT sessions, for example, and helped incentivize people to come to the office and get tested. Dating games could segue into more serious discussions of STDs and safe-sex practices. An exception were group activities that were only conceived of as play and took place outside of the office, such as outings to the countryside to go hiking and eat dinner at commercialized, faux pastoral "peasant family paradises" (*nongjiale*), which have become a popular means of escape for many urban residents in postsocialist China.

Work activities that occurred outside of the office fell into the category of "community outreach" (*waizhan*, literally "external development"). These activities were often part of HIV testing projects sponsored by the Chinese CDC and global health initiatives like the Global Fund and the Gates Foundation. During outreach activities, Tong'ai volunteers wearing tasseled red velvet sashes with the group's name embroidered on them in large gold letters visited local gay bars, bathhouses, and cruising areas in public parks to hand out condoms, packets of personal lubricant, informational pamphlets about HIV/AIDS, and "testing cards" (*jiance kapian*) containing the group's name, address, hours, and telephone number. In addition to distributing materials, volunteers also attempted to engage people in discussions about HIV/AIDS and other STDs, stressing rising incidence rates in the local MSM community and the importance of wearing condoms and regular testing. Some outreach activities in gay bars and bathhouses involved on-site HIV testing, although this practice gradually grew less frequent for reasons that will be explored in the next chapter.

A final category of work activities that took place both inside and outside the office was occasional meetings with local and regional China CDC officials. Starting or ending in either the Tong'ai or CDC offices, where project contracts were signed or project expenses and reports submitted, these meetings almost always included a lunch or dinner in a private banqueting room at a nearby restaurant, during which copious amounts of food, alcohol, and cigarettes were consumed. During these banquets, discussions between Tong'ai members and CDC officials were unfailingly casual and never touched on work-related issues; however, under the playful surface serious work was being done in the form of expressing and exercising relations, or *guanxi*, between Tong'ai and the China CDC.

Relations between Tong'ai and the China CDC were decidedly unequal, with the CDC acting as a representative of the state exercising power and authority over the members of Tong'ai who were present. This unequal power dynamic was reflected by the fact that the CDC almost always footed the bill for meals, placing Tong'ai in the role of guest. During meals, the highest-ranking CDC official present directed where everybody sat, controlled what food was ordered and the order in which it was served, and led the conversation. They would also invariably and repeatedly "urge" (*quan*) everyone to drink glass after glass of a strong liquor called *baijiu* (literally "white spirits"). Declining to drink was virtually impossible due to the insistence of the CDC host and the fact that decorum required guests to drink every time they were urged to in order to demonstrate their gratitude for their host's generosity and how much they valued the guanxi that existed between them. On numerous occasions one or more Tong'ai staff members or volunteers would be forced to drink themselves sick. One high-ranking female CDC official in a certain regional city was so feared for her ability to consume baijiu in enormous quantities that Tong'ai staff members would endeavor to time their meetings with her in order to evade the dreaded post-meeting banquet, usually to no avail.[4]

To give a more detailed look into the kinds of queer spaces and identities being created by grassroots queer activism in northwest China, I now present ethnographic snapshots of three Tong'ai activities over the span of a single year, including an office event, an outreach trip to a gay cruising site at a local public park, and a meeting with regional CDC officials.

"WE WANT PEOPLE TO BE HAPPY WHEN THEY COME IN, AND HAPPY WHEN THEY LEAVE"

One cold Friday night in late February I arrived at the Tong'ai office to find more than twenty mostly younger queer men assembled around the large table in the front room. After a round of self-introductions, Yuanzi turned off the lights and began his usual presentation. As he spoke, people took turns getting tested for HIV and other STDs in the group's VCT room. After a few slides about the history of Tong'ai, Yuanzi discussed the difference between HIV and AIDS, stating that "from the time you are infected [with HIV] until you develop AIDS or die there are ten or fifteen years." He explained that it can take up to three months for HIV to show up in a test, during which time an HIV-positive person will be highly infectious, and emphasized the need to always use condoms and to get tested every three months. After showing tables and graphs charting the rise in HIV infection rates in mainland China, Yuanzi discussed common fears, including whether HIV-positive queer men will still be able to get married and have children. Yuanzi then explained how when a person's CD4 count drops to below three hundred they become eligible to receive free generic AIDS medications under the "Four Frees and One Care" (*Si Mian Yi Guanhuai*) policy.

Yuanzi then moved on to talk about eight other common STDs. Describing syphilis, which had a 30 percent incidence of infection among the MSM tested by Tong'ai, Yuanzi described how easily it spread, saying that in the early stages of infection it can even be transmitted by sitting on a contaminated toilet seat. An older man in the audience expressed shock at this information, exclaiming, "That fast? It's like catching a cold!" A younger man chimed in, saying, "No one would dare use the toilet after you say things like that!" and everyone laughed. After several slides featuring grotesque pictures of advanced stages of syphilis that elicited strong reactions from the audience, Yuanzi wrapped up his presentation by reemphasizing the importance of using condoms and regularly getting tested for HIV and also warned against people having "one-night stands" (*siyaojiu* or 419, a play on words where the English words "four one nine" sound like "for one night"). Although it is easy to find a sexual partner that way, Yuanzi said, "You don't know what things he has growing inside him." Yuanzi asked for questions, but the audience had gone silent. We then started to play the dating game *If You Are Gay*, which was led by a volunteer who remarked that we needed something fun after such serious talk about AIDS and STDs, saying, "We want people to be happy when they come in, and happy when they leave (*kaixin jinlai, kaixin zouqu*)."

This sentiment illustrates the challenges facing groups like Tong'ai, which often attempted to package its serious message about increasing infection rates of HIV/AIDS and other STDs and the importance of regular testing together with a more playful or lighthearted gay dating game. Apart from a strategy to draw more people into the office for testing, this volunteer's remark is also an example of a "happiness imperative" that was common among grassroots queer NGOs in postsocialist China, for whom cultivating a more "healthy," "positive," and "sunny" queer community was often regarded as part of a strategy of increasing the acceptance of queer people in Chinese society by demonstrating their responsibility and dispelling stereotypes of queers as depressed and diseased.[5] Far from encouraging queer men in postsocialist China to embrace their individual sexual desires, Tong'ai volunteers like Yuanzi and Xiao Shan were often somewhat sexually conservative or even prude, encouraging local queer men to take care of themselves and each other by practicing safe sex or abstaining from sex altogether. These dynamics complicate portrayals of postsocialist Chinese society as overwhelmingly selfish and individualistic and expressions of queer activism as inherently antinormative.

BIG SISTER ZHU: DEALING AND DRINKING
WITH THE CHINA CDC

One beautiful spring day in early April, Tianguang drove me and several other volunteers along a mountainous highway outside Xi'an. We were heading to a meeting with officials at a regional China CDC with whom Tong'ai was cooperating on a Global Fund project. Tianguang's boyfriend, Xiao Bao, was in the passenger seat, and Yuanzi and I sat in the back. Despite Tianguang's cheerful assertions that we were making good time, it became clear that we were running extremely late, and Yuanzi, who was responsible for managing the project and arranging meetings with the regional CDC, was becoming increasingly agitated.

After a few wrong turns we finally arrived at the regional CDC building. Several officials were standing by the side of the road waiting for us, and after exchanging greetings we walked to a private room in a nearby restaurant where we all stood around a circular table. Yuanzi introduced me to the director of the Infectious Diseases Department, a fierce yet friendly middle-aged woman who told us to call her Big Sister Zhu. Apart from Big Sister Zhu there were three other CDC officials present, an older woman called Doctor Liu and two younger officials. There was a clear status hierarchy, with the younger officials acting very deferentially toward Big Sister Zhu, arranging our chairs, and pouring tea. Big Sister Zhu had already ordered our food; when it started to arrive, she directed us all to sit down.

Instead of discussing the Global Fund project, we engaged in small talk. With a mischievous grin, Big Sister Zhu ordered a small porcelain bottle of baijiu; I glanced at Yuanzi, who ordinarily did not drink and wore an expression of resignation on his face. Big Sister Zhu led us in a toast, and we all stood, raising our small glasses and saying "cheers" (*ganbei*) before downing the strong alcohol (figure 4.1). Throughout the meal we all took turns offering toasts to one another. Big Sister Zhu toasted Yuanzi several times, as if she was testing him; his face had turned a deep shade of red, but he had no choice but to accept her entreaties and to return them in kind. Despite our feeble protests, when the first bottle was empty Big Sister Zhu ordered two more bottles of baijiu and we continued to drink; when one of the younger CDC officials did not empty his entire glass after a toast, Big Sister Zhu mocked him.

After lunch we walked to the nearby Infectious Diseases Department, a clean, airy room in the regional CDC building full of gleaming desks, computers, and glass cabinets containing educational materials about HIV/AIDS. Big Sister Zhu left for another meeting and a different CDC official brought copies of the Global Fund project contract for Tianguang to sign as Doctor Liu busily poured us fresh cups of hot green tea. Looking queasy, Yuanzi quietly excused himself as Tianguang discussed the details of the project agreement with Doctor Liu, arguing that some of its goals, such as increasing condom use among local MSM by 50 percent over the next year, were unrealistic. Doctor Liu only nodded, saying that higher-level officials set the goals and she had no control over them. Tianguang

FIGURE 4.1. Yuanzi (left) being toasted by Big Sister Zhu (middle). Photo by author.

seemed mollified, and he signed the contract. Looking worried, Doctor Liu asked about Yuanzi, and I went to look for him. The men's room at the end of the hall was empty, but the women's room was occupied. I softly called his name and Yuanzi emerged, looking disheveled, and admitted he had been sick. When I asked why he was in the women's room he laughed, saying that he had not noticed the sign on the door.

Several days later, Yuanzi told me why he drank so much that day, saying, "I wanted to make the CDC think that the people at Tong'ai are all right, that we can get things done without dragging our feet." That Tong'ai activists often cooperated with (and were literally wined and dined by) representatives of the Chinese state in no way compromised their status as part of an emerging queer civil society in postsocialist China. Rather, such rituals were understood as simply the price of doing business. Apart from these infrequent and usually rather brief interactions, Tong'ai was largely able to conduct its affairs as it wished without the overly intrusive involvement or supervision of the state.

"MISTER XI, YOU ARE BRAVE!"

One mid-summer's evening in early August, just before dusk, a large group of eleven Tong'ai volunteers and I set out to conduct an outreach activity at a gay cruising area in a nearby public park. Although volunteers were often sexually harassed in the parks after dark, this was also when the parks were most active. One new volunteer, a gay university student named Tianhao, was so excited that he practically skipped down the street carrying a large plastic shopping bag full of condoms and personal lubricant that the local Family Planning Commission had donated to Tong'ai along with informational pamphlets on AIDS and testing cards.[6] With a curt "tsk-tsk," Yuanzi chided Tianhao, saying that we would never be able to hand out so many condoms in a single night. Bats circled over our heads as we walked to the park, and I reflected on how they are often regarded as good omens in China because of how the word "bat" (*bianfu*) is a partial homonym for "good fortune" (*fu*). Everyone seemed to be in unusually high spirits, with Xiao Wai even holding hands with Xiao Xing, his new boyfriend, something I rarely saw queer men do in public. After darting through the traffic, which was still heavy even this late in the evening, we all climbed through a narrow gap between the iron park gates and walked in a single file, balancing atop the steep embankment around the moat that encircled Xi'an's tall city walls.

Inside the park it was dark under the trees. Around us stood the silhouettes of dozens of men in clumps of twos and threes; as if curious about what we were doing, they slowly moved out of the shadows toward our group. Yuanzi gathered us in a huddle and said in a low voice, "Listen to me tell you what you should say. It's actually very simple; there are only three things. One: Who we are, where we come from. Two: Practice safe sex. Three: If you are ever in trouble, come find us." We split up into pairs containing one new and one veteran volunteer who each grabbed handfuls of supplies from the shopping bag. I was assigned to Tianhao and Xiao Xi, a shy twenty-five-year-old gay man who had been a Tong'ai volunteer for almost a year. One pair of volunteers turned down a narrow trail that wound its way underneath a stand of pine trees toward the moat; another peeled off and took the wide, paved walkway that ran deeper into the park. I trailed behind Tianhao and Xiao Xi, who were headed down a narrow path leading into a dense bamboo grove that was almost pitch-black inside.

Because it had recently rained, the path was slick with mud and riddled with large puddles that were hard to see in the gloom. Standing at the entrance to the grove, we paused uncertainly. Inside the darkness we could make out a few shadowy figures. After debating who should go in first, Xiao Xi finally took the lead and boldly entered the bamboo forest, Tianhao and I following behind as we carefully picked our path forward. Above us the sky was running through darker shades of blue and purple to dusk. All was quiet inside the bamboo grove, except for the faint noise of rustling leaves and the soft sound of sandals on mud.

The first pair of men we encountered in a small clearing greeted us warily. Undeterred, Xiao Xi introduced us as Tong'ai volunteers and they relaxed and smiled, slowly taking the condoms and lubricant we offered and even accepting a pamphlet. As we felt flushed with success, our next few encounters were easier. Soon we were almost running through the dim bamboo forest, laughing and passing out condoms and testing cards to the groups of men inside who had gathered in small bunches, negotiating quietly, all searching for something in the dark.

We worked our way toward the deepest part of the bamboo grove, where the paths became more branching and narrower. Ahead of us in the gloom two men stood near to one another. As we approached, one of them faded into the inky blackness and I could see the other turning toward us and zipping up his pants. The man angrily refused the condoms that Xiao Xi offered, saying "I don't use those!" When we tried giving him a pamphlet, he hit our hands away, snapping, "I don't read that stuff!" We retreated, exchanging downcast glances and shrugging our shoulders.

Suddenly we were back into the open air, the sky above us now almost completely black. Ahead we rejoined the others, who were also smiling and laughing, and exchanged stories of our adventures. I told everyone how Xiao Xi tried to hand out condoms to a guy even as he was still zipping up his pants, and everyone commended him for his courage, saying, "Mister Xi, you are brave!" Xiao Xi blushed, the red on his face barely visible in the fading light. I recalled how shy and timid he was the first time he attended an outreach activity in a Xi'an gay bar six months ago and inwardly marveled at the transformation.

We pressed deeper into the park, staying away from the lit-up path along the city walls and sticking to the shadows by the edge of the moat where men congregated in small, silent groups or stood apart like lonely, expectant sentries of the shade. Soon we were out of supplies, and Tianhao proudly exclaimed that he had not brought too many condoms after all. Chirping crickets serenaded us as we made our way out of the park. When we reached the main gate, we found Yuanzi, who had become separated from the group and looked relieved to see us, laughing and saying, "I was afraid you had all been lured away!"

Activities like this demonstrate how grassroots queer NGOs like Tong'ai are contributing to the development of a local queer civil society in northwest China. Xiao Xi's transformation from a bashful introvert to an increasingly confident queer activist illustrates how volunteering provides opportunities for queer people to make new friends, develop new skills, and work as part of a team of fellow-minded activists that are dedicated to improving the health and vitality of their local queer community. Such examples further challenge arguments about the increasing individualization and privatization of postsocialist Chinese society.

AIDS AND ACTIVISM: CIVIL SOCIETY AND THE POLITICS OF CHINESE QUEER NGOS

These three ethnographic vignettes offer glimpses into the vibrant queer civil society that is developing in postsocialist northwest China. Several Chinese expressions can be translated as "civil society," each with a slightly different meaning (S. Wang 1991). *Wenming shehui* ("civilized society") denotes the civilizing forces that a well-governed state is believed to exert upon society. *Shimin shehui* ("city people's society") emphasizes the autonomous, self-interested commercial pursuits of urban entrepreneurs. Influenced by Western civil society scholarship from the 1980s and 1990s, *gongmin shehui* ("citizen's society") imagines an ideal society in which all citizens participate equally in government, and individual autonomy and self-development are linked to the advancement of the common good (Des Forges 1997, 70–73).

Most queer activists in northwest China were unfamiliar with any translation of the term "civil society." Those who were usually understood it as an idealized future in which NGOs like Tong'ai worked with the Chinese government as equal partners and queer people enjoyed more civil and political rights. Xiao Shan defined civil society as "a social philosophy that there shouldn't be a single government with autocratic rule, but that every citizen in a country or society should participate in guiding its development." According to Zhiming, the ideal civil society was "one in which citizens possess every kind of right, one in which citizens, through NGOs, can fill in the blanks in places where the government can't reach." When I asked him how he viewed the relationship between NGOs and the government, Zhiming replied, "I think the government and NGOs should be equal."

Even if they were often unfamiliar with the idea of civil society, most queer activists in northwest China had strong opinions about the role and importance of grassroots NGOs. Many understood the term for "grassroots" (*caogen*) as expressing an essentially Chinese concept. As Xiao Wai explained, "'Grassroots' is an old expression in China meaning something that has started from the lowest levels [of society]." The Chinese word "grass" (*cao*) also connotes that which is wild, uncultivated, and disorganized. Zhiming explained that, in contrast to GONGOs like the Red Cross, which receive support from the government, "A grassroots NGO is a volunteer organization that doesn't have any support. It has no [state] background. . . . It is *grown from the ground*. 'Grass' means *nobody to take care* [of]; it is *wild*. 'Grassroots' can also mean not professional enough, because it is 'grass,' and not 'flower' or 'corn.' Nobody is taking care of you. You are wild."

This idea of grassroots NGOs as "wild" or "uncultivated" reflects local understandings of civil society, which stress the desirability of cooperation between civil society organizations and the state. Most Tong'ai volunteers believed that queer NGOs should work with the government in ways that would be beneficial for both state and society. Some viewed community-based organizations as needing government support because they lacked the capabilities and resources to act effectively on their own. Others acknowledged the realities of the political climate in postsocialist China. As Wenqing said, "I don't think it's realistic to be independent. Because after all, we are operating inside a governmental framework. The government and NGOs should try their hardest to harmoniously coexist." Similarly, Lao Wang argued that "In China, things are government centered. The grassroots do whatever is in their power, but they still follow the leadership of the government."

Several government officials I interviewed stressed the state's role of providing leadership and supervision to community-based NGOs. Yet they also recognized the dependence of the state on groups like Tong'ai to effectively carry out its mandate to prevent and treat HIV and AIDS. Director Zhang was a confident and business-like woman who directed the HIV/AIDS clinic at the Shaanxi CDC and had been cooperating with Tong'ai since 2002. She described the state's HIV/AIDS prevention and treatment policy as "government-led, multisectoral participation" and saw the role of the government as providing "professional guidance" and "encouragement" to community-based NGOs, as well as "assessing" how well they were doing their work. "This isn't to say that what the government is able to do, NGOs shouldn't do," Director Zhang concluded. "Right now, we need to utilize all of our resources in order to do this work." The director of a regional CDC cooperating with Tong'ai in a Global Fund-sponsored HIV/AIDS testing project told me that, in the case of "major public health projects" like those centered on HIV/AIDS, the state policy was for "the government to guide the way, public health administration to take the lead, and for every citizen to participate." He acknowledged, however, that "it is probably more difficult for government-established organizations to earn the trust of high-risk communities. If you say the CDC is coming, whether it is homosexuals or other high-risk communities, they will probably be wary of you. But Tong'ai is a civil society organization, so they are much more suitable."

Many queer volunteers also seemed to understand that, just as they needed to work with the government in order to achieve their goals, the state also had to cooperate with them in order to meet its own objectives. "There are some problems that the government cannot solve through official channels," Yangyang remarked. "So there is a need for civil society organizations." Tian'e pointed out that "people in government are not necessarily gay. If they have absolutely no understanding of this community, how would they be able to do a good job?" Although their familiarity with and proximity to the queer community afforded organizations like Tong'ai a certain degree of respect and autonomy from the state, queer volunteers also saw their work as supporting the state. Even Tianguang, who often found fault with the CCP, said, "We can criticize the government, [point out] what it should be doing that it isn't doing or that it isn't doing well. But we cannot only criticize. If we have the circumstances and the abilities, we can do things ourselves, do as much as we can. This is also a kind of support for the government." The acknowledgment of both queer activists and government officials of their mutual interdependence demonstrates an alternative cultural understanding or definition of civil society in which, rather than civil society primarily existing in order to serve as a check on state power, the state and civil society organizations ideally can and should work together, whenever possible, in order to support one another and achieve their common goals.

Like most grassroots queer NGOs in China (Hildebrandt 2011a, 975), Tong'ai was not legally registered with the state. One night as we ate dinner in the Tong'ai office, Tianguang explained the three types of NGOs that exist in postsocialist China. The first he described as "those organizations that have already registered with and are vigorously supported and assisted by the government. We call them 'under the sunlight' (*yangguang xia*) or 'open' (*gongkai*) organizations; they don't have any restrictions." Tianguang paused to eat a bite of food before continuing. "There is another kind of organization that is illegal, that cannot officially register; those types of organizations are under attack by the government, for example those so-called 'evil cult' (*xiejiao*) or 'reactionary' (*fandong*) organizations, like the Falun Gong." Tianguang laughed nervously as he said the name. "These are called 'underground' (*dixia*) or 'dark' (*hei'an*) organizations." Tianguang explained that Tong'ai belonged to a third category of so-called "gray" (*huise*) organizations, saying, "They are neither open and under the sunlight nor in the dark. If we were a dark organization the government would come and attack us. Yet the work that we do is beneficial to society, beneficial to the people, so the government cannot attack us, cannot suppress us, cannot come and close us down. But in terms of policy, in terms of law, the government doesn't support us. We describe organizations that are in this state of affairs as 'living in the gray zone' (*chu zai huise didai*)." The situation of unregistered community-based queer NGOs like Tong'ai illustrates the complex nature of state-society relations in postsocialist China. While the "gray zone" that Tianguang describes could be seen as an example of the mode of state governmentality that Aihwa Ong and Li Zhang (2008, 3) call "socialism from afar," the quasi-legal status of groups like Tong'ai also enabled them to operate relatively independently without much direct supervision by the state.

Despite its indeterminate legal status, Tong'ai developed strong working relations with local and provincial government agencies. In the late 1990s, when Tong'ai was a new organization, Tianguang actively sought out the support of local and provincial officials. Provincial CDC leaders, some of whom had already begun conducting HIV/AIDS prevention outreach in local gay cruising areas, were very supportive. "At that time, the director of the provincial CDC would attend many of our activities himself, including [HIV] testing in [gay] bars. There was a lot of basic support," Tianguang recalled. Tong'ai was relatively fortunate; not all queer NGOs in postsocialist China enjoy such official support.

In part because of his own past political activism, Tianguang took great pains to downplay the political nature of Tong'ai in order to maintain good working relationships with the state. Echoing comments I heard from queer NGO leaders across China, Tianguang argued that their immediate focus should be on HIV/AIDS, rather than on gay rights:

> There are two reasons why we put the relationship between the gay community and HIV/AIDS first. The first reason is that HIV/AIDS is a matter of life and death. . . . There is another reason: right now, the only kind of work that the Chinese government will support is HIV/AIDS-related work, and it is only through

doing HIV/AIDS-related work that we are able to obtain a few resources. If we did any other work, not only would the government not give us any support, they also probably wouldn't allow us to do it.

Tianguang also argued that avoiding politics was also necessary for groups like Tong'ai to maintain their relationship with the local queer community:

The people who we work for and provide services to, if you talk to them about health or things like that, they probably wouldn't have anything to worry about. They will communicate with you, cooperate with you, and support you. [But] if you go and talk to someone from the community about human rights, they will probably get really scared, they will probably stay far away from you. Because they know what it means to talk about human rights in China. It means political risk. It isn't safe.

Despite such efforts to avoid the appearance of political activism, queer activists in northwest China sometimes do acknowledge the political nature of their work. Tianguang himself often emphasized that their mission extended far beyond fighting HIV/AIDS:

The China CDC only cares about this community because of health problems like AIDS and sexually transmitted diseases. But what this community needs even more is to have our rights and interests protected, to have our own unique culture, to be respected and recognized by the law. . . . Doing AIDS-related work is actually the same thing as doing [human] rights work. Because everyone knows that AIDS isn't merely a public health problem. Ultimately, AIDS is a political problem, it is a human rights problem. So, you could say that the AIDS-related work we are doing is itself also human rights work.

Although genuinely dedicated to HIV/AIDS prevention and treatment, queer NGO leaders across China often frame this work as a way of achieving larger social and political goals like increasing awareness and support for homosexuality, strengthening civil society, and even one day legalizing same-sex marriage.[7] By preventing the spread of HIV/AIDS in their communities, activists like Tianguang believe they would demonstrate that they were good citizens and social attitudes toward homosexuality would gradually improve. This strategy resembles what Lucetta Kam calls "the politics of public correctness," or the idea that queer people will only gain greater acceptance by displaying "healthy" (*jiankang*) and "sunny" (*yangguang*) lifestyles (2013, 90).

Queer NGO members routinely downplay the political nature of their work, preferring the more neutral term "volunteer" instead of "activist" (*jijifenzi*). However, many volunteers see preventing HIV as a way of preserving the relative freedom and autonomy of the queer community. In recent decades, the PRC has

frequently cracked down on unruly sexualities, especially during politically sensitive periods. In September 2010, in the run-up to China's National Day holiday,
the Public Security Bureau in Beijing made several nighttime raids at a popular
gay cruising area in a public park, detaining at least eighty men (G. Wong 2010).
Rumors spread through the queer community in Xi'an that the men were forced
to get tested for HIV while in detention. Not long after the raids in Beijing, Xiao
Shan remarked how "until now the government hasn't paid much attention to us"
but speculated this would change if the HIV infection rate among MSM got too
high. Yuanzi often concluded his presentations on HIV/AIDS and STDs in the
Tong'ai office by saying, "We can only be happy when we are healthy, and we must
be happy in order to be free." Remarks like these not only demonstrate the essentially political nature of queer HIV/AIDS activism in postsocialist China but are
also a prime example of how many queer activists view achieving greater social
acceptance and political rights for queer people as dependent on creating and
maintaining healthy and happy queer communities.

UNITE: NORTHWEST CHINA'S FIRST QUEER WOMEN'S NGO

When I began fieldwork in 2007, Tong'ai was the only queer NGO in northwest
China. However, by 2010 many new queer groups had formed. One of these was
UNITE, northwest China's first queer women's NGO, which was founded in
December 2009 by three lesbian women in their late twenties. By 2011, UNITE
had between fifteen and thirty core volunteers and over two hundred people who
regularly attended its activities. Although I sought out every opportunity to interact with UNITE and gather as much information about it as I could, because the
group was not yet as active as Tong'ai was during my primary fieldwork the amount
of data about grassroots lesbian activism I was able to collect was comparatively
limited.

All three of UNITE's founders were born in the 1980s, well after the start of
China's economic and social reforms. Jiajia described how she initially did not
know anything about queer grassroots groups or activism. "I always thought that
I needed to do something" for the Chinese queer movement, she told me. "I had
already come out and I wanted to do whatever I could. But I didn't know where to
start." Jiajia eventually discovered Tongyu, a queer women's NGO in Beijing that
was founded in 2005, and became a volunteer, helping to edit the group's website.
In 2009, Jiajia attended Lala Camp, a training conference organized by the Chinese Lala Alliance that was formerly held in a different location in mainland China
every year and served as a seedbed for community organizing among queer women
(Bao 2018, 84–85; Kam 2013, 21). "While I was there," Jiajia said, "I met a lot of
other lesbian groups, and I realized that you didn't need to have a lot of money or
things in order to do some basic work. I thought that was pretty cool, and that we
could also do this. So, when I got back, we started [UNITE]."

After "graduating" from Lala Camp, Jiajia returned to northwest China and recruited two other queer women to help her start UNITE. One was Xiao Bang, another Xi'an local whom Jiajia knew from university. The other, Douzi, was a twenty-two-year-old Xi'an university student from Beijing who had also recently become a Tongyu volunteer. In what they described as a collaborative process, the three women arrived at a common understanding of what they wanted to accomplish with their new organization. As Jiajia explained:

We founded this group in order to do something for lesbians in the [northwest] region. Because there were no activities, their self-identity wasn't very good, especially those who were under economic and family pressures. A lot of lesbians are forced to marry. They are very unhappy.... We wanted to make lesbian women have greater self-identity, as well as make the lesbian community come together. In the past, things were very disorganized and there was a lot of hostility between people. We hoped that through some activities and exchanges we would be able to come together and have a little bit of power.

When I asked Jiajia why they had chosen to give the group an English name, Jiajia just laughed and explained that it would not have sounded as good in Chinese.

Xiao Bang described UNITE as "a local lesbian organization that advocates for the rights and interests [of homosexuals] and for the broader support of homosexuality." Xiao Bang told me she was inspired to start a group like UNITE because

there were a lot of gay organizations in Beijing and Shanghai, including lesbian organizations, and they had been around for a long time. But in the northwest, there were no such organizations. Also, we thought that gay bars are very unhealthy; if a straight person went and saw gay people spending the whole day inside a dark bar getting drunk, this doesn't give a good impression. We wanted to form a sunny, healthy organization; at that time, we weren't thinking about power and rights and those kinds of things, we just wanted to get some lesbians to come together and do something meaningful, that was all.

Xiao Bang's comments again underscore the ubiquity of the "happiness imperative," or the belief that queer people and communities will only achieve greater social acceptance and political rights if they are perceived as "sunny" and "healthy," among queer activists in northwest China.

Several differences existed between Tong'ai and UNITE, chief among them the increasing focus of the former on HIV/AIDS prevention, testing, and treatment. Because HIV/AIDS was not regarded (by themselves or others) as an issue affecting queer women, UNITE was free to pursue a more overtly political and cultural agenda than Tong'ai. UNITE was also more connected to national and international queer activist networks and culture than Tong'ai. The group frequently collaborated with queer NGOs based in Beijing like Tongyu and Aibai, a national queer information and advocacy organization, and participated in national activities such as the Lala Camp and the China Gay and Lesbian Film Festival (both held for the first time in northwest China in 2011 and organized by UNITE) as well as international events like the International Day against Homophobia, Biphobia, and Transphobia (IDAHOBIT), observed every year on May 17.[8]

When I asked Jiajia how UNITE was different from gay NGOs like Tong'ai, she replied:

> We probably pay more attention to advocacy and culture. In my own opinion, I think that we should make more people see us and know about us; therefore, we probably have more activities that are directed outside of the community. We also have activities inside the lesbian community. But I think if you want change, you must start by making outside people see you. You first must be willing to stand up; only then will they be able to know you, only then will they understand you and ultimately accept you. If you only play inside your own small circle, people will never know that you exist.

Xiao Bang expressed a similar opinion, arguing for the need for queer Chinese NGOs to address broader cultural and political aims and to not focus solely on HIV/AIDS:

> There are large differences between gay and lesbian organizations. In [the northwest] I only understand Tong'ai. I think that all they do is HIV/AIDS. Other things, including advocacy, they do very little of. They just tell everyone, don't go and have high-risk sex, wear a condom. But I think that isn't enough. . . . If you do some other activities, like watching movies or lectures, you can make people change their sexual behaviors from their hearts, instead of just pressuring them to change.

These comments encapsulate the challenges and opportunities of queer women's groups like UNITE in postsocialist China, who often struggle with a lack of visibility and resources compared to queer men's groups like Tong'ai. Although their lower visibility allowed UNITE to pursue broader political and cultural goals, their inability to participate in HIV/AIDS prevention and treatment projects also deprived them of a major source of funding. "If you do HIV/AIDS," Jiajia explained, "it is really easy to apply for international projects and resources. But lesbians don't have that." Unlike the well-established and better-funded Tong'ai, UNITE initially lacked an office space and held its meetings and activities in a variety of locations like local lesbian bars and private homes. Sometimes Tong'ai and UNITE organized joint events like film screenings, in part because UNITE could not afford to purchase an expensive video projector. Unable to access national or international funds earmarked for HIV/AIDS prevention and treatment, UNITE volunteers raised money by selling items like homemade rainbow flag bracelets at their events.[9] In August 2011, UNITE launched a ¥2000 ($300) online fundraising campaign to purchase their own video projector; by January 2012 they had finally raised their target amount, mostly through small donations from UNITE volunteers and supporters.

Exclusion from HIV/AIDS work also denied UNITE a valuable source of political cover and legitimacy enjoyed by their queer male counterparts. In Xiao Bang's words, "The government isn't terribly supportive of NGOs, [especially] organizations that have to do with human rights. They won't flagrantly attack you, but they definitely won't support you." Unlike Tong'ai, which Xiao Bang said could "wave the big flag of AIDS," the government did not have a reason to support queer women's groups like UNITE, which made it more difficult for them to navigate the social and legal "gray zone." "The attitude of the government is very unclear right now," Jiajia argued. "The government doesn't allow you to say that you want political rights or whatever. You can go out and play, like see a movie or have a party, but you can't talk about anything too sensitive." UNITE also struggled with the relative social and political invisibility of queer women, which Jiajia attributed to gender discrimination and exclusion from HIV/AIDS work:

> Because of AIDS, gay organizations are more able to be public, but not so with lesbian groups. Also, women themselves are a group that does not like to make their voices heard. Compared to men, women are also probably more averse to politics.... Therefore, because of AIDS, gays will be able to attract more people's attention, and gays will also be able to make their voices heard. But not women. First of all, they don't have something to attract people's attention. Secondly, they cannot cause a social panic.

Despite these limitations, UNITE's dedicated and energetic leaders and volunteers managed to organize an impressively wide variety of activities aimed at increasing the visibility of queer women in northwest China, one of which I describe in detail below.

"GAYS ARE GOOD: UNITE GOES TO CAMPUS"

One June, Jiajia and Douzi invited me to participate in a "gay-straight discussion forum" (*zhiren tongzhi jiaoliu hui*) they were organizing at a local university called "Gays Are Good: UNITE Goes to Campus." The description of the event read:

If your roommate is gay
He might be the first homosexual you meet, but he won't be your last.
Tomorrow you might run into a gay professor, a lesbian boss, a bisexual coworker.
If you seize this opportunity, learn how to hold your head held high and get along
    with gays and lesbians
Then, in your future life, you will be able to be at ease with all kinds of people.

Maybe you don't know what a lesbian is?
Maybe you don't know that June is Gay Pride Month?
Then let me tell you
Our love has no difference. In fact, we are the same.
Come, you don't have to sympathize, we are not different; let us devote ourselves
to eliminating discrimination and prejudice.

My role in the event was to give a brief presentation on "the history of the U.S. gay and lesbian movement and its current situation." Other UNITE members would also give presentations, and then we would take questions from the audience.

On the day of the event, my then-boyfriend (who was visiting me at the time) and I were to meet Jiajia at a nearby bus stop at 3:30 P.M. Jiajia was already waiting for us when we arrived, and I marveled at how she somehow managed to be both excited and relaxed at the same time. When I mentioned how nervous I was, Jiajia only laughed and said everything would be fine. "Just being able to have an activity like this is already not bad," she remarked. Xiao Bang got on the bus at a stop near her home, and we all chatted as the bus rumbled its way toward the university. When we finally reached the university gates, we all milled around waiting for the others to arrive. Eventually Douzi (who was a student at the university), her girlfriend, and a few other UNITE volunteers joined us.

As we entered the campus, Douzi pointed out a poster on a bulletin board advertising today's event. The large poster, printed on red and white paper with large, bold black Chinese characters, stood out from the other announcements. Douzi pointed out my own name, in Chinese, on the poster: "VIP: U.S. PhD student Casey Miller." A lump started to form at the back of my throat as I began to feel more nervous. When I asked how many people they were expecting, Jiajia guessed that maybe fifty people might come. Walking through campus we passed more advertisements for that night's activity posted on bulletin boards, walls, and lampposts. As we passed by a dormitory building, Douzi's girlfriend pointed out a vivid green banner draped from its open windows on which large characters spelled out "Pride starts with you. Gay love come out! Gay love has no borders." I stopped to admire the sign and expressed my amazement about its visibility to Douzi's girlfriend. She just nodded, proudly saying that the banner had already become a very "hot" (re) topic of discussion on campus. The lump in the back of my throat grew even larger.

Suddenly, Jiajia received a text message informing her that a member of the university's Communist Youth League Supervisory Committee had gotten wind of the event and was "sending a student to spy on us." Douzi's girlfriend remarked that we did not even know who the student was. "That's really rotten" she said, wrinkling her nose in disgust. More texts followed. Instead of going through the Youth League, UNITE had organized the event with the university psychology club; now that the Youth League was sending someone to observe us, the psychology professor who was sponsoring the event was nervous that I might say some-

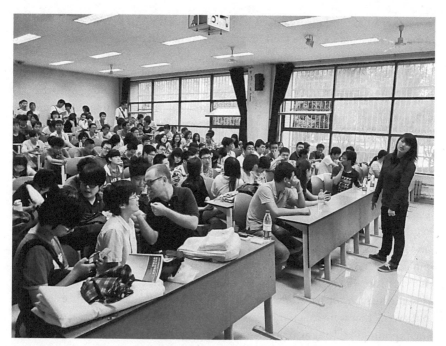

FIGURE 4.2. UNITE volunteers confer before the gay-straight discussion forum. Photo by Yan Kung.

thing critical about the PRC. After a hasty discussion, the UNITE volunteers agreed that in order to avoid further angering the Youth League it would be best if I did not mention either the United States or LGBTQ issues at all. "What should I talk about?" I asked. Douzi pursed her lips and frowned before suggesting that I talk about HIV/AIDS instead. "The Chinese government isn't very tolerant; they don't want students talking about politics," she said. "AIDS is something you can talk about; it's a global problem." But, she added, "It's best if you don't say anything negative. Chinese people like to hear good things."

As I pondered how I was going to give an extemporaneous ten-minute presentation on AIDS without mentioning any sensitive or negative topics, we arrived at the 200-person lecture hall where the activity was being held. Every chair was taken, and people were even sitting in the aisles and standing at the back of the room. More students were coming, and those who could not get inside thronged outside the windows trying to catch a glimpse of what was going on. Even Jiajia started getting nervous as the reality of what we were about to do slowly sank in. At 7 P.M., before the activity started, Douzi went around to everyone, whispering fiercely, "Be tactful! Don't be too direct!" The atmosphere in the room was one of excited anticipation; the people in the audience were looking around to see who else was there and chatting nervously in a dull roar (figure 4.2). Once the event began everything went by in a blur. Ignoring Douzi's frantic facial expressions, Jiajia threw caution to the wind and spoke very openly about homosexuality, and my rather vague and disorganized remarks about HIV/AIDS were well received. After our presentations, the UNITE volunteers engaged the audience in a long and surprisingly frank discussion about homosexuality. Two hours later, as we rode the bus back into town, everyone was relaxed again; some of the volunteers were chatting about which girls in the audience were the cutest, laughing uproariously and talking over each other. I asked Jiajia how she thought things went and she said, more seriously this time, "Actually, just being able to have an activity like this is already not bad."

This vignette illustrates several aspects of queer activism and civil society in northwest China. It shows how UNITE volunteers dealt with having less funding and visibility than queer men's groups like Tong'ai by organizing highly visible, well-publicized, and well-attended events at local university campuses that required very little money other than buying bus fares and printing some posters and a banner. It reveals how UNITE navigated both the "gray zone" and the "happiness imperative" of queer activism in postsocialist China and how even lesbian activists sometimes used HIV/AIDS as a cover issue. It also demonstrates how, despite the many obstacles they faced, UNITE was still able to organize and carry out events that were much more overtly political than those organized by queer men's groups like Tong'ai, demonstrating the depth and complexity of queer activism and civil society in northwest China.

QUEER(ING) CIVIL SOCIETY IN CHINA

Unregistered grassroots queer NGOs are an important example of the dynamic civil society taking shape in postsocialist China. By exploring the new spaces of political participation and individual identity being created by queer activists in northwest China as well as their attitudes toward and relationships with the state and society, this chapter continues "the effort begun by others to apply concepts of 'civil society' and 'public sphere' to the Chinese case in a more nuanced way" (Wasserstrom and X. Liu 1995, 392). While neither grassroots gay or lesbian NGOs or their volunteers in northwest China view themselves as opposing the postsocialist state, their efforts to broaden citizen participation in China's expanding public sphere, and to increase the awareness and acceptance of homosexuality in Chinese society, contest the hegemonic powers of the state as well as heteronormative gender and sexual norms in postsocialist China.

Although the disciplinary power of the state is never far from the thoughts and actions of queer activists and NGOs, the state is also never in complete control; indeed, the state is itself reliant upon queer men's groups like Tong'ai to successfully implement national and international HIV/AIDS prevention and treatment priorities and programs. As a result, queer NGOs enjoy a certain degree of leeway to pursue their personal, political, and cultural goals in the "gray zone" at the margins of Chinese state and society.

HIV/AIDS has played a similar role in catalyzing the emergence of queer social movements around the world. According to Dennis Altman, "The [AIDS] epidemic has allowed for a new openness about not just homosexuality but also about the growth of self-conscious homosexual identities in much of Asia" (1995, 101). Similarly, Richard Parker relates how in Brazil "AIDS provided an important basis, as well as a significant source of funding, for increasingly visible gay organizing and mobilization" (1999, 45; also see Wright 2005). HIV/AIDS is also a mixed blessing for queer women's activism. On the one hand, because they are not associated with AIDS, queer women's groups like UNITE are denied valuable sources of political legitimacy, visibility, and funding, both domestically and internationally. On the other hand, the relative anonymity they enjoy also brings some benefits to queer women's organizing, including less government interference as well as greater latitude to pursue more explicitly cultural, social, and political goals.

I continue exploring grassroots queer activism in northwest China in the next chapter by taking a critical look at the relationships between grassroots queer men's NGOs, the state, and global health initiatives. Examining internal divisions and conflicts within and among local queer men's NGOs, as well as an increase in competition between local and nonlocal NGOs in the area of HIV/AIDS prevention and treatment, I show how these changes have furthered the creation of an "(un)civil society" that is partially the result of a neoliberal public health model in which global health initiatives and the state increasingly outsource the provision of HIV testing and treatment services among MSM to NGOs, which are then forced to compete with one another for future rounds of funding. I also explore the positive and negative effects that such pressures are having on grassroots queer men's NGOs, their ability to respond effectively to the threat of HIV/AIDS in their communities, and their broader political and social objectives of increasing awareness and acceptance of homosexuality in China.

5 · "DYING FOR MONEY"
Conflict and Competition among
Queer Men's NGOs

One sweltering summer afternoon, I stood with a group of Tong'ai volunteers in the dust beneath a highway overpass in Xi'an.[1] We chatted nervously as cars rushed by overhead, and there was a palpable feeling of tension and excitement in the muggy air. Over the past several weeks, something strange had been happening in Tong'ai. People seemed increasingly agitated and began having hushed conversations that would end as soon as I entered a room; when I asked what was going on, they simply shrugged and replied, "Nothing," while exchanging meaningful looks. I eventually confronted Xiao Jun, a core Tong'ai volunteer who, like me at the time, was a PhD student in his late twenties. Although he would not tell me what was happening, Xiao Jun assured me I would soon find out. Meanwhile, I noticed a growing antagonism between some group members and Lao Huang, an older volunteer who managed the group's telephone hotline and possessed one of the few coveted sets of office keys. I wondered if what was happening had anything to do with him. What I did I not know was that tensions that had been simmering in the group long before my arrival were about to boil over.

Earlier that morning, I had received a cryptic phone call from Xiao Jun instructing me to meet him later that afternoon at his university, where I would be given further information. It was all very mysterious, and I felt certain that I was about to be let in on the secret. When I arrived at the campus, I was greeted by Xiao Jun and two other Tong'ai volunteers. Xiao Jun hurriedly briefed us on the details: for some time, Tianguang, the founder and leader of Tong'ai, had suspected that Lao Huang was secretly working for the Yi De Foundation, a rival queer men's NGO based in Hong Kong and directed by Chengji, a Hong Kong queer activist and Tianguang's nemesis. According to Xiao Jun, these suspicions had recently been confirmed: in exchange for a personal monthly salary, his own office, and a new laptop computer, for the past several months Lao Huang had covertly been helping Chengji establish a new branch of Yi De in Xi'an. What was more, Xiao Jun continued, Lao Huang had also been trying to persuade other Tong'ai volunteers to leave the group and join Yi De. Today, the new Xi'an branch of Yi De was holding its first meeting at a secret time and location somewhere in the city. However, a spy from inside the new group was going to tell us when and where the meeting was being held. Additionally, Tianguang, whom everyone thought was attending a national HIV/AIDS conference in Beijing, had secretly returned to Xi'an and was planning to crash the clandestine Yi De meeting and personally confront Lao Huang.

Xiao Jun had received a text message directing us to meet Tianguang under the baking highway overpass where we were now waiting. When Tianguang arrived, we set off toward the Yi De meeting, which turned out to be in a nearby karaoke lounge. Ignoring the startled women at the front desk, we stormed up several flights of stairs and made a rather dramatic entrance into the cramped, smoke-filled room, where a surprised Lao Huang had just begun speaking. A long red banner hung on the wall with large white characters that proclaimed the event as the first meeting of the Yi De Foundation in northwest China. After a few moments of chaos, Tianguang began interrogating Lao Huang in front of everyone, demanding to know when and why he had started secretly working for Yi De.

After almost an hour and a half of verbal sparring, Tianguang finally concluded the confrontation by officially expelling Lao Huang from Tong'ai and confiscating his office keys. "From now on," Tianguang said, "in front of our volunteers here, if the majority has no objections: Lao Huang, you are no longer a Tong'ai volunteer. You need to take out your keys and hand them over. Take out all your keys." There was a long silence, followed by the sound of jingling metal, as Lao Huang finally handed over his office keys. Tianguang quietly asked him, "Now, are there any of your things left inside the office?" to which Lao Huang responded, very quietly, "No." "Are any of your personal things there?" Tianguang asked again. "No," Lao Huang said a second time, his voice barely audible. "If they are, we can arrange a time for you to come and collect them," Tianguang said. And with that, we quickly exited the room and hurried Tianguang to his car so that he would not miss his flight back to Beijing.

In the previous chapter, I explored how social and economic reforms and a looming AIDS crisis in the late 1990s and early 2000s created opportunities for queer activists to begin organizing to fight the spread of HIV among their peers and advocate for increased awareness and acceptance of homosexuality in Chinese society. The ethnographic vignette at the beginning of this chapter, an example of what Carina Heckert (2018, 126) calls a "biopolitical drama," illustrates how relationships between queer civil society actors are often anything but civil. In my many years of fieldwork among queer activists in northwest China, while I was continually impressed and inspired by their hard work, dedication, and sacrifice, I was also struck by the growing degree of distrust, discord, and disillusionment that existed within the community.

When I began fieldwork in July 2007, Tong'ai was a cash-strapped community-based NGO operated by a small but dedicated group of volunteers with a vision that far outstripped its meager resources. In addition to offering community programming and a free telephone hotline that dispensed support and advice to queer men, Tong'ai was one of the only NGOs in northwest China providing HIV/AIDS testing and prevention services to MSM, or "men who have sex with men." After the arrival of large global health initiatives like the Bill and Melinda Gates Foundation and the Global Fund to Fight AIDS, Tuberculosis, and Malaria in northwest China in 2008, the availability of resources expanded, but so did the number of organizations providing services to MSM. Relations between these groups ranged from collaborative to combative, with local queer community-based NGOs like Tong'ai struggling to survive in the face of stiff competition from various regional, national, and international organizations, many of whom had no prior experience with either queer men or HIV/AIDS prevention.

In this chapter, I take critical look at what some have called the "dark side" (Mudde 2003) of civil society by examining the changing and often contentious relationships within and between grassroots queer men's NGOs, other local and nonlocal NGOs, the state, and global health initiatives in northwest China. Drawing on Max Weber's theories of charismatic authority and bureaucratization, I show how a temporary and sudden increase in HIV/AIDS funding provided by global health initiatives like the Gates Foundation and the Global Fund exacerbated existing tensions between rival charismatic NGO leaders who were already engaged in contests over territory, followers, and resources. Working with the Chinese government, global health initiatives purposefully promoted a neoliberal process whereby public health services were increasingly outsourced to NGOs, which were then required to "compete" (*jingzheng*) with one another to secure "projects" (*xiangmu*) and "funds" (*zijin*) to continue providing HIV prevention services to MSM in the future. This increase in competition between NGOs also encouraged processes of bureaucratization and medicalization within Tong'ai, shrinking its volunteer base, weakening its connections with the local queer community, and channeling its activities away from broader political and social objectives toward a narrower, more entrepreneurial emphasis on HIV testing. These findings help us better understand processes of depoliticization among queer NGOs in postsocialist China. They also show the harmful consequences of market-based HIV/AIDS prevention programs in which "competition" becomes synonymous with "progress" and underline the need to better understand the complex and perhaps unintended effects of global health initiatives on local health systems and civil society.

THE PROMISE AND PERIL OF GLOBAL HEALTH INITIATIVES

Over the past several decades, scholars from a variety of academic disciplines have turned an increasingly critical eye toward the organization, implementation, and effects of global health initiatives (Cohn et al. 2011; Hanefeld 2010, 2014; Heckert 2018; Kapilashrami and McPake 2013; Kapilashrami and O'Brien 2012; Khanna

2009; Spicer et al. 2010). One of the newest and perhaps most momentous evolutions of the global "AIDS service industry" (Patton 1990), global health initiatives are complex international humanitarian organizations that raise and disburse resources for the prevention and treatment of infectious diseases. Global health initiatives have proven especially effective in rapidly mobilizing the "scale-up" of HIV/AIDS prevention and treatment. By 2010, the three largest global health initiatives—the Global Fund, the President's Emergency Plan for AIDS Relief, and the World Bank Multi-Country AIDS Program—provided the majority of external HIV/AIDS funding for low-income countries, supporting the "roll-out" of antiretroviral treatment for over four million people living with HIV (Cohn et al. 2011, 688; Hanefeld 2010, 94).

In addition to increasing funding for fighting HIV/AIDS and other infectious diseases, global health initiatives have also been credited with increasing political attention and commitment to disease control and prevention, broadening the participation and engagement of community "stakeholders" (Hanefeld 2010, 99; 2014, 55–56; Spicer et al. 2010;), and lowering overall morbidity and mortality rates for target diseases (Cohn et al. 2011, 692). However, global health initiatives have also been critiqued for further burdening already weakened country health systems (Cohn et al. 2011, 69; Spicer et al. 2010, 2); hampering national and subnational coordination of HIV/AIDS prevention and treatment due to the complexity of aid infrastructure, overlapping programs, and competition for scarce resources among NGOs (Hanefeld 2014, 55; Spicer et al. 2010, 12); prioritizing the rapid "scale-up" of HIV/AIDS prevention and treatment over long-term sustainability (Hanefeld 2010, 99); and encouraging depoliticization and donor dependency among recipients (Kapilashrami and O'Brien 2012, 448). For example, exploring what she calls the "fault lines of care" in the work of global health initiatives, Heckert (2018) documents how, despite their stated commitments to empower local stakeholders and prioritize vulnerable communities, Global Fund programs in Bolivia worsened existing inequalities by directing funding for HIV prevention and treatment toward "high-impact" and "cost-effective" interventions among MSM and excluding vulnerable women from testing, prevention, and care.

Although academic attention to global health initiatives has been increasing, most studies focus on the effects of global health initiatives at the national level. Detailed ethnographic investigations of global health initiatives (Heckert 2018; Khanna 2009; Pfeiffer 2013; Whyte et al. 2013) are less common, especially those that investigate the complex interactions between global health initiatives, government agencies, and civil society actors at the subnational and local levels. Therefore, ethnographic approaches are of crucial importance in critiquing global health initiatives by questioning the epistemic assumptions underlying them and broadening our understanding of the effects of these initiatives on local communities. As João Biehl and Adriana Petryna argue, "Ethnographers are uniquely positioned to see what more categorically minded experts may overlook: namely, the empirical evidence that emerges when people express their most pressing and ordinary concerns, which then open up to complex human stories in time and space" (2013, 19).

This chapter contributes to a deeper and more nuanced understanding of the complex consequences of global health initiatives by presenting an extended critical ethnographic case study of the changes that took place in Tong'ai before, during, and after the arrival of global health initiatives in northwest China. Scholars have long lamented the many problems and challenges facing queer men's NGOs in China, including high turnover rates, a lack of professionalism among volunteers and staff, and endemic infighting between NGO leaders. Joan Kaufman (2009, 169) argues that:

> There is damaging infighting among groups, especially within the MSM community, with sometimes unfounded allegations publicized on listservs. This basic lack of trust, compounded by desire for visibility and competition for scarce funding, has fragmented rather than unified groups working on similar issues, playing into the hands of the central government by preventing the needed alliance building among these groups.

While Kaufman predicts that "new influxes of donor funding with specific focus on NGOs and AIDS will help to build the capacity of the sector" (170), I show how the abrupt and ultimately fleeting infusion of cash that accompanied the arrival of global health initiatives in northwest China in 2008 had the opposite effect, worsening infighting between queer men's NGOs and leading to increased turnover, burnout, and alienation within Tong'ai.

Other scholars have also critiqued the effects of global health initiatives on queer men's NGOs and activism in postsocialist China. Elsa Fan (2014) criticizes global health initiatives for "reproducing the social and political marginalization of MSM" (95) by regarding them as "almost always already infected" (92) with HIV and extending invasive forms of state surveillance into their lives. Timothy Hildebrandt describes the "splintering" effects of global health initiatives on queer Chinese NGOs, writing that "due to the availability of HIV/AIDS funds, the number of groups in many locales has increased to the point where they are overlapping in their work; this redundancy has further fueled competition" (2012, 858). Lynette Chua and Timothy Hildebrandt (2014) further report that external HIV/AIDS funding can exert a depoliticizing and "de-pinking" influence on Chinese queer NGOs, steering them away from other forms of advocacy toward an exclusive focus on HIV/AIDS.

Here I build upon and extend this earlier work by analyzing the causes and consequences of "conflict" (chongtu) and "competition" (jingzheng) among queer men's NGOs in northwest China. Examining changes and tensions within Tong'ai over more than a decade, as well as increasing competition between Tong'ai and other NGOs (both queer and nonqueer, local and nonlocal), I trace the causes of incivility to several factors, including long-standing rivalries between Chinese queer and AIDS NGOs and activists; the charismatic leadership style of Tianguang, the founder and leader of Tong'ai; and the competitive outsourcing of public health services from the state to civil society groups that was promoted by global health initiatives like the Gates Foundation and the Global Fund.

FEUDS AND FACTIONALISM AMONG QUEER MEN'S NGOS

Conflict and competition within and among queer men's NGOs in northwest China predated the arrival of global health initiatives in 2008. Many of my informants told me that the biggest obstacles groups like Tong'ai faced were not negative social attitudes toward homosexuality, restrictive state policies regarding civil society, or a lack of HIV/AIDS funding, but rather endemic infighting between queer NGOs and the "despotic" (baquan) management styles of their leaders. Many of these conflicts, such as the feud between Tianguang and Chengji, started long before any increase in funding for HIV/AIDS prevention.

By the time of my fieldwork, queer men's NGOs in postsocialist China were divided into three major factions. One was comprised of community-based queer NGOs, including Tong'ai, that had been established with the help of Zhang Beichuan, one of the first people to respond to the spread of HIV among MSM in the 1990s. A second faction was made up of groups sponsored by Chengji and the Hong Kong-based Yi De Foundation. The third faction included groups affiliated with another leading Chinese AIDS activist named Wan Yanhai.[2] Unlike Zhang Beichuan and Chengji, who were not well known outside of Chinese queer and AIDS activist circles, Wan Yanhai has achieved a measure of global renown for the trailblazing role he played at the very start of China's AIDS epidemic by calling attention to the blood-selling scandal in Henan and the spread of HIV among MSM in Beijing, after which he lost his job and was detained by the PRC authorities. He has since taken refuge in the United States.

A queer Chinese scholar named Xingshan, who has written several books on Chinese queer culture and HIV/AIDS activism, described to me during an interview how the conflict between these three factions first started. During the 2000s, Chengji, who mainly fundraised in Hong Kong and on the U.S. West Coast, and Wan Yanhai, who raised money primarily on the U.S. East Coast, both reached out to Zhang Beichuan looking for contacts among Chinese queer men's NGOs with whom they could collaborate. Zhang Beichuan was happy to oblige, Xingshan told me, seeing this as a chance for Chinese queer men's NGOs to secure much-needed international funding and connections. However, Xingshan said, not only did Chengji and Wan Yanhai turn out to be controlling and stingy with their financial support, they also started to compete for donors in the United States and for influence and territory in the PRC. This increasingly divided the community, as various leaders and groups fought with one another, spreading rumors and attacks through online bulletin boards and e-mail lists and attempting to increase their own power through the elimination of their rivals.

Although largely anecdotal, the above account corroborates similar descriptions of feuding and factionalism among Chinese queer men's NGOs and AIDS activists that I heard from community members across China as well as events I personally witnessed during fieldwork. Many people complained to me that both Chengji and Wan Yanhai had a lack of respect and consideration for queer men's NGO leaders and activists in mainland China, and that they used their international backgrounds and connections (as well as their superior English language skills) to bully and outcompete grassroots Chinese queer men's groups rather than cooperate with and support them.

Another reason why many grassroots queer men's NGOs were wary of collaborating with Wan Yanhai was because of how politically "sensitive" (*minggan*) he is due to his history of criticizing the government. Such political sensitivity could cause problems for queer NGO leaders who worked hard to cultivate good working relationships with local officials. In November 2010, Wan Yanhai (who was then based in the United States) organized a national conference of Chinese AIDS NGOs to be held in Xi'an. Tianguang told Yuanzi and me in the Tong'ai office that Wan Yanhai had telephoned him to ask if he would host the meeting, but that he had refused. The State Security Bureau ended up canceling the conference a few days before it was scheduled to begin, possibly because careless announcements that the conference organizers had posted online may have attracted the attention of the authorities.

The cancellation of Wan Yanhai's national AIDS conference in Xi'an caused several complications for Tong'ai, even though it had no affiliation with the event. Starting at 8 A.M. that morning, Tianguang began receiving calls from the State Security Bureau and the Shaanxi Center for Disease Control and Prevention (CDC), both of which were convinced, despite Tianguang's repeated denials, that Tong'ai had somehow been involved in organizing the canceled conference. Tianguang angrily complained that he had worked for many years to develop good working relationships with the local authorities, relationships which were now threatened. Tianguang also worried that after this incident Tong'ai (and possibly my research) would come under greater state scrutiny. Fortunately, after several days the incident seemed to blow over. However, the event underscores the political precariousness of local queer men's NGOs in postsocialist China, as well as how many years of careful work could be threatened overnight by a single careless misstep or outside actor.

"ONE MOUNTAIN CANNOT CONTAIN TWO TIGERS": CONFLICT AND CHARISMATIC AUTHORITY

Conflicts like the one between Tianguang and Chengji can be understood as contests among rival charismatic leaders over territory, followers, resources, and authority. According to Weber, charismatic leaders emerge in response to extraordinary circumstances or challenges due to their holding "specific gifts of body and mind" that ordinary people do not possess. With an authority that is highly transient, individualized, and bound to a specific social or political group, the charismatic leader "seizes the task for which he is destined and demands that others obey and follow him by virtue of his mission" (1968a, 1111–1112). Kaufman's observation that Chinese queer men's NGOs are "usually started by a visionary champion willing to take risks and navigate local politics" (2009, 169) resonates with Weber's description of charismatic authority and with my own impressions of Tianguang, whose charm, eloquence, and zealous devotion to grassroots queer and AIDS activism made him well-equipped to attract followers and navigate the uncertain political waters of postsocialist China.

Weber argues that charismatic authority is absolute and cannot be shared between rival leaders. "When such an authority comes into conflict with the competing authority of another who claims charismatic sanction," he writes, "the only recourse is to some kind of contest, by magical means or even as an actual physical battle of the leaders. In principle only one side can be right in such a conflict" (1968b, 51). Queer men's NGO volunteers used several expressions to describe the bitter rivalries between their leaders that illustrate Weber's description of the absolute nature of charismatic authority. One such phrase was *shantou zhuyi* or "mountaintop ideology," which like the English expression "king of the hill" describes a situation in which everyone wants to occupy the top position. Another idiom used by volunteers to explain struggles for power and prestige among queer NGO leaders was *yi shan bu rong er hu* or "one mountain cannot contain two tigers." This idiom refers to the notion that in any given social group there is only room for one leader. Volunteers also argued that NGO leaders were not willing to share power or territory with others, each wanting to be the *laoda*, which literally refers to the eldest sibling but can also describe someone who is the "number one" or "boss."

In addition to factionalism among queer men's and AIDS NGOs, another ongoing source of conflict came from within Tong'ai itself and was largely the result of the rather unorthodox management and leadership style of its leader. Tianguang was a complex and controversial figure within both the local queer community and the broader Chinese queer men's movement. Known for being an early and vocal advocate who tirelessly worked for the cause of HIV/AIDS prevention among MSM, especially in the northwest, Tianguang had many supporters and fans around China and the world. But many people also regarded him as someone who could be crafty and controlling, mendacious and manipulative. One of the main complaints I heard from current and former Tong'ai volunteers concerned how Tianguang wielded absolute power within the organization. This sentiment was often communicated by the expression *yi ge ren shuo le suan* or "whatever one person says goes," which is consistent with Weber's description of charismatic authority.

One former Tong'ai volunteer argued that sometimes such tactics were necessary to get things done in postsocialist China. To support his claim, he cited the proverb "you cannot raise fish in clear water" (*qing shui bu yang yu*), a management philosophy that is the *sine qua non* of charismatic authority. According to Weber, "Genuine charismatic justice does not refer to rules; in its pure type it is the most extreme contrast to formal and traditional prescription" (1968a, 1115). As another member of Tong'ai put it, "If we don't have any rules, then [Tianguang] is the ruler; he can decide everything. [In] this group, whatever he says goes." The same Tong'ai member also pointed out the hypocrisy of queer men's NGO leaders like Tianguang, who extolled the virtues of democracy but ran their own groups in an undemocratic fashion, saying, "They say that China doesn't have democracy, that we ought to be democratic. But the things they themselves do are fundamentally undemocratic. What he says is completely different from what he does."

Another ongoing source of tension within Tong'ai was its lack of organization and efficiency. Staff and volunteers routinely groused about Tianguang's poor management and communication skills, especially when group meetings were scheduled with little or no advance warning, which happened regularly. Tianguang himself was routinely late for appointments, which often caused embarrassment and frustration for staff. On any given day, no one knew whether or when Tianguang would show up at the office, which kept everyone on alert. The electricity, water, phone, and Internet connections to the Tong'ai office were often disconnected due to lack of payment. Tianguang's habit of "procrastination" (*tuoyan*), which often resulted in all-night emergency work sessions before project deadlines, was another bone of contention among Tong'ai volunteers and staff. According to Weber, while this type of unpredictability and unreliability is common among charismatic leaders, it is inconsistent with the stable and dispassionate enactment of authority under a bureaucracy: "Precision, speed, unambiguity, reduction of friction . . . these are raised to the optimum point in the strictly bureaucratic administration" (1968a, 973).

Another common complaint among Tong'ai volunteers and staff was a lack of transparency in the group's finances. According to Weber, "followers" or "disciples" of charismatic authority figures do not receive regular wages or compensation from their leader, but rather "share in the use of those goods which the authoritarian leader receives as donation, booty or endowment and which he distributes among them without accounting or contractual fixation" (1968a, 1119). A similar state of affairs held sway in Tong'ai and created much of the conflict between Tianguang and his volunteers. As one former volunteer explained, "The finances are not transparent. That is to say, exactly how much income there is, we don't know. This is because the finances are completely controlled by Tianguang." Even though volunteers were not normally paid, many HIV/AIDS prevention and testing projects included money in their budgets to give "subsidies" (*butie*) to volunteers for minor expenses like bus fares. Although the amounts were small (¥10 or $1.20 per person), for many volunteers this represented a significant sum over time. Several people complained that Tianguang promised to give them subsidies but never followed through, which caused a great deal of resentment and led to accusations of financial mismanagement or even corruption. Some even speculated that Tianguang had paid for a new car and an apartment with project monies; as one group member said, "I think that this money ought to be used to empower more gays, to bring them more democracy, to make more gays get sick less. It shouldn't be used so that other people can have a car to drive, have money to buy a house."

It should be said that not all Tong'ai members suspected Tianguang of financial mismanagement. One group member forcefully defended Tianguang against such allegations, saying "If you have never been in charge of expenses, you will never know how expensive the 'daily necessities' (*chai mi you yan*, literally "fuel, rice, oil, and salt") can be. . . . A lot of expenses are hidden. It's a dog-eat-dog world; in China it costs a lot to deal with people and to maintain relationships." However, in part due to these various grievances, the volunteer turnover rate was high, as people who were initially enthusiastic later became disillusioned with Tianguang and left Tong'ai. By 2010, many disgruntled former Tong'ai members had begun volunteering with one of the numerous rival organizations that by then had begun competing with one another to offer HIV/AIDS testing services to local MSM.

"THERE WILL ONLY BE PROGRESS WHEN THERE IS COMPETITION": FOREIGN FUNDING AND THE FRACTURING OF CIVIL SOCIETY

Increasing dissatisfaction among queer men's NGO volunteers created fertile conditions for the rapid expansion and fracturing of civil society following the arrival of global health initiatives like the Gates Foundation and the Global Fund in northwest China. Taking advantage of the sudden increase in funding, many current and former Tong'ai volunteers joined or even founded rival organizations, resulting in sometimes fierce competition between NGOs. This competition was encouraged by government officials and by the way that HIV/AIDS prevention and testing funds and projects were distributed and administered by global health initiatives themselves.

Although the Gates Foundation and the Global Fund began operating in China as early as 2003 and 2007, respectively, they only began funding HIV/AIDS projects in northwest China in 2008. These projects were jointly administered by the China CDC and GONGOs like the Chinese Association of STD and AIDS Prevention and Control. Because grassroots queer NGOs like Tong'ai were unable to legally register with the state, they could not accept funds directly from foreign donors; GONGOs therefore acted as "trustees" (*tuoguan*) on their behalf, funneling funds from global health initiatives to local NGOs while diverting some of the resources to support themselves.

By 2012, the Global Fund planned to invest $369 million in the PRC (Global Fund 2012), while the Gates Foundation had allocated an additional $50 million over a five-year period (Jacobs 2009). While most of these funds were captured

TABLE 5.1   List of NGOs Involved in HIV/AIDS Work among MSM in Xi'an

Founded	Group name	Group type
1998	Tong'ai Working Group	Local queer community-based organization
2007	Yi De Foundation	International HIV/AIDS charity organization
2009	Brotherly Love	Local queer community-based organization
2009	Jishi Aid	Regional charity organization
2009	Reproductive Health International	International sexual and reproductive health organization
2010	Qingtian Working Group	Local queer community-based organization

by government agencies and GONGOs, they nevertheless represented a significant increase in funding for Chinese queer men's NGOs. One result of the sudden spurt of foreign funding was a swift growth in the number of NGOs involved in HIV/AIDS prevention, especially among MSM, the fastest-growing risk group in China's AIDS epidemic and the sector toward which most of the new resources flowed. In Xi'an, between 2009 and 2010 the number of NGOs providing services to MSM quickly grew from two organizations to six (table 5.1). Similar changes also took place in other cities across the PRC.

Two of these new NGOs were nonqueer organizations whose previous work had not focused on either HIV/AIDS prevention or MSM. One was a regional branch of Reproductive Health International (RHI), a global NGO headquartered in London focusing on family planning and women's reproductive health. The other was a regional charity, the Jishi Aid Association or Jishi, which worked with elderly nursing home patients, the children of prison inmates, and mentally handicapped children. Two other new NGOs were both local queer men's groups started by disgruntled former Tong'ai volunteers. The first, Brotherly Love, was led by Xiao Jun. Brotherly Love started out as a queer social networking group but later partnered with nonqueer NGOs like RHI and Jishi to help them with their HIV testing projects in the local MSM community. The second, Qingtian Working Group, was founded by Da You, who previously directed Tong'ai's community outreach activities but left the group after a dispute with Tianguang over unpaid reimbursements and began managing the largest gay bathhouse in Xi'an.

The fierce competition between NGOs was actively encouraged by the way HIV/AIDS projects and funding were structured and allocated by the China CDC and global health initiatives. Gates Foundation and Global Fund projects heavily prioritized HIV testing over other forms of community outreach, prevention, and treatment. NGOs that received project contracts were paid a certain amount of money for each vial of blood they collected during their HIV testing drives, with cash bonuses for blood samples that tested positive for HIV. The

Gates Foundation paid civil society groups ¥62 for each HIV test they conducted, with a further "reward" (*jiang*) of ¥300 for each HIV-positive blood sample they discovered. Global Fund projects were structured in a similar way. These practices were controversial, with the *New York Times* running a story about the Gates Foundation titled "H.I.V. Tests Turn Blood into Cash in China" (Jacobs 2009). Many local queer activists also pointed out the problems that such reward structures caused. Tianguang argued that "the main problem with the Gates Foundation project is that how much money they pay you depends on how much blood you collect. After this, many groups stopped doing anything; all they did was collect blood. Also, when collecting blood, they would fake their results." Although ostensibly intended to incentivize NGOs to focus their testing efforts on MSM who were thought to be at high risk for contracting HIV, market-based reward structures promoted by global health initiatives caused groups like Tong'ai to scale back other forms of community outreach and also encouraged fraud.

Another result of paying NGOs for every HIV test they performed was to increase competition for HIV tests among civil society groups. Xiao Jun, the leader of Brotherly Love, explained it to me this way: "To do an [HIV] intervention you need to write a project proposal. How many people will your intervention reach? How many tests will you perform? Someone who gets tested in one place isn't likely to go get tested in another place. . . . This is where the competition for funding lies."

The way projects were administrated also encouraged competition among NGOs. Every year, the China CDC arbitrarily increased the target number of HIV tests stipulated in new project contracts, regardless of whether groups like Tong'ai had managed to meet their previous targets. At the end of each project cycle, the CDC ranked NGOs according to the number of HIV tests they had performed and the percentage of HIV-positive blood samples they had produced, with groups who performed more tests and handed in more HIV-positive blood samples given larger, more lucrative contracts in the future. Rather than promoting a strong and independent civil society, HIV testing projects funded by global health initiatives like the Gates Foundation and the Global Fund encouraged competitive clientelism among NGOs, who were forced to vie for state approval in order to secure future financial resources. As Dongdong, the thirty-one-year-old director of the MSM program at Reproductive Health International, told me, "If you have done more tests, if you have discovered more infected people, that means you have performed really well. I think this is the reason why there is this kind of competition."

In addition to encouraging NGOs from outside the queer community to work on HIV/AIDS prevention projects, the China CDC also promoted competition among civil society groups by actively recruiting former Tong'ai volunteers like Xiao Jun and Da You to start their own organizations and giving them projects. CDC officials often argued that increased competition among NGOs would yield better results. As Director Zhang of the Shaanxi CDC AIDS Department told me,

"Regarding the development of NGOs, I believe that there will only be progress when there is competition." She also claimed that competition was necessary for the development of grassroots queer NGOs like Tong'ai, saying, "I think that an organization's normal development should include competition. Otherwise, they won't know if they are doing a good job or a bad job."

Director Li, the leader of Reproductive Health International, also expressed enthusiasm for increased competition among NGOs. Using the language of consumer choice and describing MSM as customers, she argued that more competition among NGOs would result in MSM receiving better services. "From the perspective of the target community it is a good thing," she asserted. "If you go to an organization and they are very busy, or the service that they give you isn't very good, if you have to wait for a long time to receive the results of your test, then you can go to another organization. This type of competitive relationship is beneficial for customers." Director Li dismissed the possibility of groups like RHI and Tong'ai working together. Comparing them to Kentucky Fried Chicken and McDonald's, whose eateries dotted the postsocialist urban Chinese landscape and were an easily accessible archetype of capitalistic competition, she said, "If people are willing to eat garbage, then they can go to McDonald's. It would be better if there were no McDonald's. But then how would people choose KFC? So I think that competition is better."

Tong'ai members expressed a more ambivalent attitude about competition between NGOs. While many welcomed competition, they often questioned the methods and motivations of their nonlocal and nonqueer competitors. Many objected to their use of "illegitimate" (bu zhengdang) competitive practices, including "scooping" (wa) volunteers away from established queer community-based NGOs. RHI and Jishi attempted to poach each of the three trained Tong'ai staff members by offering them a ¥3,000 ($360) monthly salary, more than twice what they were making at Tong'ai, along with other benefits that Tong'ai could not afford to pay. However, despite receiving such lucrative offers, they all remained at Tong'ai, partially due to their sense of loyalty to the queer community and partially due to their distrust of the long-term dedication of these nonqueer NGOs to the work of HIV/AIDS prevention. Xiao Pu was a physician from Xinjiang in his thirties and a full-time Tong'ai staff member who directed the group's voluntary counseling and testing program. When I asked Xiao Pu why he did not move to an organization like Jishi, he replied, "They are only in it for the money. As soon as the projects are over, they won't do it anymore. I would rather work for Tong'ai, work for my own people, even if I didn't get any money all month, even if all I had to drink was the northwest wind."

Perhaps the most egregious example of illegitimate competitive practices was RHI's strategy of paying kickbacks to the owners of local gay bars and bathhouses in exchange for exclusive access to their venues to carry out HIV testing. According to several people familiar with the situation, the practice started when RHI had to quickly complete a large number of HIV tests for a Gates Foundation project. Having no established connections within the local MSM community, RHI allegedly negotiated an agreement with the owner of one Xi'an gay bar to pay him ¥40 per blood test carried out on the premises.[3] Such practices not only excluded other groups from carrying out HIV prevention and testing activities in the same venues, they also damaged the relationships that grassroots queer men's NGOs like Tong'ai had cultivated over many years with local gay business owners. As Tianguang explained, "They had been cooperating with us for such a long time, and we had never given them any money before. Now they think that all this time we have been keeping all the money for ourselves." Such practices also threatened the long-term sustainability of HIV prevention work after global health initiatives like the Gates Foundation and the Global Fund left northwest China. As Tianguang put it, "When the resources have run out, how are we going to give the bosses their money? How will we do our work?"

Tong'ai members also complained about the lack of a level playing field between them and nonlocal, nonqueer NGOs. Because larger national and international NGOs like Yi De and RHI could communicate in English, they had greater access to international funding sources than smaller, queer community-based groups like Tong'ai. Chengji, Yi De's chairman, was a fluent English speaker educated at Harvard who worked as an investment banker and held a U.S. passport, all of which Tianguang argued gave him and his NGO much greater access to international resources than Tong'ai. Not only were Tianguang and the other members of Tong'ai unable to communicate in English, which prevented them from applying for many international grants and projects, it was also difficult and expensive for them to travel abroad. "He can go compete for international resources," Tianguang said of Chengji. "But not us. We can only compete locally . . . and then perhaps obtain a little bit of resources through the government." Well-connected national and international NGOs were also able to legally register with the state and receive funds directly from global health initiatives without relying on government agencies or GONGOs to act as middlemen, giving them an even greater financial advantage over grassroots, unregistered queer NGOs like Tong'ai.

Perhaps unsurprisingly, the leaders of Jishi and RHI saw things rather differently. When I interviewed the director of Jishi, he downplayed or denied the existence of competition among NGOs offering HIV/AIDS services to MSM. "Many different spheres exist within this community," he maintained. "We serve one sphere, they serve another, and there is no competition." While Director Li, the leader of the local RHI branch, admitted their competitive relationship with Tong'ai, she argued that if anything the playing field was tilted in Tong'ai's favor, not theirs. "They have been in this circle longer; we only just entered. It is very unequal. They have a lot of advantages that we don't have," she said. "They regard us as competitive rivals. In fact, we only want to complete the task given to us by the [China] CDC." Director Li also defended the payments that RHI gave to gay business owners for conducting HIV tests, arguing that other groups, including

Tong'ai, were essentially already doing the same thing when they purchased alcohol during their community outreach activities. "When they would go to bars, they would buy a bottle of beer or whatever, which counts as paying the bar a fee," she said.

Perhaps the biggest complaint voiced by members of Tong'ai about nonlocal and nonqueer NGOs was that they were only interested in HIV/AIDS prevention and testing projects among MSM because of the money. "They are certainly not thinking about the health of this community," Tianguang said about RHI. "They are only working for this community because of a Global Fund project [from the] Chinese government. They are utilizing their dominant position to come and plunder these resources. They have already very frankly and openly said that if it weren't for this project, they wouldn't be doing this work." Lao Wang, who had volunteered at both Tong'ai and RHI, made a similar argument. "Working for RHI made me bitterly disappointed," he told me. "Because RHI—how do I say it—when you are doing [HIV] tests, it is just like a cake. Everyone is happy when there is cake. If that cake didn't exist, people wouldn't keep doing this work." Even Director Zhang from the Shaanxi CDC admitted that she thought RHI was only doing HIV/AIDS work among MSM for financial reasons. "Even though they are doing this work, they are only doing it because the Bill Gates project encouraged them to do it," she said. "One day, when the Bill Gates project is over, I don't know whether or not they will keep doing the work." Contrasting outside organizations like RHI with local queer NGOs, Director Zhang said, "Because Tong'ai is an MSM community organization, they will do this work whether or not there is money. RHI isn't like that."

Many Tong'ai members worried about the effects that unfair competition from national and international NGOs like Yi De and RHI would have on their future ability to offer HIV/AIDS prevention and testing services to the local queer community. "They shouldn't come and contend for resources with Chinese community-based organizations," Tianguang argued, "because these community-based organizations have very few channels through which to obtain resources, and the resources that they are able to obtain are also very few." Not only would outside groups with a short-term, financially driven commitment to HIV/AIDS prevention and testing not do a very good job, Tianguang argued, but they would also divert scarce resources away from grassroots queer groups like Tong'ai with a vested interest in the long-term health of local MSM. "After they have taken the project funds, after they have walked away with these resources, who is then going to be responsible for their health? Who is then going to do the work that needs to be done?" Tianguang asked. These findings reveal how, instead of building capacity and promoting the long-term sustainability of HIV/AIDS prevention efforts among MSM in northwest China, the market-based reward structures promoted by global health initiatives and the state actually undermined existing community-based queer men's NGOs by encouraging competition between NGOs and promoting the further fracturing of civil society.

"WE HAVE TO DEVELOP": BUREAUCRATIZATION AND MEDICALIZATION

The arrival of global health initiatives not only had a disruptive effect on relations between queer men's and AIDS NGOs in northwest China, but also had a profound impact on Tong'ai itself. Within only a few years of receiving funding from the Gates Foundation and the Global Fund, the organization had started to change in fundamental ways. Some of the changes were positive; Tong'ai had more resources than ever, which enabled it to move from its crowded and rundown office to a much larger space in a newly constructed eighteen-story residential and commercial complex several blocks away. In August 2010, Tianguang was able to hire three volunteers, Yuanzi, Xiao Shan, and Xiao Pu, as full-time staff members, rewarding their hard work (which before was purely voluntary) with a small monthly salary. But I also detected a darker side to the changes that were taking place within Tong'ai, an impression that grew stronger the more time I spent with the group. Most of the volunteers I met in 2007 and 2008 had left, and fewer new people were coming to take their place. Indeed, the large, clean, sterile rooms of the new office were often empty and quiet, a far cry from the cramped and boisterous conditions of the past.

According to Tianguang, the decreasing number of Tong'ai volunteers was a sign of the group's "development" (*fazhan*) from a "volunteer organization" (*zhiyuanzhe zuzhi*) to what he proudly described as a "professional service agency" (*zhuanye fuwu jigou*). "The changes between now and when you came in 2007 and 2008 are actually very large," Tianguang said. "Back then you probably felt that we were a very lively organization, that our foundation in the community was very good. But even though it seemed like there were a lot of people, the work [we] were able to do for society was very limited." The problem with volunteers, Tianguang argued, is that they are "unreliable" (*bu kaopu*), only showing up when it suits them and more interested in "having fun" (*wan*) and looking for "one-night stands" (*siyaojiu*) than doing work. "The efficiency of that type of work was actually insufficient to meet the needs of the community," Tianguang said. "For example, in 2007 and 2008 we were able to provide roughly 200 to 300 people with [HIV] tests. Now, in one year we can provide tests to between 2,000 and 3,000 people. Think about it: our efficiency has increased tenfold." This quote reveals how, after the arrival of global health initiatives, queer men's NGOs and leaders like Tianguang increasingly used the number of HIV tests they could perform as the primary metric for measuring both the quantity and the quality of their work for the local queer community.

For their part, some of the group's new paid staff members also seemed pleased with these changes. Speaking about 2007 and 2008, Xiao Pu recalled, "Back then I was doing [HIV] testing in my spare time. I didn't get an allowance. Back then, in order to survive, in order to fill my stomach and smoke a cigarette, I could only do it in my spare time. Now Teacher Tian can give me a living allowance of ¥1,500 [$180] a month." Like Tianguang, Xiao Pu also saw the organization's decreasing number of volunteers as a sign of its professionalization. "If you want to do this work, you have to invest all of your energies into doing it," Xiao Pu argued. "You have to be really serious." Describing the shift from volunteers to full-time staff as "a result of us becoming more mature," Xiao Pu remarked, "we have to develop."

However, not everyone was as enthusiastic about the changes that were taking place within Tong'ai. One former volunteer argued that with the loss of its volunteers, Tong'ai was no different from outside groups like Yi De and RHI. "In the past, one difference was that Tong'ai had a group of capable and knowledgeable volunteers," he said. "Now, I don't think that there is any difference. The only difference is in how much money you can bring in."[4] He argued that the professionalization of Tong'ai had come at a high cost, saying, "In 2007, everyone was a volunteer, no one was making money. . . . We all had a sense of enthusiasm and responsibility when we did this work. Now it more resembles a professional organization."

The replacement of its previous ethos of volunteerism with one that valorized professionalization is an example of bureaucratization, or the rationalization of charismatic authority within Tong'ai. According to Weber (1968b, 54), as soon as the extraordinary social or political conditions that created it have subsided, charismatic authority becomes increasingly routinized in order to gain access to more permanent sources of material resources and followers. Weber's observations about the routinization of charismatic authority are reflected in Tianguang's attempts to relaunch Tong'ai as a commercial enterprise, which in turn were driven by the group's need to compete with other NGOs for the market-based HIV/AIDS testing projects that were being awarded by global health initiatives and administered by the Chinese state. In November 2010, Tianguang described how Tong'ai had begun to provide a "one-stop service" (*yi tiao long de fuwu*), offering HIV/AIDS prevention, testing, and treatment all in one convenient location. In March 2011, Tianguang rebranded Tong'ai as the "Tong'ai Community Development and Service Center" (*Tong'ai Shequ Fazhan yu Fuwu Zhongxin*), arguing that "right now we need to consider a more entrepreneurial model in order to develop." He also drafted new "aim" (*zongzhi*) and "mission" (*mubiao*) statements for the group, which he had me translate and then printed out in large, three-dimensional Chinese characters and English letters that were displayed prominently in the front room of the Tong'ai office:

AIM: Expanding scientific knowledge, advocating for human rights, promoting health, and building community.
MISSION: To work hard to construct an equitable, healthy, civilized, and harmonious LGBT community.

When I asked him why he thought these statements were necessary, Tianguang replied, "We need to consider a model like that of a private enterprise in order to develop, in order to operate." The transformation of Tong'ai from a vibrant community-based volunteer organization into an increasingly professional enterprise focused on testing as many MSM for HIV as possible reveals the sweeping effects neoliberal global health initiatives can have on local civil society.

The bureaucratization and professionalization of Tong'ai, while perhaps intended to enable it to survive in the face of stiff competition from nonlocal and nonqueer NGOs, had a significant impact on the tenor and spirit of the organization. Almost all of the original volunteers who had been with the group since its early days in the 1990s and 2000s were gone. As one middle-aged former volunteer told me rather wistfully, "I think that Tong'ai is very different now. . . . They have lost all the older people. They don't care about them anymore. Before, there were people of all ages, of all kinds. But now there are only young people." When I asked him why he thought this was, he replied, "It is probably a strategic decision made by the leader. . . . Young people probably have more social connections, more contacts. Also, it is more convenient [for younger volunteers] to send messages over the Internet." This older former volunteer argued that there was a trade-off between professionalization and enthusiasm and that Tong'ai had lost something valuable in its efforts to become more professional, saying:

> Right now, the director, Teacher Tian, is basically saying, "I give you this much money, and you have to finish this amount of work by a certain time." . . . It's not like how it used to be with volunteers; back then everyone relied on their enthusiastic hearts to do this work. Even though the amount of the subsidies that were given was very small, a dozen *kuai* [$1.50] or so, everyone was very active. You remember; in the evenings everyone would go to do community outreach in the bars. Lots of people would go.

As another former Tong'ai volunteer observed, "I think [Tong'ai] is gradually becoming more like a service organization than a volunteer organization. . . . Now, most of their volunteer work has been retired to do projects. Ordinary community outreach and hotline work has all been suspended. So the amount of true volunteer work that they are doing right now is very small."

This last observation reveals another important change that took place within Tong'ai after the arrival of global health initiatives. Instead of providing general services to and engaging with the local queer community and advocating for greater rights and equality for queer people, the new full-time staff members and dwindling volunteers increasingly devoted their time and energies toward competing for and completing HIV testing projects from the Gates Foundation and the Global Fund. "It has to do with projects, and it also has to do with financial and economic interests," one former volunteer observed. "You only have money if you have projects." Tianguang himself seemed to confirm this during a staff meeting in February 2011, where he announced, "Speaking frankly, HIV tests are a lifeline for social organizations like ours. Right now, we have no choice but to rely on tests."

As the group increasingly focused on HIV testing and treatment, I watched as more comprehensive HIV prevention activities like community outreach events in local queer bars, saunas, and cruising areas slowly ground to a halt. People from outside the group increasingly complained that Tong'ai had lost its connection to the local queer community. "Tong'ai is no longer doing its fundamental work very well," one former volunteer said. "They have become divorced from the community. They only play with themselves; they no longer truly go down to the bars, the parks, the bathhouses and make friends." Some people even began comparing what Tong'ai had become to a "vampire" (*xixuegui*), an undead monster or ghost that survives by consuming the blood of its living victims. Rather than trying to eliminate HIV/AIDS, many within the local queer community seemed to think that Tong'ai was now drawing nourishment from it. "Some people say that they rely on HIV/AIDS to support themselves," one former volunteer said. "A lot of people think that they feed off of HIV/AIDS."

Yuanzi, then a full-time staff member, expressed similar concerns when I asked him how he thought the group had changed. "I think that our largest and most fatal change is that we have lost our roots," he said, before continuing:

To use a metaphor I was thinking of a few days ago, when everyone is doing something together, it is like planting a seed. If you don't pick a good seed, if you don't put it in fertile soil, if you don't water it, if you don't give it fertilizer, it won't bear fruit. For example, if you plant a bed of flowers, if you are very attentive, when the flowers open, they will be very beautiful. I think that if we don't organize activities, if we don't interact with everyone, if we just sit here, then no one will know about Tong'ai.

Whereas in 2007 and 2008 Tong'ai volunteers would organize community outreach events in queer bars, bathhouses, and cruising areas several times a week to engage with MSM, raise awareness about HIV and STIs, and pass out packets of condoms and personal lubricant, by 2010 these outings had become much scarcer. By 2011 they had stopped almost completely.

The alienation of Tong'ai from the local queer community and its increasingly narrow focus on HIV/AIDS testing and treatment came at the expense of a more comprehensive approach to HIV prevention. The narrowing of the group's original social and political goals was also the direct result of the actions and priorities of the government and global health initiatives like the Gates Foundation and the Global Fund. For the Chinese state, as well as the international donor agencies who were working with it, combating a disease like HIV/AIDS may have seemed more acceptable than acknowledging and confronting problems like homophobia and discrimination against queer people.[5] This is an example of medicalization, the process whereby an ordinary biological phenomenon or a social, economic, or political problem becomes understood and addressed primarily as a medical problem that can be treated or cured through medical intervention.[6] As Irving

Kenneth Zola observes, "The labels health and illness are remarkable 'depoliticizers' of an issue. By locating the source and the treatment of problems in an individual, other levels of intervention are effectively closed" (1972, 500). By directing financial rewards and incentives toward HIV/AIDS testing, the Chinese government and global health initiatives encouraged or even compelled local queer men's NGOs like Tong'ai to become increasingly medicalized and abandon their broader social and political aims or risk being outcompeted by rival organizations for the funding they needed in order to survive.

One similar example is the medicalization of poverty and hunger in northeast Brazil described by Nancy Scheper-Hughes, in which symptoms of starvation were treated as signs of a personal psychological illness called *nervoso* or "extreme nervousness" that the state and local medical establishment then "treated" with pharmaceuticals. "In this way," Scheper-Hughes argues, "hunger is isolated and denied, and an individualized discourse on sickness comes to replace a more radical and socialized discourse on hunger" (1992, 169). Of course, there are important differences between the situations in northwest China and northeast Brazil; HIV/AIDS is an unquestionably urgent medical and public health problem (as well as an important political and human rights issue), and my informants gave many reasons to justify their concentrating on fighting HIV/AIDS rather than addressing other issues, at least in the short term. However, as the focus of Tong'ai increasingly turned toward HIV/AIDS testing and the group became more detached from its roots in the local queer community, its initial goals of creating social change and constructing an "equitable, healthy, civilized, and harmonious LGBT community" seemed to recede ever further into the horizon.

"THERE IS A DEMON IN MY HEART": ENERVATION AND ALIENATION

One poignant example of Tong'ai's increasing alienation and medicalization is the fate of its free telephone hotline. Wenqing, who began managing the hotline after Lao Huang moved to the Yi De Foundation in 2007, shared his memories with me during an interview in August 2011, several months after he had also left to join Yi De. Wenqing recalled how he first called the hotline in 2006, which is how he became a Tong'ai volunteer. "At that time, I thought that it was really good," he said. "There were a lot of volunteers. Things were very systematic and orderly." When I asked him to describe what things were like back then, Wenqing replied, "Tong'ai still had many dedicated volunteers. Even though we didn't have any full-time staff, everyone was very dedicated. There was the hotline, so I applied to be an operator. Everyone was organized into five groups who came to the office to answer the hotline after work. We were all very responsible."

I asked Wenqing if during all the years he had answered the hotline there were any calls that had stuck with him. "Yes," he replied, before continuing:

Some people thought of the hotline as a part of their lives. They would call every week and chat with me about their situation, and when they hung up their hearts would be more comfortable. It was like I had completed a mission. The person I remember the most would call every week, and when he called he would thank us, saying how hard we worked to answer the hotline every day. He was in Xinjiang, working in a railroad construction team. He called often. Where he worked was very far from the city; he said when he went outside he was in a desolate wilderness. Therefore, he had a lot of loneliness in his heart.

I asked Wenqing what kind of difference he thought the hotline had made in people's lives, and he replied, "As far as I am concerned, our hotline [made people feel like] someone accepted them. Even though you couldn't solve any of their big problems, you could still give them some suggestions, help them with their lives. Because of the work we did, [they felt like] someone accepted them. It gave them a lot of comfort." When I asked Wenqing how many calls he thought he had answered during his time as a hotline operator, he laughed, his face breaking into a broad grin. "Oh, there were a lot of hotline calls!" he said. "Several people would help out with answering the hotline, each person coming in on a different day of the week. When they were busy, I would cover for them. I answered the hotline like this from 2006 until 2011. And then it was over." As he said this, Wenqing laughed again, this time more quietly and sadly. He sipped some water, then set his glass down and continued his story:

Through the latter half of [2010], no one paid the telephone bill. I started coming in less and less often. A few months after the [2011] New Year the hotline finally closed down. They told me that they were going to use the office for something else, and that they weren't going to answer the hotline anymore. Because I was the director of the hotline, I wrote down who had answered the hotline from 2006 to 2010 and on what days, including a year and several months when subsidies were given out, and who hadn't been given their subsidies. I went and gave a copy to Teacher Tian. He said that we weren't going to be doing the hotline this year, that it had been canceled. I said that if there wasn't going to be a hotline anymore, then I would stop answering the phone. He didn't give me a direct reply. The next day I didn't come back.

For a while, the former hotline office was used for storage. It was eventually converted into another space for HIV/AIDS testing.

In addition to the increasing estrangement of Tong'ai from the local queer community, I also observed growing feelings of enervation and alienation among its full-time staff. As Tong'ai became more professionalized and medicalized, its staff appeared to grow more downtrodden and discouraged as the distance between what Yuanzi described as the "ideal" and the "reality" of their work grew more apparent. Late one night as we were working together in the Tong'ai office, Xiao Shan suddenly remarked on the growing pressure he faced to complete HIV testing projects on time. "Our work, it's not only exhausting on the outside, but it's also exhausting on the inside," he said. Such feelings are an example of alienation. According to Raymond Williams (1983, 33), alienation describes an act or state of estrangement or refers to the action of transferring rights or ownership from one person or thing to another. These two meanings are synthesized in Karl Marx's theorization of alienation in "Economic and Philosophic Manuscripts of 1944" (1978a, 74–77), in which Marx describes alienation as a process of "estrangement" by which workers in a class-based society are separated from their essential human nature as economic producers by "the division of labor, private property, and the capitalist mode of production in which the worker loses both the product of his labor and his sense of his own productive ability, following the expropriation of both by capital" (Williams 1983, 35).

Xiao Shan and Yuanzi increasingly felt disenchanted, powerless, and exploited in their work at Tong'ai. As they struggled to complete ever more HIV testing projects, often with little or no help or support from Tianguang, they both grew increasingly frustrated and bitter. Yuanzi in particular often remarked on how tired the work was making him, and how his "heart had less and less energy." One night, after working all day in the office, Yuanzi and I went out to eat dinner together at a nearby street lined with inexpensive food carts and small restaurants. After wandering up and down the street, Yuanzi still could not find anything that whetted his appetite. We finally ended up in a small mom-and-pop eatery that served dumplings and *youbing*, a soft, oily and slightly sweet deep-fried pancake served warm in a plastic bag. Yuanzi seemed even more stressed than usual; he had spent the entire day entering information from a large pile of wrinkled receipts into a project reimbursement form for a regional CDC, only to lose the information when he accidentally tripped on his laptop power cord before saving his work. We ate in silence for a long time until Yuanzi, staring down at his steaming plate of dumplings, suddenly said, in a dejected tone of voice, that he felt like "there is a demon in my heart" (*wo de xinli you mogui*).

Xiao Shan and Yuanzi's increasing feelings of alienation and depression were caused in part by the difficult and often frustrating nature of their jobs. They worked long and odd hours, ostensibly from 2 P.M. to 10 P.M. every day except Tuesday, although they often had to stay at the office late, especially during the weekends when activities at the office could stretch into the early hours of the morning. These work hours were designed to overlap with the times when the queer community was the most active and it was easiest to mobilize people to come into the office and get tested for HIV; however, they also made it difficult for Xiao Shan and Yuanzi to carry on any kind of normal social life outside of work. "*Aiya*, it's had a huge influence on my life," Yuanzi told me when I asked him how working at Tong'ai had affected him. He continued:

Everything is in chaos. There is already no way for us to have normal contacts with people inside or outside of the circle. For example, we work from 2 P.M. until 10 P.M. But by 10 P.M. everyone is already asleep! And during the weekends we organize activities. . . . *Aiya*, it's too exhausting. I want to go and play badminton, go and work out, go out and have fun, go hiking—but we basically don't have time for any of that.

Yuanzi was single at the time. When I asked him if he wanted a boyfriend, he just laughed, saying, "No. Even if I wanted to find one, I wouldn't have the time!"

Despite working such long hours, Xiao Shan and Yuanzi received very little compensation, and money was a constant source of worry for them, as they both came from working-class backgrounds. At only ¥1,500 ($183) a month, with no benefits like health or retirement insurance, their salary was barely enough to cover basic living expenses like food, clothing, rent, and transportation. As we worked together in the office, Xiao Shan would frequently bemoan his lack of money, comparing himself to friends who were making two or three times as much. "1,500 is really too low," he complained one day. "We are starving to death. Only the two of us are stupid enough to work for so little." Their low pay hampered Xiao Shan and Yuanzi's ability to take part in postsocialist China's growing consumer economy, a source of constant humiliation. Xiao Shan also worried about making enough money to start saving for an apartment of his own, a requirement for most urban Chinese men who wanted to marry. "Casey, next year I have to start making money," Xiao Shan wailed one day. "If I don't start making money next year, I'll die. Look at how poor I am. I don't even have enough money to buy a washing machine. I am too sad like this. I need to start making money. . . . If I don't have money, other people will shame me. If I keep going on like this, I will be humiliated my entire life. . . . Look how pitiful I am!"

Tianguang was often several months late in paying his workers' salaries, which made Xiao Shan and Yuanzi's financial situation even more fragile. Things got especially difficult during the holiday season. One afternoon, as we were working in the office, Xiao Shan suddenly heaved a deep sigh, scrunched his face up into a frustrated grimace, and leaned back in his chair, exclaiming, "Casey, I want to do this work well, but how can I go on like this? We still haven't received our salary from February, and it's already April. . . . I think if things go on like this, I truly will lose hope. . . . I'm already feeling very unhappy. . . . *Aiya*, what am I going to do?"

The nature of Xiao Shan and Yuanzi's work was difficult and disheartening, adding to their feelings of frustration. It was often challenging to persuade people to get tested for HIV, especially members of the post-90s generation. One day, after a young man came to the Tong'ai office to get tested, he began having second thoughts. After speaking with him for a long while, Yuanzi finally convinced him to go through with the test, only to have him change his mind again at the last minute and leave. Yuanzi sat down in his chair and heaved a deep sigh, shaking his head and saying, "Those post-90s children, it's impossible to intervene with them."

FIGURE 5.1. Yuanzi and Tong'ai volunteers burn incense at a Buddhist temple in Xi'an. Photo by author.

When I asked him why he thought this was, he simply replied that their attitude toward life and HIV was to just "accept their fate." Xiao Pu emerged from the HIV testing room, snapping on a pair of latex gloves and barking in his usual gruff voice, "Where is he?" Without looking up from his laptop, Yuanzi said in a resigned tone of voice, "He won't do it." "Why not?" Xiao Pu asked incredulously, telling Yuanzi to go talk to the guy again and to try to make him change his mind. Yuanzi, looking exasperated and irritated, simply replied, "I'm not a supernatural being, you know."

Even with all the hard work and long hours that they put in, the HIV infection rate among MSM in Xi'an continued to climb month after month, year after year. This only deepened Xiao Shan and Yuanzi's growing feelings of frustration and despair.[7] One year during the Lantern Festival, the fifteenth day of the first lunar month and the last day of the Lunar New Year celebrations, a group of Tong'ai volunteers along with Yuanzi and I spent a glorious day at a local Buddhist temple (figure 5.1). Together we burned yellow incense sticks, turned golden prayer wheels, watched people light long strings of bright red firecrackers, attended a chaotic temple fair, and purchased packages of *zongzi*, the triangular, sweet glutinous rice dumplings that symbolize family harmony and are traditionally eaten during the Lantern Festival, which we brought back to share with everyone at Tong'ai. When we arrived at the office, however, we found that Xiao Shan and Xiao Pu had spent the entire day administering HIV tests to a dozen or so people. Xiao Shan told me that a young man had tested positive for HIV, and that he had had unprotected sex with many other young men, several of whom had tested positive themselves. Xiao Shan, who was despondent and looked even more tired than usual, told me that the events of the day had put him in a bad mood. What was the point of working so hard to spread awareness about HIV/AIDS if so many young men could test positive in one day? Although it was a holiday, Xiao Shan said, he did not think it was a good day anymore. All the people who tested positive would be really sad, he said, and from now on they would always hate the Lantern Festival, because that was the day they found out they had HIV.

Despite these difficulties, most of the frustration and alienation Xiao Shan and Yuanzi experienced in their work resulted from Tianguang's chaotic and charismatic leadership style, which remained firmly in place at Tong'ai despite its moves toward professionalization and bureaucratization. Because of Tianguang's overall lack of support and oversight, his tendency toward procrastination, and his complete control over the group's finances, including monies that were supposed to be used to complete HIV testing projects but were often never given to those in charge of them, Xiao Shan and Yuanzi were often left holding the bag when projects were not completed on time. These kinds of dysfunctions within the organization also led to varying levels of last-minute forgery the night before project reports were due. Many times, I was witness to or even drafted into these desperate acts of deception, which sometimes included various volunteers being gathered into assembly lines to methodically create doctored documents by faking signatures, fingerprints, ID-card numbers, and the like.

Xiao Shan and Yuanzi greatly resented being put in such a position, feeling that Tianguang was using them to commit fraud, but they argued that there was nothing they could do about it. One time Xiao Shan said that it was because of "you crazy foreigners" (referring to global health initiatives like the Gates Foundation and the Global Fund) requiring things like fingerprints and signatures on expense reports that he and Yuanzi had found themselves in this predicament, saying that "you are killing us Chinese" and that "we don't have any choice, because you have the money."[8] On another occasion, Xiao Shan argued that it was because of Tianguang's "procrastination problem" that they had no choice but to commit fraud. "We could have done these things for real," he asserted. "But every time Teacher Tian finds some excuse [to delay], and then there is no more time left. Yuanzi is really angry, but he doesn't like to speak up. . . . Because he wants to keep working here. But I probably won't be doing it anymore. I don't want to help falsify things; I'm afraid that I will go to hell."

External bureaucratic accountability measures and internal leadership problems were not the only cause of such fraud, however; in at least one instance that I witnessed, the China CDC itself compelled Yuanzi to produce fake documents. One day when I arrived at the office, I saw that Yuanzi looked even more anxious than usual. When I asked him what was wrong, he explained that a district-level CDC official had just called him about a Global Fund project that Tong'ai was ostensibly doing for them. The work was supposed to have started months ago, but the project contract had never been signed, so Yuanzi assumed that it had been canceled. Now the CDC wanted him to pretend that Tong'ai had been working on the project all along. Yuanzi heaved a deep sigh and leaned on the desk, his cheek resting on his right fist, and gave me a tired look. "We will have to fake things," he said in a tired voice. "We have no choice." Several days later Yuanzi received another call from the same district-level CDC official, who gave him a detailed list of the various project reports and other forms of documentation she wanted him to produce. When Yuanzi hung up the phone he turned to Xiao Shan and angrily recounted what the CDC official had told him, saying that she even wanted him to provide photographs of events she knew had never taken place. "Who does she think she is?" Xiao Shan asked angrily. But Yuanzi just shook his head and started producing the fake documents that the official was demanding. The growing feelings of enervation experienced by Tong'ai staff, as well as the group's increasing alienation from the local queer community, further demonstrate the many harmful effects that neoliberal, market-based HIV/AIDS prevention projects funded by global health initiatives and administered by the state have had on grassroots queer activists and NGOs.

DYING FOR MONEY: THE COMPLEX AND CONTRADICTORY EFFECTS OF GLOBAL HEALTH INITIATIVES

In the summer of 2008, everyone in Tong'ai was discussing the imminent arrival of the Gates Foundation and the Global Fund in northwest China. To my surprise, instead of being excited, many people were concerned about what a sudden increase in funding for HIV/AIDS testing and prevention among MSM might mean for the local civil society. Some, like Tianguang, worried that, because many NGOs were not yet equipped to handle large amounts of money responsibly, the extra resources might cause more trouble than they were worth. In hindsight, many of these worries were prophetic. Several years later, Tianguang argued that the increase in competition among queer men's and AIDS NGOs was caused in part because "the current state of affairs or stage of development of Chinese community-based organizations is still not advanced enough." If the resources came a few years later, Tianguang postulated, "when NGOs were a bit more mature," some problems could have been reduced or altogether avoided. However, Tianguang continued, not all of the blame could be apportioned to Chinese civil society. "The other reason has a lot to do with the funding agencies themselves," he asserted. "Because there are a very large number of international agencies and institutions who are investing resources into China right now, a lot of the money they are spending is being used irresponsibly."

As I show in this chapter, the arrival of global health initiatives in 2008 had complex and contradictory effects on community-based queer men's NGOs and activism in northwest China. In many ways, the temporary increase in foreign funding was a boon for groups like Tong'ai. "Right now, all of our resources come from international society," Tianguang often reminded me. "Civil society organizations rely on those funds to survive; if you removed them these community-based organizations would all collapse." Additional funding allowed cash-strapped grassroots queer men's NGOs like Tong'ai to begin expanding and professionalizing their operations, reaching more local MSM with HIV testing services, and providing a small but significant source of income for dedicated full-time staff members whose past volunteer work had been largely uncompensated.

However, the manner in which HIV/AIDS projects and funds were administered by global health initiatives and the Chinese state also had negative effects. A sudden increase in foreign funding exacerbated existing divisions among and between queer and nonqueer NGOs by encouraging them to compete for project contracts and monies that they became increasingly reliant upon to survive. This competition in turn fueled processes of bureaucratization and medicalization within Tong'ai, which increasingly narrowed its focus from working toward long-term social and political change to simply performing ever-greater numbers of HIV tests. As Yuanzi told me in November 2010, "I thought it would be a good thing that there were a lot of resources; then we could really get some practical work done. But sometimes having a lot of resources isn't a very good thing." When I asked what he meant, he said, "China has an old saying: 'Men will die for money, just as birds will perish for food (*ren wei cai si, niao wei shi wang*).'"

Global health initiatives "incorporate a moral discourse of saving lives and improving health, making their actions appear righteous and unquestionable" (Heckert 2018, 144). However, this chapter highlights the crucial importance of ethnography in investigating and understanding the complicated and perhaps unintended effects that global health initiatives can have on civil society. It also focuses attention on the ways that marginalized communities like queer activists and people living with HIV interact with and are affected by global health initiatives and the neoliberal logic and discourses that they represent and reproduce. While it would appear that increasing HIV/AIDS funding and testing among MSM are obvious goods, depending on how it is administered and distributed increased foreign funding can sometimes create as many problems as it solves. In northwest China, the problems queer Chinese activists and NGOs had to contend with included worsening infighting and factionalism; the depoliticizing, medicalizing, and bureaucratizing of their organizations and activities; and increasing alienation from their former goals, their workers and volunteers, and the local communities that they serve. Rather than blaming queer Chinese activists and NGOs alone, I demonstrate how these consequences are the outcome of complex interactions between global health initiatives, the state, and local civil society actors.

The prediction made by many Tong'ai members in 2008 that global health initiatives would soon leave northwest China soon came true. In May 2011, the Global Fund temporarily suspended payments to its HIV/AIDS projects in the PRC after an internal audit of a $283 million grant revealed that the state had failed to meet its commitment to allocate at least 35 percent of the funds to civil society organizations (LaFraniere 2011). Suspension of the grant was particularly detrimental to community-based queer men's NGOs like Tong'ai, which had come to rely on

Global Fund projects for approximately 50 percent of its annual budget. Although payments resumed in August 2011 (*New York Times* 2011), in November 2011 the Global Fund announced that its HIV/AIDS projects in the PRC would be ending in 2013 (Jia 2012). While the Chinese government pledged to make up any shortfall in funds for NGOs involved in the fight against HIV/AIDS (Shan 2011), after the sudden withdrawal of global health initiatives in 2013 queer men's groups like Tong'ai faced an even more uncertain and precarious future.

6 · FROM RAINBOW FLAGS TO MR GAY WORLD
Transnational Queer Culture and Activism

In April 2008, as I prepared for a second summer of fieldwork, I received an e-mail from Xiao Jun, who at the time was still a volunteer at Tong'ai. Xiao Jun wanted to know if I could bring a few rainbow flags with me to give to the group. In the decades since it was created in 1978 by the queer American artist Gilbert Baker, the rainbow flag has become a transnational symbol of queer identity, pride, and activism. Because my fieldwork coincided with International Lesbian, Gay, Bisexual, Transgender, and Queer (LGBTQ) Pride Month, observed around the world in June, I reasoned Xiao Jun thought some new rainbow flags could help Tong'ai celebrate the occasion. Apart from the one large rainbow flag that hung proudly on the wall in the front room of the Tong'ai office, the group had no other rainbow flags that I knew of. Excited by the opportunity to show my gratitude to my hosts, I quickly agreed to bring the rainbow flags.

After a few days I received another email from Xiao Jun asking for additional rainbow flags. Several days after that, another email arrived, again requesting more rainbow flags, and then another email, and another. . . . The number of requested rainbow flags quickly increased from a few to a few dozen, in as many different shapes and sizes as possible. Not only was the cost of the flags starting to weigh on my modest graduate student stipend, but I was becoming increasingly concerned about whether my suitcase would even make it into the PRC. Border security was especially tight due to the upcoming 2008 Summer Olympics being held in Beijing and recent social and political unrest in Tibet. Getting a travel visa had been more difficult than usual; mine had been approved by the Chinese consulate in New York City just before the PRC had announced that no additional visas would be issued. I worried about what would happen if someone at customs inspected my suitcase and found it stuffed full of rainbow flags. Would they think I was helping to organize some form of protest? Would I be denied entry into the country?

Thankfully, my suitcase and all of the rainbow flags it contained made it safely from Boston to Xi'an, where the flags and I were excitedly received at Tong'ai

FIGURE 6.1. Rainbow flags being delivered to Tong'ai by the author. Photo by author.

(figure 6.1). It was not until several weeks later that I discovered what was behind the ever-escalating requests for rainbow flags that summer: word had gotten out to other queer NGOs all around the PRC that Tong'ai had an anthropologist coming from the United States who was bringing rainbow flags, and apparently everyone wanted to get in on the action.

I often recall this early moment from my fieldwork to reflect on what it might reveal about the globalization of sexuality, or the movement of certain symbols or expressions of queer activism and affect from one part of the world to another. Why did my queer friends and informants in Xi'an ask me to bring them so many rainbow flags that summer? Why could they not simply purchase their own rainbow flags in the PRC? Was there something especially significant about rainbow flags from the United States? How did they intend to use the flags? What does the rainbow flag represent to queer activists in postsocialist China? And what might this transnational traffic in rainbow flags reveal not only about the globalization of sexuality but also about queer culture and activism in northwest China and elsewhere?

Benedict Anderson (1991) suggests that the idea of "the nation" is nothing more than an "imagined community." Nations, Anderson argues, are imagined in the sense that their citizens do not all know one another personally and therefore must somehow come to think of themselves as sharing a common identity. According to Anderson, the invention of the printing press and the emergence of mass media were crucial steps in the formation of these imagined communities, as the ritual of reading the same newspaper every day helped make people feel like part of a collective. Invoking Anderson's notion of imagined communities, Donald Donham (1998, 15) observes that, despite important differences in race, class, and culture among queer people around the world, "there is still in the background a wider imagined community of gay people with which all of these persons are familiar and, at least in certain contexts, with which they identify. How this imagined community becomes 'available' for persons variously situated across the globe is a major analytical question." In their analysis of the queer Taiwanese publication *G&L Magazine*, Andrew Wong and Qing Zhang (2001, 248) show how its contributors and readers deploy various linguistic resources "to construct an imagined Chinese gay community with its own distinctive style." But how do queer activists in the PRC use transnational symbols like the rainbow flag to indicate their membership in an imagined global queer community? And, returning to Donham's original question, how might this help us better understand how an imagined global queer community is created, accessed, and sustained by queer people around the world?

In this chapter, I expand my focus from northwest China to explore how queer activists and NGOs from across the PRC use and understand transnational symbols and rituals of gay identity and pride. Analyzing two specific examples of the local circulation of what might be called "global gay culture," rainbow flags and video clips of the Mr Gay World pageant, I reveal the specific ways in which queer activists in postsocialist China use them to index their belonging and participation in an imagined transnational queer community or circle of queer people around the world.

In postsocialist China in the 2000s and 2010s, rainbow flags were a coveted commodity among queer activists and NGOs that were at once foreign and domestic, globally circulated and yet often locally unavailable. As I soon discovered, one reason why I had been asked to bring so many rainbow flags with me to Xi'an was that, before the late 2010s, rainbow flags were not widely available for purchase inside the PRC.[1] This is ironic because, although the first mass-produced rainbow flags were made in American factories, today most of the global supply of rainbow flags is produced inside China. Unable to obtain domestically manufactured rainbow flags in their own country, from the 1990s to the late 2010s queer activists and organizations from all around the PRC used a variety of means to acquire them, including sourcing rainbow flags from contacts abroad or making their own out of locally available materials.

Queer activists in postsocialist China have historically also had a hard time participating in another symbol of global queer culture, the annual Mr Gay World pageant. Held in a different country every year, the pageant features finalists sent from individual participating countries' own national contests who compete to claim the coveted title of "Mr Gay World." Despite the Chinese government trying to shut down the first "Mr Gay China" contest in 2010, and even though they were unable to travel abroad, my queer informants in northwest China neverthe-less managed to participate virtually in the event, evading the PRC's ever-present Internet censors in order to watch unofficial video clips of the Mr Gay World finals that were circulating online. Examples like these reveal both the limits and extent of the globalization of sexuality by showing how many queer people around the world are simultaneously excluded from yet able to find creative and resourceful ways to participate in the kinds of transnational circulations that constitute an imagined global queer community. I argue that, like the Chinese queer concept of the circle, analyzing how queer activists from across postsocialist China in the 2000s and 2010s reinterpreted, refashioned, and repurposed these symbols and rituals of global queer culture may help us resolve old theoretical tensions between sameness and difference that have long bedeviled queer anthropology and the anthropology of globalization. By demonstrating how tokens of transnational queerness like rainbow flags and the Mr Gay World pageant can be used to both signify their belonging in an imagined global queer community and enact locally meaningful and specific forms of queer culture and activism, queer activists in the PRC blur the boundaries between East and West, local and global, in ways that emphasize simultaneity and coincidence rather than sameness or difference.

MOVING BEYOND SAMENESS AND DIFFERENCE IN THE GLOBALIZATION OF SEXUALITY

The circulation of objects like rainbow flags and video clips of the Mr Gay World pageant are just two examples of the kinds of global "flows" of people, money, goods, media, and ideas that have been widely discussed in the anthropology of global-ization. Jonathan Inda and Renato Rosaldo (2002, 2) describe "a world where bor-ders and boundaries have become increasingly porous, allowing more and more peoples and cultures to be cast into intense and immediate contact with each other." Queer anthropologists have made similar assertions. Citing how "gay and lesbian lifestyle products, from pink triangles to rainbow flags . . . are more frequently bought as identity markers by queers around the globe," Arnaldo Cruz-Malavé and Martin Manalansan (2002, 1) proclaim that "queerness is now global." Dennis Altman (1996, 77) even speculates that global flows of queer people, commodities, and iden-tities may be having a homogenizing effect by replacing local queer cultures with a global queerness that emphasizes "an in-your-face attitude toward traditional restric-tions and an interest in both activism and fashion."

However, Anna Tsing (2000, 327–328) argues that some scholars may have pre-maturely announced the birth of a new "global era" without questioning the many assumptions contained in such "global rhetoric." Although the extent and degree of global flows enabled by modern transportation and telecommunication tech-nologies may make globalization seem new, examples like European exploration and colonialism in the so-called "Age of Discovery" from the fifteenth to eigh-teenth centuries and the surge in migration to North America in the nineteenth and twentieth centuries suggest that this is not the case. Many anthropologists also point out that, despite its name, globalization is not a truly global phenomenon. While some people and communities are becoming increasingly connected, others are being left out and left behind. As James Ferguson (1999, 243) argues, "What we have come to call globalization is not simply a process that links together the world but also one that differentiates it," creating "new, up-to-date ways not only of connecting places but [also] of bypassing and ignoring them." Analyzing "flexible citizenship" practices in the Chinese diaspora, Aihwa Ong (1999, 6–7) observes that "the art of government has been highly responsive to the challenges of transnationality." Indeed, many states around the world seem to be exerting ever more control over their national borders, erecting physical walls or constructing digital barriers like the PRC's "Great Firewall" to block or filter Internet traffic and information that is deemed harmful to national security.

Queer anthropologists have also pushed back against Altman's argument that local queer cultures around the world are being increasingly "internationalized." Lisa Rofel (1999, 454–455) argues that Altman "merely reads globalization as the spread of Western models of homosexuality" and criticizes him for espousing a "notion of culture as timeless, bounded, homogenous, and unchanging." Writing about queer men in Beijing, Rofel argues that "Chinese gay identities materialize in the articulation of transcultural practices with intense desires for cultural belonging, or cultural citizenship, in China" (453). This, according to Rofel, leads to a kind of "doubled" queer identity that is marked by both cultural difference and sameness. In a similar vein, Tom Boellstorff (2005) proposes the concept of "dubbing culture" as an analogy for understanding the concurrent cultural similitude and alterity of *gay* and *lesbi* identities in Indonesia. "In dubbing culture," Boellstorff writes, "two elements are held together in productive tension without the expectation that they will resolve into one—just as it is known from the outset that the speaker's lips will never be in synch with the spoken word in a dubbed film" (5). As important as these kinds of anthropological interventions are, they may ultimately do little to help us move beyond conceptualizations of non-Western queerness that are based on *either* sameness *or* difference. As Naisargi Dave (2012, 16) points out, many queer anthropologists continue to emphasize "an underlying difference between Western queers and their non-Western counterparts: gay men in China 'double' so that they can be gay but still Chinese; Indonesian *gay* and *lesbi* people 'dub culture' so that they can be simultaneously queer and Indonesian."

The queer Chinese concept of the circle, in which a person can belong to multiple, overlapping imagined queer communities and identities at the same time, might help to resolve long-standing theoretical debates over sameness and difference within queer anthropology. The inventive ways in which queer activists and NGOs in postsocialist China obtain, interpret, and use rainbow flags and Mr Gay World videos signify both their exclusion from and belonging to an imagined global queer community. By imbuing these symbols with new meanings like "tolerance" and "harmony," queer Chinese activists incorporate them into local instantiations of global queer culture and activism. Rainbow flags, gay pageants, and the queer subjects and strategies that they both reveal and help to create are not reducible to a single set of significations—similar or different, American or Chinese, global or local—rather, they are flexibly and creatively used by queer Chinese activists to simultaneously imagine, express, and reconcile these seemingly contradictory meanings and identities. By doing so, they emphasize how local understandings of what it means to be queer in a particular time and place always reflect even as they also help to construct an imagined transnational queer community.

"A SYMBOL THAT GIVES ME HOPE": QUEER CHINESE UNDERSTANDINGS OF THE RAINBOW FLAG

Gilbert Baker's first rainbow flag contained eight horizontal bars of color: pink; red; orange; yellow; green; turquoise; indigo; and violet, which symbolized, respectively, sexuality; life; healing; sun; nature; art; harmony; and spirit (Vezeris 1995). The rainbow of colors was designed to represent "the theme of unity in diversity" (Conner, Sparks, and Sparks 1997, 279). Baker dyed and stitched the original flag by hand, earning him comparisons to Betsy Ross, the legendary creator of the first American flag (Perry 1989). Thirty volunteers later assisted Baker in creating two huge 40′ × 40′ rainbow flags for the 1978 Gay Freedom Day Parade in San Francisco (Ferrigan 1989; Haggerty 2000; Vezeris 1995). The flags were made using 1,000 yards of white cotton fabric imported from China (Ferrigan 1989, 116), revealing how the rainbow flag has always been the product of transnational flows between the PRC and the United States.

After the 1978 parade, which was attended by some 250,000 people, the San Francisco–based Paramount Flag Company began to produce and sell a version of Baker's rainbow flag. The pink stripe was omitted due to a lack of commercially available dye (Ferrigan 1989; Haggerty 2000; Vezeris 1995). Following the assassination of Harvey Milk, San Francisco's first openly queer city supervisor, the 1979 Gay Freedom Day Parade committee decided to fly the rainbow flag again "to demonstrate the gay community's strength and solidarity in the aftermath of this tragedy" (S. Anderson 1993). To make the rainbow flag symmetrical, the indigo stripe was eliminated, giving rise to the six-color version (S. Anderson 1993; Ferrigan 1989). The rainbow flag continues to evolve, including the addition in 2017 of black and brown stripes by Philadelphia's Office of LGBT Affairs to recognize queer and transgender people of color; the "Progress Pride Flag" by Portland-based designer Daniel Quasar, which included black and brown stripes in a chevron alongside the colors of the transgender pride flag; and a version recently released by Intersex Equality Rights UK "featuring a yellow triangle and purple circle to represent the intersex community" (Green 2021).[2]

During fieldwork I discovered that queer Chinese activists have a variety of understandings and interpretations of the rainbow flag. While some have no idea what it represents, others are relatively familiar with its origins and the symbolic meaning of its colors. Most simply regard the rainbow flag as a generic queer "sign" (*biaozhi*) or "symbol" (*xiangzheng*). Xiao Bang told me, "The rainbow flag is the flag that represents queer people." Recalling when UNITE began in December 2009, Xiao Bang remarked, "We didn't have any rainbow flags. We also didn't think about making them. We just knew about rainbow flags, and when we went to buy something [for the group] we would specially pick things with rainbows." When I asked her why, she simply answered, "Because they represent the homosexual community."

Opinions about the rainbow flag's design also vary considerably among my queer Chinese informants. While some think the design is "pretty" (*piaoliang*) or "sexy" (*xinggan*), others feel it is too "showy" (*xianyan*). Xiao Feng said, "I think that the colors are very bright. They give people a positive and progressive feeling. It can warm people's hearts." In contrast, Paopao told me, "The first time I saw one, I thought the design was a bit too conspicuous. It didn't have an ounce of subtlety. Once you see it, you'll never forget it. The several colors are dark, without any harmony, and it just transitions straight from cool to warm hues. . . . The first time I saw it, I didn't think it was very pretty." Some people report developing a deeper appreciation of the rainbow flag over time. "Before I became involved in UNITE, I thought the rainbow flag was OK," recounted Jiajia. "But after you see [gay pride] parades around the world, and you see so many rainbow flags, it's very different. You think it is very pretty, very beautiful. But it is not only that kind of beauty; it's more in your heart. . . . You feel a type of belonging, a kind of self-representation."

For many queer activists in the PRC, it is local interpretations of the rainbow flag as representing Chinese concepts and ideals like "abundance" (*fengfu*) and "harmony" (*hexie*) that give the symbol its affective depth and resonance. Xiao Lei, a thirty-three-year-old volunteer at a queer men's NGO in northeast China, expressed how, in his eyes, "The rainbow represents different communities; the different colors stand for different mentalities. The rainbow flag embodies all of these differences coming together to do the same work." "Every color under the sun represents the rich colors of life," said Xiao Chang, a thirty-year-old staff member at a queer men's NGO in southwest China. "It communicates how we want to live together with everyone under the multihued sun." "I really like the rainbow flag," said Xiao Kai. "It's a symbol that gives me hope, that lets me see the day that I dream of, as beautiful as a rainbow, with freedom and peace, no discrimination, the exchange of truth, and everything else in my dreams."

While some queer Chinese activists see the rainbow flag as foreign, many regard it as a Chinese or global symbol. Yangyang said the rainbow flag represented being "inside the circle" (*quan'er nei*), a phrase that often describes local, regional, or national Chinese queer communities but can also refer to an imagined global gay community. Similarly, Xiao Feng remarked that while the rainbow flag primarily represented Chinese queer people, "It can also be said that it belongs to the entire world." Others argue that when or where the rainbow flag originally came from does not matter as much as the power that it has to bring people together in the here and now. As Zhiming put it, "One time I heard the story of the rainbow flag, where it came from. But I think that its origins aren't important. What is important is that it is a flag, it is a kind of symbol. It has a kind of cohesive force." In the context of queer culture in postsocialist China, it is often people's relative unfamiliarity with the semiotic history and significance of the rainbow flag that makes it such a potent and flexible symbol, able at once to symbolize positive local Chinese meanings like "abundance" and "harmony" and signify membership in an imagined transnational queer community.

"IN CHINA, SENSITIVE THINGS AREN'T SOLD": IMPORTING AND IMPROVISING RAINBOW FLAGS

The irony of the unavailability of rainbow flags within postsocialist China in the 2000s and 2010s was not lost on my informants. According to Dandan, the leader of a queer men's NGO in the eastern Chinese city of Tianjin, "These rainbow flags are all manufactured in China. They go abroad and then they come back." Many queer activists argued there simply was not a big enough domestic market for rainbow flags in China at the time. "I think it's probably because the queer movement still hasn't entered the mainstream," Jiajia reasoned. "People haven't realized that this is a community." Similarly, Da Xiong, the leader of a queer men's NGO in Sichuan, stated, "I think the reason you can't buy them inside the country is that there is no market for them; businesspeople don't know who would want these things. . . . Understanding of the rainbow flag is still not universal among domestic gay organizations, so rainbow flags are also not very widespread."

Other queer activists speculated that the unavailability of rainbow flags in postsocialist China could also be a political issue rather than a purely economic one. When I asked Zhiming why he thought rainbow flags were unavailable, he replied, "They don't make them." When I pointed out that all the rainbow flags I had purchased or seen for sale in the United States were manufactured in the PRC, he said, "Yes! But those are made for foreigners!" "Couldn't they be made for Chinese people?" I asked. "Impossible," Zhiming said. "In China, sensitive things aren't sold." Although he thought it was unlikely the state understood the significance of the rainbow flag, Zhiming argued that it did not matter. "The government is afraid of everything," he said. "They don't care what kind of flag it is, a rainbow flag, a sun flag, a moon flag—if it isn't a [Chinese] flag, they don't let you use it. They are afraid. Because flags have a kind of cohesive force. They are a kind of summons. They have a political meaning."

Zhiming's argument that flags of all kinds serve as powerful political symbols draws support from vexillology, the study of flags. Robert Shanafelt (2009, 16) argues, "The simple act of lifting aloft a symbolic token (any symbolic token) is a gesture whose meaning is easily grasped both within and across political domains. The fact that flags are raised continuously above the head also gives them power. Not only does the display of a flag suggest social solidarity, it simultaneously demands political deference." Drawing from Émile Durkheim's theorization of totemism, Carolyn Marvin and David Ingle (1999, 63) suggest that the American flag, by symbolizing the bodies of people who gave their lives for their country, simultaneously signifies, creates, and sustains the very idea of the nation, arguing that "the flag is the sign and agent of the nation formed in sacrifice." The rainbow flag, rather than symbolizing a nation-state like the PRC or the United States, instead indexes an imagined global community or "nation" of queer people. As Marvin and Ingle point out, the rainbow flag also "has a sacrificial history" in that the flag only gained international popularity as a symbol of queer identity follow-ing the assassination of Harvey Milk in 1979, when the flag was used "to commem-orate Harvey Milk's sacrifice" (363–364).

Despite the unavailability of rainbow flags in postsocialist China in the 2000s and 2010s, queer activists developed several strategies to obtain them. One com-mon method was to smuggle rainbow flags into the country in the suitcases of travelers and foreign friends. Tianguang told me the large rainbow flag that hung on the wall in the Tong'ai office was brought to Xi'an many years ago by the brother of a friend who was studying abroad in France. When I asked Jiajia about the ori-gins of UNITE's single rainbow flag, she explained how it was donated by Tongyu, a Chinese lesbian NGO in Beijing. When I asked how Tongyu obtained the flag, she said, "I think they got it from abroad. When people go abroad, they bring them back."

When they could not source rainbow flags from abroad, queer Chinese activists would make their own. One method was to order rainbow flags from local print-ing shops. As Xiao Bang explained, "Ready-made [rainbow] flags are very rare. So, you have to place a custom order." However, there were downsides to this solution; because rainbow flags had so many colors, they were relatively expensive, costing as much as ¥100 ($15) each depending on the size. Custom orders also had to be placed in bulk, a high cost that was out of reach for most community-based queer NGOs. Furthermore, the colors often did not turn out quite right, making Xiao Bang and others argue that custom-made flags were not as "authentic" (zhengzong) as the mass-produced Chinese rainbow flags made for export. Another solution was for queer activists to make their own rainbow flags from scratch. Reminiscent of Baker and his volunteers in San Francisco in 1978, Jiajia and her mother, who was retired, handcrafted bracelets and key chains in Xi'an out of nylon rainbow fabric donated by Les+, a Beijing-based Chinese lesbian culture and media organ-ization. UNITE volunteers sold these colorful items, along with other rainbow-emblazoned paraphernalia including stickers, buttons, and postcards, to raise money for the group (figure 6.2).

In the process of making their own rainbow flags, Chinese queer activists often imbued them with new meanings that reflected local queer culture. One June

FIGURE 6.2. Rainbow flag items being sold by UNITE volunteers. Photo by author.

night, some Tong'ai volunteers and I attended an event celebrating International LGBTQ Pride Month in a Xi'an gay bar. When we arrived, a young man approached our group holding a small green flag fashioned from a roughly cut piece of nylon cloth that had been glued to a bamboo skewer. Through the dim light and smoke, I could see many men seated at other tables who were excitedly waving similar yellow, red, and green flags. As loud dance music played and spotlights swept the room, I noticed large, rectangular swaths of the same yellow, red, and green fabric hanging from the ceiling. A man standing nearby informed us that they represented the rainbow flag. Later an MC took to the stage and announced that the three colors represented gay sexual roles: yellow stood for "big-old bottoms," red indicated "pure tops," and green symbolized men who were "versatile" (*ling dian'er wu*).[3] The MC later told me he wanted to hang a "real" rainbow flag behind the bar and asked if I knew where he could find one. Examples like this show both the creativity of queer activists in postsocialist China and the semiotic capaciousness of the rainbow flag. When they were unable to find or purchase "real" rainbow flags that were made in Chinese factories, queer activists and community members turned to locally available resources including inexpensive nylon cloth. At the same time, rather than being limited by the color symbolism of Baker's original rainbow flag, Chinese queers, like the people at the gay bar in Xi'an that night, assigned them their own meanings drawn from the local queer sex/gender system.

THE RAINBOW FLAG AND THE
POLITICS OF SEMIVISIBILITY

As with the globalization of sexuality, academic discussions of queer Chinese activism also frequently feature questions of sameness and difference. Chinese queer activism is often described as nonconfrontational, silent, and covert and is either implicitly or explicitly compared to a Western queer activism that is supposedly more antagonistic, vocal, and public. Chou Wah-shan (2000) juxtaposes a queer Western politics of confrontational individualism with what he describes as a queer Chinese activism that emphasizes preserving social harmony and familial relationships.[4] Lucetta Kam (2013, 90–94) describes Chinese queer activism as a "politics of public correctness" in which "destigmatization assumes priority before other goals" and Chinese queers are encouraged to construct themselves as "model homosexuals" in order to "bring about positive recognition by one's family, and eventually, acceptance by the general public." Contrasting it with "a Western-originating politics of public visibility," Elisabeth Engebretsen (2014, 126) similarly characterizes queer Chinese activism as embracing a "politics of community, where the primary strategy is to establish a collective consciousness within queer communities, raise general awareness, and ultimately consolidate popular support and mainstream acceptance."[5]

Questions of public visibility and political efficacy also feature prominently in academic discussions of queer Chinese AIDS activism. As I show in chapter 4, although the HIV/AIDS epidemic has catalyzed the development of increasingly organized forms of community-based queer activism in postsocialist China, rather than frame their activities in overtly political terms queer Chinese activists often keep a relatively low public profile while focusing on areas of overlap between their agendas and those of the state, including providing HIV/AIDS prevention and treatment to "men who have sex with men" (MSM).[6] Not only are less confrontational or visible forms of Chinese queer activism just as authentic, but, as Lisa Rofel (2013, 156) writes, "In the current moment in China, there is no way for lesbian and gay activists to create a full-blown social movement that would demand rights from the state." To do so would not only be counterproductive but would also pose significant risks for queer activists and NGOs.[7]

Queer people and activism in postsocialist China both exist in states of precarity. Although homosexuality was decriminalized in 1997 and is no longer officially considered a mental illness, the state does not officially recognize homosexuality, and queer people continue to face widespread social prejudice and discrimination. Although some government agencies like the Ministry of Health support queer AIDS activists and NGOs, other state organs like the Public Security Bureau harass and detain them. Queer activists must manage their visibility accordingly, keeping a low profile in most public spaces while being more visible in public health settings like World AIDS Day events or HIV testing campaigns. While the Internet has emerged as a crucial space for queer people to meet, organize, and express themselves more openly, queer activists and organizations have to carefully manage their online visibility to avoid unwelcome state interference, including avoiding politically sensitive topics like human rights and not broadcasting the time and location of events in advance.

Transnational queer symbols like the rainbow flag are often strategically deployed by queer activists in postsocialist China to enact what I call a queer politics of semivisibility.[8] Although mass-produced rainbow flags may have been a rare commodity in the 2000s and 2010s, rainbow flag imagery is ubiquitous in Chinese queer spaces and media, appearing in the names, logos, and websites of queer organizations; queer movie titles and posters; and flyers, pamphlets, and even condoms distributed by queer activists. However, outside of the queer community, the rainbow flag is not widely recognized or understood as a queer symbol in postsocialist China. This relative degree of public misrecognition is precisely what makes the rainbow flag so useful to queer Chinese activists, as it enables them to partake in both local and global forms of queer activism while simultaneously avoiding unwelcome state attention or interference.

There are two primary ways that queer Chinese activists use rainbow flags. One is to transform neutral, semipublic areas into queer spaces. This transformation can occur on a long-term basis, such as when an otherwise ordinary apartment or office is turned into a permanent queer space. This process is almost invariably achieved by hanging a rainbow flag, usually in a prominent place near the entrance or on a main wall; indeed, every Chinese queer NGO office I visited had at least one rainbow flag prominently on display. More often, rainbow flags are used to temporarily turn unmarked commercial venues into ad hoc queer activist spaces. I witnessed this several times when I accompanied Tong'ai members on trips to smaller northwest Chinese cities and towns to conduct HIV/AIDS outreach activities in hotel, restaurant, or karaoke rooms. During such events, rainbow flags were always hung alongside a traditional red banner (hengfu) displaying the names of the NGO and donor agency sponsoring the event. The use of the rainbow flag in these contexts is significant because it allows queer Chinese activists to briefly occupy semipublic spaces without alerting building supervisors, hotel managers, and public security officials.

Queer Chinese activists also use rainbow flags to enact a politics of semivisibility in more public spaces like parks, squares, and monuments. Displaying the rainbow flag during organized events allows activists to openly express their queer identities while managing the amount of public attention they receive. One common expression of semivisible Chinese queer activism involves flying rainbow-colored kites at monuments like the Great Wall during International LGBTQ Pride Month (Cui 2009; Engebretsen 2015, 99). Such displays are significant because they combine the rainbow flag, a token of global queer identity, visibility, and pride, with the kite, a symbol of traditional Chinese culture. As one informant explained, "Kites were originally used [in China] to disseminate information. By chance, the rainbow signifies the information of being queer."

FIGURE 6.3. Queer activists at an IDAHOBIT activity organized by UNITE in downtown Xi'an. Photo by author.

In examples like this, the significance of publicly displaying the rainbow flag is enabled, rather than prevented, by the flag's relative obscurity in postsocialist China.

Queer Chinese activism involving rainbow flags can sometimes also be quite visible and confrontational. On May 17, 2011, I attended an activity in downtown Xi'an organized by UNITE marking the International Day against Homophobia, Biphobia, and Transphobia (IDAHOBIT). Early in the morning, I joined a group of about twenty queer activists sporting rainbow flags of every shape and size. We rode bicycles through the broad streets and avenues of Xi'an, pausing at public squares and landmarks to disseminate leaflets like "The ABCs of Homosexuality" and engage passersby in frank and explicit discussions of sexuality (figure 6.3). As soon as our activities attracted the attention of public security officials, we hopped back on our bikes and rode to our next destination to repeat the process all over again.

In many ways, the event was like a miniature, highly mobile and visible queer pride parade. While many passersby were curious and receptive to our overtures, we also encountered some negative reactions. At one point along our route, a lesbian UNITE volunteer named Xiao Mei and I were passing out leaflets when a young man approached us to see what we were doing. As soon as he heard the word "homosexual" he wrinkled his nose in disgust and shook his head, saying that homosexuality was "abnormal" (*bu zhengchang*). "Anyway," he continued, "how could two women make love?" "With their hands!" Xiao Mei loudly exclaimed with a grin. Not only was this expression of queer Chinese activism highly visible and even confrontational, but its extensive use of rainbow flags, even if their significance was not immediately understood by the average pedestrian, was deeply meaningful to the queer activists who participated, as it symbolically linked them to an imagined global community of other queer activists who were engaging in similar IDAHOBIT events around the world that day.

Semivisible expressions of queer activism involving rainbow flags not only give queer Chinese people a relatively safe way to proudly assert their identities in public spaces, they also enable them to enact forms of belonging in an imagined global queer community that makes them feel more powerful and less vulnerable and isolated. Recalling her participation in IDAHOBIT, Jiajia said, "You feel that you are a part of the movement. It's a really good feeling, like the work you are doing is helping yourself, that you are expressing some of your power." As Hongwei Bao (2018, 40) argues, "Imagination has performative dimensions and often translates into social realities through people's lived experiences." While queer Chinese activists often avoid open confrontation and overt public visibility, this does not mean that queer Chinese activism is always nonconfrontational, silent, or invisible. The relative anonymity of the rainbow flag in postsocialist China allows queer activists to walk a fine line between confrontation and nonconfrontation, visibility and invisibility. Just as the rainbow flag itself is simultaneously both Chinese and Western, local and global, the forms of queer activism it enables and expresses in postsocialist China cannot be constrained within simple and reductive binaries like antagonistic or silent, public or hidden.

OF QUEER ACTIVISM AND APATHY: LIU XIAOBO AND MR GAY WORLD

Like the rainbow flag, the Mr Gay World pageant exemplifies both the limits and extent of the globalization of sexuality in postsocialist China and the creativity and resilience of queer Chinese activists. The following ethnographic vignette reveals how, despite their frequent exclusion from many symbols and rituals of global queer culture, queer Chinese activists nevertheless find resourceful ways to index their membership in an imagined transnational queer community while also expressing local forms of queer identity. It also highlights disagreements over political activism between queer activists of different generations, demonstrating the many different and equally valid forms of queer activism that exist in postsocialist China, even within a single queer men's NGO.

Just before sunset one evening in October 2010, I was seated at the large table in the front room of the Tong'ai office. Xiao Shan and Yuanzi sat beside me, hunched over their laptops busily recruiting people for HIV testing. No one else was there, and things were quiet except for the sound of fingers tapping on keyboards and the ever-present noise of construction filtering in from the darkening cityscape outside. Pulling my own laptop out of my bag, I began typing notes while waiting for something to happen. After two hours, I suddenly received a message from Tianguang. "Good news!!!" he said, the electronic characters brimming with excitement and exclamation points. "A Chinese person has finally won a Nobel Prize!!! Liu Xiaobo has won the Nobel Peace Prize!!!"

For several days the Western news media had been full of speculation that Liu Xiaobo, an imprisoned Chinese dissident and democracy advocate, might be selected to receive the honor. I quickly typed my congratulations to Tianguang, who replied, "Hehe, it's really something that's worthy of a national celebration!" That news of Liu Xiaobo's honor would become an occasion for national celebration seemed unlikely to me, given the increasingly repressive political climate in the PRC and recent international news reports that claimed that "Liu is almost unknown in China except among political activists" (McDonald and Ritter 2010). Wondering if Xiao Shan and Yuanzi had heard of Liu, I quickly told them the news. Looking up from their computers, they both gazed at me expressionlessly. Xiao Shan, in a slightly embarrassed tone, confessed he did not know who Liu Xiaobo was. Yuanzi just laughed, saying "This is the first time I've heard that name."

I could not help but feel a bit disappointed at their responses. After all, as full-time professional activists who worked at a quasi-legal grassroots queer men's NGO, shouldn't they be among the most likely people in the PRC to have heard of Liu Xiaobo? I messaged Tianguang back, telling him that Xiao Shan and Yuanzi had not heard of Liu. He replied, "Hehe, it makes me feel depressed, too. I don't know what those two care about. . . . Most Chinese people are all the same way, it's the result of being brainwashed." When I told Xiao Shan and Yuanzi what Tianguang had said, they rolled their eyes. I pressed them further, asking them if they were indeed queer activists—an assertion to which they reluctantly nodded their assent—shouldn't they have at least heard of Liu Xiaobo? Yuanzi grew serious, and, with a frown, told me that China's recent economic development had mostly been very equal, that if there was political trouble or unrest many people could get hurt, and that things should stay the way they were: "peaceful." When I asked Yuanzi to explain, he simply recited the idiom: "The happiness one receives from enjoying music alone is less than the happiness one receives from enjoying music with others" (du yue le buru zhong yue le).[9] Yuanzi's choice of idiom was selected to convey the classical Confucian notion that the importance of social harmony and the greater good outweighs that of individual happiness or personal interests. By extension, Yuanzi was arguing that China's current peace and prosperity were not worth risking by supporting the kind of political activism practiced by Liu Xiaobo.

As I opened my mouth to respond I was brusquely shushed by Yuanzi, who had just finished downloading an unofficial video clip of what turned out to be the final round of competition of the 2010 Mr Gay World contest. By coincidence, Mr Gay World had taken place several months earlier in Oslo, Norway, the same city where Liu Xiaobo's selection as the recipient of the ninety-first Nobel Peace Prize had just been announced. Same city, very different contest. If either Xiao Shan or Yuanzi realized the irony of this coincidence, they did not show it; instead, we clustered around Yuanzi's laptop and excitedly watched the grainy, low-resolution video.

It was hard to make out what was happening in the clip, as the unsteady video fell in and out of focus and was accompanied by scratchy and distorted sound. But Xiao Shan and Yuanzi were riveted. As the various Mr Gay World pageant participants took to the stage, dancing and sashaying to Celine Dion's international smash hit, "My Heart Will Go On," Xiao Shan and Yuanzi kept a sharp lookout for Mr Gay China. The 2010 Mr Gay World contest marked the first time that the PRC had sent a representative to the event. In January 2010, the Mr Gay China contest was supposed to have taken place in Beijing but had been unceremoniously shut down by the police (Jacobs 2010). The contest was later held anyway, in a less publicized venue, and the winner, a gay man from northwest China named Xindai Muyi, had flown to Oslo to take part in the Mr Gay World competition despite fears that he might be punished for doing so (E. Wong 2010). When Yuanzi finally spotted Mr Gay China among the other scantily clad contestants, he let out a scandalized sigh. "Oh my god," he said, as if he could not believe what he was seeing.

The 2010 Mr Gay World finals resembled an international runway fashion show, with most contestants dressed up in ethnic outfits ostensibly representing their home countries. One man wore a plaid kilt ensemble; another sported nothing but short white briefs and a magnificent white feathered Native American headdress. They were quickly followed by a man dressed as a cowboy, a man wearing an Asian conical hat, and a man in a tight-fitting New Zealand All Blacks rugby team kit. The exuberant proceedings were suddenly halted for a somber video montage depicting scenes of homophobic violence from around the world. There were pictures of "God Hates Fags" signs as well as more disturbing images of people being attacked and killed. After passively observing for a moment, Xiao Shan asked Yuanzi to skip ahead. Yuanzi quickly agreed and advanced the video to the swimwear competition. They both squealed with glee as they watched the various contestants prance around the stage wearing an assortment of revealing swimwear.

Later that evening when Tianguang finally arrived at Tong'ai, I followed him into his private office. We chatted about international reports that the news of Liu Xiaobo's Nobel Peace Prize was being blocked inside mainland China. (I was only able to access these stories using my virtual personal network or VPN, which allowed me to circumvent the Great Firewall.) Some of the reports said that even text messages with Liu Xiaobo's name in them were being blocked. Tianguang suggested that I try to send him a text. I composed a message containing Liu Xiaobo's name and sent it to Tianguang. After a few moments, when he still had not received it, Tianguang complained, "This demonstrates how perverted this government is." Tianguang described how he and Liu Xiaobo were good friends, telling me about how he had visited Liu Xiaobo once in Beijing when he was out of prison, and how in 1993 Liu Xiaobo had come to Xi'an after he had just been released from prison again. When Tianguang had taken him to visit the Shaanxi

Provincial History Museum, they were shadowed by plainclothes policeman. After visiting Xi'an for three or four days, Liu Xiaobo returned to Beijing and was imprisoned once more. "The Nobel Peace Prize is not Liu Xiaobo's alone," Tianguang remarked. "It is a prize for all the forces for democracy in China."

Later, as I watched the video of the 2010 Nobel Peace Prize ceremony, I could not help but be struck by the seeming incongruity of the two events. The Nobel Peace Prize ceremony, in which Liu Xiaobo was famously represented by an empty chair, was stuffy and formal, while the Mr Gay World pageant finals were much more energetic and significantly less clothed. Apart from both taking place in Oslo in 2010 and both being international competitions of sorts, the two events initially appear to have nothing else in common. However, both videos are marked by telling absences and presences, inclusions and exclusions, visibility and censorship. The empty chair in the Nobel Peace Prize ceremony is symbolic of both the absence of Liu Xiaobo, who was unable to accept the award in person because he was imprisoned in the PRC, and the broader oppression of activists and dissidents in postsocialist China.[10] Similarly, the unlikely presence of Xindai Muyi in the 2010 Mr Gay World competition symbolized the growing confidence and visibility of queer Chinese people, many of whom, like Xiao Shan and Yuanzi, may not have been able to travel to Oslo but could nevertheless still participate vicariously in this periodic (and problematic) ritual of global gay culture by watching unofficial videos of the event that, despite the Great Firewall, were circulating widely online.

It is tempting to interpret this story as one of "progress"; indeed, both events featured a first for China—the PRC's first Nobel Prize and the first time that a Chinese contestant had participated in the Mr Gay World contest. It is also tempting to interpret the story as one of "difference," in terms of political and sexual freedom in the West versus political and sexual repression in China, or even as representing a Western queer activism of confrontation, visibility, and pride versus a Chinese queer activism emphasizing social harmony, discretion, and personal responsibility. However, embracing such narratives of progress or difference would be a mistake. Depicting queer Chinese people as essentially apolitical is an example of what Naisargi Dave (2012, 16) describes as the tendency to assume "that most non-Western queer people are preoccupied not with the politics of identity, but with commensurating their sexuality with culture, religion, or nation." Under such a view, which Dave rightly criticizes, non-Western queer people like Xiao Shan and Yuanzi "do not, or more importantly, cannot" embrace Western identity politics, and are therefore incapable of becoming genuine queer activists. Engebretsen (2015, 91) similarly points out "the limited ability of Western models to accurately describe and analyze realities beyond the cultural contexts in which they were produced" and calls attention to how "these models reproduce a Eurocentric and monolithic version of sexuality and gender."

One important difference this story does reveal is that between generations of queer activists in postsocialist China. Older queer activists like Tianguang, who had lived through some of the worst excesses of revolutionary Maoism, often favored more direct political action and were more openly critical of the CCP and the state. Younger queer activists like Xiao Shan and Yuanzi, who had come of age in the era of economic and social reforms, often favored more tacit, less disruptive forms of activism, and tended to be more supportive of the CCP and the state. However, rather than interpret this story as one of either progress or difference, in which Chinese democratic and queer activists are being recognized for their efforts to help China become more like the West, we should instead read this story as one of *coincidence*, or what Tom Boellstorff describes as "copresence without incorporation" (2007b, 232), a particularly queer form of temporality that, like the queer Chinese concept of the circle, allows for and even celebrates moments of incongruity, serendipity, and apparent contradiction.

The story of Liu Xiaobo's Nobel Peace Prize and the 2010 Mr Gay World pageant reveals how queerness and queer activism in the PRC are just as diverse, messy, and contested as they are everywhere else. Even as they shun more visible, confrontational, and individualistic expressions of queer activism in favor of a more low-key, pragmatic, and relational approach that emphasizes physical well-being and social harmony, many younger people like Xiao Shan and Yuanzi still conceive of themselves as activists dedicated to improving the awareness and acceptance of queer people in postsocialist China. And while they may have been unfamiliar with Liu Xiaobo and uninterested in the 2010 Nobel Peace Prize, they were actively engaged with what in their eyes was a much more interesting and consequential international contest: the 2010 Mr Gay World competition. Queer moments of ethnographic coincidence like this emphasize the importance of moving beyond simple assumptions and narratives of sameness or difference in both queer anthropology and the anthropology of globalization and the necessity of seeking greater understanding within what Boellstorff (2007b, 236) calls "this messy middle ground of complicity and imbrication." By reminding us that not all queer activists or people necessarily see things the same way, stories like these emphasize the multitude of equally valid ways of understanding and enacting queer identity and activism in postsocialist China and around the world.

"OUR GAY COUNTRY!" IMAGINING AND ENACTING NEW FORMS OF QUEER SOLIDARITY

Jiajia once told me a funny story about the public misrecognition of the rainbow flag in northwest China. The story took place after the 2010 Lala Camp, a yearly event that brought lesbian activists from around mainland China, Hong Kong, Taiwan, and the Chinese diaspora together to exchange information, share strategies, and support one another. That year, the Lala Camp was held in northwest China for the first time, reflecting the growth and success of UNITE, which had organized and hosted the event, including several days of workshops and lectures at a hotel and conference center in downtown Xi'an, without attracting the attention of the authorities. Jiajia recalled how after Lala Camp concluded the participants all went to have dinner together in a crowded, touristy part of Xi'an. "Because there were so many people, someone held up a rainbow flag so that we could all stay together, just like a tour guide," she said. "A Chinese person came over and asked us, 'What country's flag is that?' We all said, 'Our gay country!'" Jiajia's story is one more example of how the rainbow flag, as the emblem of a queer "nation" that transcends political and cultural barriers, is making an imagined global queer community "available" (Donham 1998, 15) for people in postsocialist China and around the world. This idea of a global queer nation is echoed by a slogan that was popular among queer Chinese activists during my fieldwork: "Queer love has no borders!" (*tong'ai wu guojie*).

The small subset of rainbow flags that are produced in Chinese factories, exported abroad, and slowly make their way back to the hands of queer activists inside the PRC is a perfect example of what Tsing (2004, 4) calls "friction," or "the awkward, unequal, unstable, and creative qualities of interconnection across difference." Instead of flowing freely around the world, as most commodities are often assumed to do in this supposed era of global production and consumption, these flags must take a more circuitous route before reaching their final destinations. Although the first rainbow flags may have been "made in the USA" (using raw materials imported from China), not only are most of the world's rainbow flags today manufactured inside the PRC, but the rainbow flag is increasingly being used inside postsocialist China to enact both local and transnational forms of queer affect and activism. However, rather than interpreting rainbow flags in China as examples of the globalization of sexuality or the localization of a global queer symbol, we should instead view their "back and forth movement" (Inda and Rosaldo 2002, 2) between the PRC and the United States as blurring the lines between East and West, center and periphery, sameness and difference.

Despite being unable to purchase any of the rainbow flags that were mass-produced in their own country, queer Chinese activists in the 2000s and 2010s nevertheless found various ways to reimport, reinterpret, and rework this transnational symbol of queer identity. Likewise, despite repeated attempts by the authorities to shut down the Mr Gay China pageant and the efforts of Internet censors to block any news or videos of the Mr Gay World finals, queer Chinese activists nevertheless found ways to take part in this annual ritual of global queer identity by circulating and viewing unofficial video clips among themselves. Together, these efforts are examples of what Rofel (2013, 158) describes as the "creative, thoughtful, flexible, and nimble" qualities of queer Chinese activism. Far from their strategic semivisibility indicating a lack of authenticity or efficacy, the multiple ways that queer Chinese activists deploy rainbow flags and Mr Gay World videos illustrates how "they do not remain in a fixed relationship to power" but on the contrary actively "maneuver within and around the various powers that shape subjectivities, socialities, political beliefs and economic inequality" (158) both within postsocialist China and beyond.

Like the queer Chinese idea of the circle, the use of rainbow flags and the Mr Gay World pageant by queer activists in postsocialist China suggests new ways of theorizing transnational queer affect and activism that emphasize coincidence and imbrication instead of sameness and difference. Rather than simply signifying either the globalization of sexuality, in which queer people everywhere are becoming increasingly similar, or forms of local resistance to such globalization, in which queer people in places like China assert and maintain their difference, these flexible and capacious symbols are able to combine seemingly contradictory or even conflicting meanings under a single signifier. Just as originally Western queer symbols like the rainbow flag were initially produced out of transnational flows between the PRC and the United States, so do Chinese queer activists use them today to imagine and index both local and global forms of queer culture and identity. Understanding the complex semiotic significance of rainbow flags and the Mr Gay World pageant in China reveals the limits and extent of the globalization of sexuality and helps us to imagine and enact new forms of transnational queer solidarity. As my friends and informants in northwest China often say, "We are all inside the circle" (*women dou shi quan'er nei de ren*).

CONCLUSION

My twenty-ninth birthday took place while I was in the field. Xiao Shan, who had by then become a close friend as well as a key informant, helped me celebrate by partaking in a traditional American breakfast that I prepared in my small Xi'an apartment featuring pancakes with maple syrup and home-fried potatoes. (Xiao Shan found the pancakes "too sweet" for his tastes, but he liked the spicy home fries.) Xiao Shan surprised me with two birthday presents: a decorative disc of compressed Pu'er tea and a small Yixing clay teapot that was encircled with a swarm of tiny black Chinese characters that had been hand-etched onto its smooth red surface with minute precision. Xiao Shan explained that the characters on the teapot belonged to his favorite Buddhist scripture, the Heart Sutra, one of the most popular sutras in Mahayana Buddhism that is attributed to Avalokitesvara (known in Chinese as *Guanyin* or the Goddess of Mercy), wherein he (or she) relates achieving nirvana through the realization of the fundamentally illusory and ephemeral nature of human existence.

Xiao Shan later found an English translation of the Heart Sutra online, which he shared with me. The beginning of the sutra reads: "When the holy Bodhisattva Avalokitesvara had truly grasped the transcendent wisdom, he realized that visible form is only illusion. The same applies to its perception, to its names and categories, to discriminative intellect and finally even to our consciousness. They are all illusion. With this realization he was beyond all sorrow and bitterness" (Herzog n.d.). Every time I read this Buddhist scripture, I am struck again by how accurately it describes the transitory quality of the lives led by many of the people I came to know inside the circle. Over the more than a decade I spent conducting ethnographic fieldwork on queer culture and activism in northwest China, I watched as people rotated in and out of the circle of queer life and activism, often after only a few years, months, or weeks. Many people eventually left town because they had graduated from university or moved on to new jobs in other cities or regions of the PRC. Others dropped out of queer life due to social pressures to get married and start a new family outside of the circle. Sometimes people just disappeared, with no reason or explanation, never to be seen or heard from again.

The brief career of one Tong'ai volunteer named Da Sheng is typical of the trajectory of many of the queer activists I met in northwest China. One pleasant spring evening, a handsome young man in his twenties showed up unannounced at the Tong'ai office. As he entered, I noticed the long strand of mahogany-colored wooden Buddhist prayer beads that were wrapped loosely around his right wrist. Mortified, Xiao Shan, whose black toupee he usually wore in the presence of guests was then sitting on top of the table instead of on top of his head, wailed, "It's all over!" before fleeing into the bathroom. After regaining his composure (and his hairpiece), Xiao Shan realized that he had met Da Sheng a year or two before at a Buddhist retreat in Xi'an, but at the time neither of them knew that the other was inside the circle.

Da Sheng said that he had heard about Tong'ai months before while getting tested for HIV and that for some time he had wanted to come and start volunteering himself but that he had been too busy with work until now. Yuanzi, who was also working in the Tong'ai office that day, smiled and laughed nervously before starting to explain, "Right now, Tong'ai doesn't really have volunteers anymore—" when Da Sheng politely interrupted him by simply asking, "Are there things that need to be done or not?" Xiao Shan quickly interjected, saying, "Yes, yes, there are a lot of things that need to be done!" Da Sheng soon became a regular presence in the group, helping Xiao Shan and Yuanzi organize group activities and mobilize people to come get tested for HIV. Due to his kindhearted and friendly manner, Da Sheng instantly became popular with everyone at Tong'ai. He proved to be a hardworking and dedicated volunteer, even helping Tong'ai publish its first online newsletter.

Then one evening not three months later, Xiao Shan pulled me away from the cheerful ruckus in the front room of the Tong'ai office and asked me to accompany him to the small back room where the telephone hotline had once operated but which now usually stood dark and empty. Closing the door behind him, Xiao Shan said that Da Sheng was leaving Xi'an and returning to his hometown in Anhui Province. Surprised and confused, I asked Xiao Shan when Da Sheng would be coming back. Shaking his head slowly and pursing his lips, Xiao Shan explained that Da Sheng would never be coming back, that he had gone home to get married. The reason he was telling me this, Xiao Shan said, was that before Da Sheng left he had come by the office and dropped off a present for me. Opening the small bundle Xiao Shan handed me, I found that it contained a vegetarian cookbook with a handwritten inscription inside the front cover and a small red box holding a hand-carved white jade pendant of the figure of Guanyin, the Goddess of Mercy.

I called Da Sheng on his mobile phone to thank him for his gifts, and when he realized who I was he became excited and happy. He confirmed that he was returning to his hometown to get married and start a family. "It's unavoidable," he added, by way of an explanation. We made plans to stay in touch and said our goodbyes. After I hung up, I lingered for a while in the quiet empty room, turning over the white jade likeness of Guanyin in my hands. As I watched the sun set slowly in a smudge of hazy orange and red beyond rows of newly constructed high-rise apartment buildings, I found myself wondering what the future held for people like Da Sheng and others who had already joined and left the circle.

BEING QUEER IN POSTSOCIALIST CHINA

The uncertainty and precarity confronting people inside the circle mirrors the high degree of change and unpredictability that characterizes life in postsocialist China. As Arthur Kleinman et al. (2011, 24) write, "China is clearly facing a number of challenges: the widening gap between the rich and the poor, labor unrest, rampant corruption, environmental destruction, a crisis in regulation of food and other products, the clash of values in society . . . conflict with ethnic minorities, restriction on communication of dissenting and activist voices, and continued surveillance and repression." At the same time, China is also grappling with "a looming crisis of elder care," as its aging population exerts ever "greater pressure on singleton adult children in increasingly urban settings among an exploding middle class" (24).

However, in many ways the challenges facing Da Sheng and others inside the circle are unique. Queer people in postsocialist China must navigate the conflicting and contradictory demands of economic and social change while at the same time attempting to reconcile their individual sexual identities and desires with enduring traditional parental and familial expectations regarding gender, marriage, and family. Many significant changes are taking place in postsocialist China, including expanding individual freedoms and a growing social movement in which queer activists from across the country are coming together to advocate for increased awareness and acceptance of homosexuality and fight the spread of HIV/AIDS in their communities. Despite this, most of my informants in northwest China are either already married with children or expect to be married and start having children by the time they turn thirty. Queer Chinese children like Da Sheng who leave home to go to university and seek their fortunes in the big city are still expected to eventually return home to be married, not only to fulfill the traditional filial obligation of perpetuating the family line by having children of their own, but also in order to look after aging parents, many of whom continue to rely on their children for care and financial support despite China's recent economic growth. As I discovered during numerous discussions with my queer friends and informants, especially those from the post-80s and post-90s generations, many of them are also deeply invested in seemingly normative ideals of marriage and family and are committed to maintaining harmonious relationships with parents. They often find both profound value and personal satisfaction in fulfilling their wider social and filial duties, even when they directly conflict with their own individual queer desires and personhoods.

By the fall of 2011, the demands of family and filial piety had finally caught up with Xiao Shan, whose thirtieth birthday was fast approaching. Xiao Shan was purchasing a newly constructed apartment in a suburb of Xi'an, a necessary step in the preparation for getting married in postsocialist China, where prospective brides expect to be wooed not only by new forms of romantic love but also by a set of house keys provided by the family of the groom. Xiao Shan's parents, who had located a suitable marriage partner for him, were investing their entire life savings in the small apartment, where they eventually intended to move in with Xiao Shan and his future wife, who would look after them in retirement. Construction of the apartment was nearly finished, and Xiao Shan joked that he would be married the next time I saw him. Yuanzi, who was also nearing the critical age of thirty and still lived at home with his mother, was also encountering growing pressure to settle down and begin making more money in order to support a future family. Yuanzi had recently started dating a new Tong'ai volunteer, but he anxiously told me that his mother wanted him to buy a house and to get married so that she could come and live with him for the rest of her life, a move that would vastly complicate his plans to eventually find a lesbian partner and arrange a contract marriage so that he could keep covertly dating other men and leading a life inside the circle.

Stories like these help us better understand what it means to be queer in postsocialist China and shed light on cross-culturally universal dimensions of the queer experience. Despite frequently being offered in the ethnographic literature as examples of China's "sexual revolution" and how postsocialist Chinese personhoods are becoming increasingly selfish and individualistic, the lives and experiences of queer activists in northwest China reveal how, even as they have gained new opportunities to explore and embrace their queer identities in recent decades, these freedoms often collide with deeply entrenched and enduring social and familial expectations of filial piety, including the traditional Confucian ideal of marrying and perpetuating the family line. Although many scholars argue the institutions of marriage and family are becoming increasingly privatized and deinstitutionalized, the reality faced by most queer people in northwest China is that marriage and parenthood can only be delayed for so long. As a result, queer love and kinship often take on a temporary, circular quality, which my research participants explicitly contrasted with the eternal and linear nature of heterosexual marriage and family. However, rather than analyze or critique the experiences and priorities of my queer informants in northwest China as examples of homonormativity, I instead argue that they broaden our perspectives and deepen our knowledge of what it means to be queer, not only in China but elsewhere. Despite cultural differences in understandings and practices of personhood and kinship, many queer people around the world face similar pressures as they struggle to reconcile their own individual identities with the needs and expectations of their families and communities.

QUEER ACTIVISM IN NORTHWEST CHINA: CHALLENGES AND OPPORTUNITIES

Grassroots queer activists and organizations in northwest China like Tong'ai and UNITE also face an uncertain future as the government continues to press forward on its path of promoting economic growth and development while placing additional restrictions on civil society and other forms of political expression. In the complicated and often contradictory political landscape of postsocialist

China, community-based queer activists and NGOs often find themselves trapped in the liminal "gray zone" between legality and illegality, visibility and conceal-ment, that exists at the margins of Chinese state and society. However, this limin-ality holds promises as well as pitfalls for queer activists and organizations, many of which are able to take advantage of their relative invisibility to continue work-ing to advance their political and social agendas, even as the state increasingly cracks down on dissent and civil society.

While a growing crisis of HIV/AIDS among MSM has afforded many queer men opportunities to organize, collaborate with sympathetic organs of the Chi-nese state like the China CDC, and obtain funding from international donors and global health initiatives like the Gates Foundation and the Global Fund, queer men's NGOs like Tong'ai continue to be plagued by debilitating infighting and factionalism. The temporary surge in foreign funding provided by the arrival of global health initiatives in northwest China in 2008 worsened these divisions and tensions, fostering increased competition between NGOs and activists and encouraging processes of bureaucratization and medicalization within Tong'ai. As the group became ever more focused on HIV testing and treatment in order to survive, it became increasingly alienated from the local queer community, its own volunteers and staff, and its original mission of working to create a more accepting and inclusive atmosphere for queer people in China. The sudden departure of global health initiatives and their funding several years later left many grassroots queer men's NGOs like Tong'ai in a debilitated state, with fewer volunteers, a decreased presence in the local queer community, more competition from nonlo-cal and nonqueer NGOs, and an uncertain financial future.

The experiences of Tong'ai reveal how for queer activists and NGOs in north-west China the fight against HIV/AIDS is a decidedly mixed blessing. Although queer Chinese women's NGOs like UNITE are unable to benefit from the state's concern with fighting HIV/AIDS among MSM, which deprives them of signifi-cant sources of political legitimacy, visibility, and financial support, at the same time their distance from the HIV/AIDS crisis and the relative degree of anonym-ity they enjoy compared to many queer men's groups allows them to pursue a more politically oriented agenda and also insulates them from the pressures of depoliticization and medicalization that often accompany HIV/AIDS prevention. Indeed, even as Tong'ai emerged from its dealings with global health initiatives much weaker than before, its younger queer sibling UNITE continued to grow and thrive in the years that followed. This does not mean that queer women's activism and NGOs in postsocialist China do not face challenges of their own. Indeed, they seem to be afflicted by the same sorts of infighting and factionalism that plague their queer male counterparts. The Chinese Lala Alliance, which was founded in 2007 and had organized the yearly Lala Camp for grassroots queer women's activism and organizing in mainland China every year since then (Kam 2013, 21), disbanded in 2018, partially as a result of increasing government restrictions on civil society but also, I was told, due to disagreements and divisions among its leadership.

Despite these challenges, most queer activists inside the circle express a sense of hope and optimism for the future. Citing the remarkable progress that has already been made in increasing awareness and acceptance of homosexuality in Chinese society, particularly among younger generations, many of my informants eagerly look forward to even greater advances in the coming years, such as being able to come out to friends and family and maybe even one day marry their same-sex partners. For all the difficulties it entails, many of my informants report that being a volunteer has been a profoundly moving and validating experience and is also a source of their positive outlook on the future of queer Chinese culture and activism. Xiao Feng, a university student, said that volunteering in Tong'ai had deeply affected him. "I have become familiar with a lot of others like me," he said. "It makes me feel like I am not alone." Xiao Wai, who had just graduated from high school, told me that before he joined Tong'ai he did not dare to tell anyone he was gay. "Now I don't think it's a big deal," he declared. "I am more confident. Now I believe even more that every person has their differences, that every community has their own culture. This is something we should be proud of. Some people think that being gay is a kind of sickness, but I think that we are no different from anyone else."

It was not only younger queer men who shared such stories with me. Da You, who was in his sixties by the time I left the field, said that being a volunteer had helped him to "feel much better about my identity as a gay man." When I asked him to elaborate, he replied:

> I think that after becoming a volunteer, after doing this work for everyone, my mentality became much better. Furthermore, after doing this work for a while, I felt more at peace about my identity; my heart was able to face up to my identity more calmly. I wasn't afraid of other people knowing. After being a volunteer, a lot of people knew—even a lot of my [straight] friends knew that I was this kind of person. For example, in 2008 I told my mother about myself. My father had already passed, but I went and told my mother. She is seventy-five years old. She was also able to understand me. She told me that if I had told her before, she wouldn't have forced me to get married. When she said that, I felt really light, even though I had already been married and have a kid who is this big. She told me, "You are my son, I want you to live happily." But I was already married.

I asked Da You if hearing his mother say this gave him any regrets, "Some," he replied. "But I have already made a family, had a child. I must be responsible to my family. You can have love, but you must not harm your wife." Da You's story of being able to embrace his queer identity and begin to live more openly as a gay man even while continuing to fulfill his duties and obligations to his parents and family illustrates the challenges and opportunities facing queer activists of all ages in northwest China. Queer stories and perspectives like these complicate and challenge straightforward narratives of privatization and individualization in post-socialist Chinese society, even as they also enrich our understanding of what it means to be queer in China and around the world.

Community-based queer activism and NGOs are understudied and important examples of the civil society taking shape in postsocialist China. They reveal how, instead of having no civil society or a civil society with "Chinese characteristics," members of vulnerable and marginalized communities in postsocialist China are coming together to advocate for causes that are important to them even as opportunities for political organization and expression narrow. While it may be true, as Hongwei Bao (2018, 171) argues, that "the queer public sphere is fleeting, transient, contingent and somewhat fugitive in China," nevertheless it endures. The stories in this book reveal the tenacity, creativity, and dedication of queer activists in northwest China. Seeking out opportunities to collaborate with rather than work against the state and strategically deploying a politics of semivisibility in order to evade government censorship, queer activists continue to persevere in their struggle for greater social acceptance and equal rights, despite increasingly challenging political and social conditions. By resourcefully participating in symbols and rituals of transnational queer culture and identity like rainbow flags, pride events, and the Mr Gay World pageant, queer activists and NGOs help to create and maintain an imagined transnational queer community even as they also imbue these tokens of global queer culture with new meanings and use them to enact local resistance strategies. Stories and examples of grassroots queer activism show that civil society in postsocialist China is more robust and resilient than it may appear and that, even as the state once again begins exerting a growing presence in people's daily lives, social and economic reforms continue to afford many marginalized people and groups new opportunities for individual expression and collaboration.

UPDATES FROM THE FIELD

In hindsight, the 2000s and 2010s seem like they were a "golden era" (Bao 2018, 200) of grassroots queer culture and activism in postsocialist China. Although people had to carefully manage their degree of semivisibility in order to avoid running afoul of the PRC's watchful public security apparatus, queer activists and NGOs were nevertheless able to operate with some degree of freedom. However, in the decades following president Xi Jinping's consolidation of power in 2012, the political climate has grown much less tolerant. The government has launched a widescale and systematic crackdown on lawyers, journalists, activists, and civil society organizations of all kinds, which the international human rights research and advocacy organization Human Rights Watch has described as "the most severe since the Tiananmen Square democracy movement" (Cumming-Bruce 2017).

At the same time, the PRC has also cracked down on public discussions and representations of queerness. In 2016, the government passed a new set of regulations that banned content that "exaggerates the dark side of society," including depictions of queer people, incest, extramarital affairs, and sexual assault (Ellis-Petersen 2016). In 2018, the Chinese social media site Sina Weibo announced a ban on all gay-related content but quickly reversed the decision after a backlash from millions of internet users (Hernández and Mou 2018). In 2019, Sina Weibo deleted a prominent online community for lesbian and bisexual women called "les" but again reversed itself after a similar backlash. However, in 2021, another popular Chinese social media platform, WeChat, suddenly erased the accounts and content of campus LGBTQ groups at China's top universities and gender-related academic research associations, showing how queer online content and communities continue to be targeted for censorship and erasure (R. Davis 2021). Although China's overall HIV prevalence is still relatively low compared to many other countries, rates of HIV infection among people between the ages of fifteen and twenty-four rose by more than one-third every year from 2011–2015, with most of the new infections occurring between MSM (*The Economist* 2019).

Not all recent changes have been negative. With the spread of smartphones, queer social networking apps like Blued (which was launched in 2012 and is now the world's largest queer social networking or dating app) have become popular, as have other apps and websites like www.chinagayles.com, where hundreds of thousands of Chinese gays and lesbians are arranging "contract marriages" with each other (Chen 2015). In 2014, a court in Beijing ruled in favor of a gay man who had sued a clinic for giving him electric shocks in an effort to "cure" his homosexuality after his parents had pressured him to seek treatment (Levin 2014). In 2017, Taiwan's Constitutional Court ruled that gays and lesbians had the right to marry, and same-sex marriage was legalized in 2019, making Taiwan the first (and so far only) place in Asia where same-sex couples are allowed to wed (A. Wang 2019).

In 2012, Xiao Shan got married in a traditional wedding ceremony. In 2013, he and his new wife had a baby, an adorable girl, and he excitedly and proudly texted me pictures of her. Xiao Shan had finally fulfilled his ambition of finding someone to start a family and spend the rest of his life with, "like two clasped hands." In 2013, Yuanzi also got married to a lesbian woman he met online. Yuanzi and his bride did all the things that a newlywed couple was expected to do, including taking wedding photos and hosting a wedding banquet with both families present. Yuanzi also bought an apartment, and after marrying lived there with his wife for a time, along with his boyfriend and her girlfriend. However, relations between the two couples soon soured, and Yuanzi moved back in with his mother, who was already pressuring him to have a child.

On March 7, 2015, the day before International Women's Day, Douzi, one of UNITE's founders, was arrested along with four other feminist and queer activists and charged with "picking quarrels and creating a disturbance," a vaguely worded offense that is often used to justify detaining and imprisoning activists and dissidents (Jacobs 2015). Douzi, who had left UNITE and was working for a Beijing-based human rights NGO, and the four other women were planning on handing out leaflets and stickers on public transportation to raise awareness of domestic violence, a growing problem in postsocialist China. The "Feminist Five," as they were later dubbed by the international media, were eventually released on April 15, 2015, without being formally charged (E. Wong 2015). However, the incident underscored how intolerant the state has become of public expressions of activism.

When I returned to the field in the summer of 2017, I was shocked to see the changes that had taken place within Tong'ai. The formerly brand-new office that Tianguang had once been so proud of and had argued was a sign of the group's growing professionalism looked like it had been abandoned and had largely fallen into disrepair. The Internet had long been disconnected, as had the water and the electricity, due to the utility bills not being paid for many months. The large, raised plastic letters of the group's motto and mission statement, which Tianguang previously had me translate and were prominently displayed on the front wall of the office, had started to come unglued and were falling to the floor in a disorganized heap, as if symbolizing the gradual decay and decline of the organization itself.

Although Xiao Pu had left Tong'ai at the end of 2012 after falling out with Tianguang over the mismanagement of project resources, Xiao Shan and Yuanzi were still working as full-time staff members, even though they had not received any salary in months. They described how, after the departure of the Gates Foundation and the Global Fund in 2013, the amount of funding for HIV/AIDS prevention among MSM in northwest China had declined precipitously. While the government was making up some of the difference in the form of small grants from the China CDC, the projects were much smaller than in previous years. However, after their most recent grant had been awarded, they alleged, Tianguang had taken all the money for himself and had not used it to pay the group's bills or their salaries. In order to make ends meet, Xiao Shan and Yuanzi, along with the few remaining Tong'ai volunteers, began selling T-shirts on the side of the road in one of Xi'an's many open-air markets (figure C.1). Before I left the field that summer, I met Tianguang for dinner in the city's Muslim quarter. He acted as if everything was fine and did not bring up any of the problems facing the group or its finances; our conversation was awkward, and it ended up being the last time that we spoke.

In a reversal of fortunes, UNITE seemed to be thriving when I visited the organization in 2017. They had recently moved into a gleaming office space in a newly constructed high-rise building in a northern suburb of Xi'an, and had hired several new full-time staff members. Jiajia, who along with Xiao Bang was still leading the organization, proudly gave me a tour of the UNITE office, showing off the desks, computers, workstations, and activity rooms. Although the group was

FIGURE C.1. Tong'ai volunteers sell T-shirts by the side of the road in Xi'an. Photo by author.

still involved in queer activism, UNITE had also begun working on youth advocacy, which had enabled them to secure new lines of funding, and they had more active volunteers and programs than ever before.

In the summer of 2019, during my last trip to the field, I found that UNITE had moved into an even larger office space closer to downtown Xi'an and was doing better than ever. Tong'ai, northwest China's first and oldest queer NGO, had finally collapsed some twenty years after it had begun work in 1998. However, like a phoenix rising from the ashes, Tong'ai had been reborn in the form of a new grassroots queer men's NGO founded by Xiao Shan and Yuanzi. After securing their first project contract from the China CDC, they along with several other former Tong'ai volunteers had rented a small space in an apartment building across the street from the previous Tong'ai office and were busy offering free HIV/AIDS testing services to local MSM. No one had seen or heard from Tianguang in years. Xiao Pu had left queer and AIDS activism behind and now owned his own tea shop. Yangyang had graduated from university and had become a high school English teacher in his hometown in Zhejiang Province. Yuanzi was still living with his mother, who had stopped nagging him about moving back in with his wife and having a baby. He was still dating his boyfriend, who also had a wife and child in a smaller regional city. Xiao Shan was still very much in love with his wife and baby daughter, who had only grown more adorable in the years since I had last seen her in 2017. In 2022, Xiao Shan and his wife welcomed a second baby, also a girl, into their growing and happy family.

FINAL WORDS

I choose to end this book like I began it, with the words of one of my queer Chinese informants. Late one July night, the day after Da Sheng's sudden departure from the circle, I was in my apartment putting the finishing touches on my field notes for the day. At around 2 A.M., I noticed that Yangyang had just posted a long poem in a Tong'ai volunteer group chat. Below is the full poem, which I think perfectly encapsulates the feelings of both angst and anticipation that characterize queer life in postsocialist northwest China:

When I realized that my sexual orientation was not the same as other men, when I gradually began to understand that my sexual psychology was oriented differently from ordinary people, when I clearly understood that I wouldn't be able to walk the road others travel toward an early marriage, I chose to escape, and the means of escape was to fight.

When I moved from a closed, small village to the bustling city, had my first *gay* experience, and then moved on to another metropolis, that was the start of my struggle.

Now that I knew, now that I understood my difference, I had to allow myself to be as different as possible. I, or the largest part of myself, have been constantly staggering along, constantly fighting, until the day arrived when I had a job and could support myself. But because I am *gay*, having a job is not enough. There is also protection in old age, if I really make it that far, the ability to afford a nursing home.

Because I am *gay*, I have to work even harder than others, to strive to achieve every kind of honor, so that people won't look down on me because I am unmarried.

Because I am *gay*, I have to learn to be even more kind-hearted, to never show a cold shoulder to vulnerable people, to do more good deeds when I have the chance.

Because I am *gay*, I have learned how to be a person, a person with integrity, a person whom others respect and admire.

Because I am *gay*, I have learned more than others my own age how to cherish, protect, and care for myself, because I know that often no one but me will know whether I am tired or sick, whether I am warm or cold.

Because I am *gay*, I show more love and care to my family, because I know in this world the people who love you the most are still your own kin.

Because I am *gay*, I value affection very much, because in this world the affection between friends is the only lubricant to maintain a positive state of mind. Friends occupy a huge space in my life.

Because I am *gay*, I need to learn how to undertake the responsibilities at home that would normally fall on two people, to cook and clean for myself, to look after my own finances, to pick out my own matching shirts and shoes, even to select a suitable apartment on my own.

Because I am *gay*, I have learned how to be tolerant and generous, how to not fight with people over small things like chicken feathers and garlic peels, how to not care as much about all the little ups and downs.

They say that tongzhi are just normal people; actually, to be a normal tongzhi you have to work even harder than ordinary people. Sadly, *gays* have no future. Because they have no future, they have to seize the present. For *gays*, the present is more important than the future.

Because I am *gay*, I have a *gay* love life; having a romantic life is also one of the goals I have been fighting for. Love is something you can fight for but cannot force, because it is a different kind of struggle; after all, love is a matter between two people.

Because I am *gay*, I love myself all the more!

A few moments later, Yangyang proudly posted an addendum: "I wrote this all myself!"

LIST OF NAMES

Chengji	程济	Journey; help
Da Sheng	大圣	Little Sage
Da Xiong	大雄	Big Hero
Da You	大优	Large Excellence
Dandan	蛋蛋	Egg
Dongdong	冬冬	Winter
Douzi	豆子	Bean
Jiajia	嘉嘉	Excellence
Lang	狼	Wolf
Lao Huang	老黄	Old Yellow
Lao Wang	老王	Old Wang (surname)
Li Zhuren	李主任	Director Li (surname)
Liu Daifu	刘大夫	Doctor Liu (surname)
Paopao	蝙蝠	Bubble
Tian'e	天鹅	Swan
Tianguang	天光	Daylight
Tianhao	天号	Heavenly Sign
Wenqing	文清	Cultured; peaceful
Xiao Bang	小棒	Little Stick; Little Cool
Xiao Bao	小包	Little Bun
Xiao Chang	小常	Little Ordinary
Xiao Feng	小枫	Little Maple
Xiao Hei	小黑	Little Black
Xiao Jun	小君	Little Monarch
Xiao Kai	小凯	Little Triumph
Xiao Lei	小雷	Little Thunder
Xiao Long	小龙	Little Dragon
Xiao Mei	小梅	Little Plum
Xiao Niu	小牛	Little Bull
Xiao Pu	小普	Little General
Xiao Shan	小山	Little Mountain
Xiao Wai	小歪	Little Crooked
Xiao Xi	小习	Little Habit
Xiao Xing	小星	Little Star
Xiao Yu	小雨	Little Rain
Xingshan	行善	Do Good
Yangyang	洋洋	Ocean
Yuanzi	圆子	Dumpling
Zhang Zhuren	张主任	Director Zhang (surname)
Zhengzheng	正正	Straight; honest
Zhiming	志明	Aspiration; bright
Zhujie	朱姐	Big Sister Zhu (surname)

GLOSSARY OF CHINESE CHARACTERS

ai	爱
aiya	哎呀
aizibing	艾滋病
baba	爸爸
bai shan xiao wei xian	百善孝为先
baijiu	白酒
bao sunzi	抱孙子
baorong	包容
baquan	霸权
bei charu fang	被插入方
beidong	被动
bianfu	蝙蝠
biaozhi	标志
bingzi	饼子
boli	玻璃
bu kaopu	不靠谱
bu niang bu C	不娘不C
bu xiao you san, wu hou wei da	不孝有三无后为大
bu zhengchang	不正常
bu zhengdang	不正当
bufen	不分
butie	补贴
C yi meng ling	C一勐零
cai	菜
cao	草
caogen	草根
chai mi you yan	柴米油盐
charu fang	插入方
chongtu	冲突
chu zai huise didai	处在灰色地带
chuantong	传统
chuanzong-jiedai	传宗接代
chugui	出柜
chun yi	纯一
chunhuo	蠢货
da leipi	打雷劈
da mu ling	大母零
danhua	淡化
dixia	地下
du yue le buru zhong yue le	独乐乐不如众乐乐
duanxiupi	断袖癖
erbai	二百
er sao	二嫂
erzi	儿子

fandong	反动
fazhan	发展
Feicheng Wurao	非诚勿扰
feifei	狒狒
Feitong Wurao	非同勿扰
fengfu	丰富
fentaozhihao	分桃之好
fu	福
gaige kaifang	改革开放
ganbei	干杯
gay dian	gay点
gong	攻
gong	公
gongkai	公开
gongmin shehui	公民社会
gongxian	攻陷
gongzhan	攻占
gongzuo	工作
Guangze Jiazu	广泽家族
guanxi	关系
Guanyin	观音
guifei	贵妃
gunzi	棍子
hanhu	含糊
hao niu a	好扭啊
haojuhaosan	好聚好散
hei'an	黑暗
hengfu	横幅
heshi	合适
hexie	和谐
hexin	核心
hezuo hunyin	合作婚姻
hou hou lian	猴猴恋
houtinghua	后庭花
houzi	猴子
hua qian mai xue	花钱买雪
huise	灰色
huixiexing	诙谐性
huo	货
huo	伙
huo	祸
huobi	货币
huodong	活动
huohai	祸害
huopin	货品
huose	货色
ji	鸡
jia	家
jiahuo	家伙
jiance kapian	检测卡片

jiang	奖
jiangnan zuonü	将男作女
jiankang	健康
jiaru	加入
jiating	家庭
jiazu	家族
jie	姐
jiechu dao	接触到
jiehun wenti	结婚问题
jiejie	姐姐
jijian	鸡奸
jijifenzi	积极分子
jingji wenti	经济问题
jingzheng	竞争
jiqing	激情
jiu bie sheng xin hun	久别胜新婚
jiuma	舅妈
kaifang	开放
kaixin jinlai, kaixin zouqu	开心进来, 开心走去
kouzi	扣子
kuai	块
ku'er	酷儿
la	拉
lala	拉拉
lanhuazhi	兰花指
lao chou mu wu rao	老丑母无扰
laoban	老板
laoda	老大
laogong	老公
laopo	老婆
lazi	拉子
le	乐
ling	零
ling dian'er wu	零点五
Longyangjun	龙阳君
luan	乱
lunzi-paibei	论资排辈
luoye-guigen	落叶归根
mama	妈妈
mantou	馒头
Ma shi	马师
maomao xiong	毛毛熊
mei banfa	没办法
meimei	妹妹
meiniang	媚娘
meiyou yibeizi de aiqing	没有一辈子的爱情
meizi	妹子
meng	勐
minggan	敏感
mu	母

mubiao	目标
muhou	母后
nanchong	男宠
nanfeng	南风/男风
nannan xing xingweizhe	男男性行为者
nanse	男色
nanxing	男性
nanzun-nübei	男尊女卑
neige	那个
ni you meiyou baoma	你有没有宝马
niang	娘
nongjiale	农家乐
nü'er	女儿
nütong	女同
nüxing	女性
ouran	偶然
pianhun	骗婚
piaoliang	漂亮
piaopiao	飘飘
pijing	屁精
po	婆
PP lian	PP恋
pu lai pu qu	扑来扑去
Qi Xiannü Jiazu	七仙女家族
qiangpo	强迫
qing shui bu yang yu	清水不养鱼
Qingming Jie	清明节
Qingren Jie	情人节
qinqing	亲情
qinshu zhidu	亲属制度
quan	劝
quan'er nei	圈儿内
quan'er nei de ren	圈儿内的人
quanzi	圈子
queren	确认
qun	群
qunti	群体
re	热
ren	认
ren wei cai si, niao wei shi wang	人为财死鸟为食亡
renqun	人群
renyao	人妖
rexian	热线
rou	柔
rou hou	肉猴
san bu	三不
sao ji	骚鸡
shantou zhuyi	山头主义
shequ	社区
shequn	社群

shimin shehui	市民社会
shou	守
shou	受
shou xiong	瘦熊
shoufu	收服
shuangxinglian	双性恋
Si Mian Yi Guanhuai	四免一关怀
siyaojiu	四一九
songsan	松散
T yu	T域
ta shi wo de cai	他是我的菜
ta shi wo de meizi	他我的妹子
ta shi wo xihuan chi de cai	他是我喜欢吃的菜
ta ye shi	他也是
taifei	太妃
taitai	太太
tanlian'ai	谈恋爱
tianlun zhile, ersun raoxi	天伦之乐, 儿孙绕膝
Tong'ai	同爱
Tong'ai Shequ Fazhan yu Fuwu Zhongxin	同爱社区发展与服务中心
tong'ai wu guojie	同爱无国界
tongxing lian'ai	同性恋爱
tongxinglian	同性恋
tongzhi	同志
Tongzhi Aizibing Gongzuo Zuzhi	同志艾滋病工作组织
tongzhi jiazu	同志家族
tongzhi zhi jia	同志之家
TT lian	TT 恋
tuoguan	托管
tuoyan	拖延
tuzi	兔子
wa	挖
waizhan	外展
wan	玩
wenming shehui	文明社会
wo de xinli you mogui	我的心里有魔鬼
women dou shi quan'er nei de ren	我们都是圈儿内的人
xianggong	相公
xiangmu	项目
xiangzheng	象征
xiansheng	先生
xianyan	显眼
xiao	小
xiao	孝
xiejiao	邪教
xinggan	性感
xinghun	形婚
xingshi hunyin	形式婚姻
xiong	熊
xiong hou lian	熊猴恋

xiong xiong lian	熊熊恋
xixuegui	吸血鬼
xuanchuan	宣传
yali	压力
yang	阳
yanggang	阳刚
yangguang	阳光
yangguang xia	阳光下
yao	妖
yaojing	妖精
yaonie	妖孽
yaonü	妖女
ye P niang T	野P娘T
yeman'er	野蛮儿
yi	一
yi ge ren shuo le suan	一个人说了算
yi shan bu rong er hu	一山不容二虎
yi tiao long de fuwu	一条龙的服务
yin	阴
yisheng-yishi	一生一世
yixin-yiyi	一心一意
youbing	油饼
yuanfen	缘分
yue	乐
zeren	责任
zhao caicai	找菜菜
zhao meizi	找妹子
zhende	真的
zheng	正
zhengzong	正宗
zheyang de ren	这样的人
zhijie	直截
zhiren tongzhi jiaoliu hui	直人同志交流会
zhitong-daohe	志同道合
zhiyuanzhe	志愿者
zhiyuanzhe zuzhi	志愿者组织
zhuanye fuwu jigou	专业服务机构
zhudong	主动
zijin	资金
zongzhi	宗旨
zongzi	粽子
zouhanlu	走旱路

ACKNOWLEDGMENTS

Writing this book has been a long academic and personal journey that I could not have completed without the help and support of many people and organizations along the way. This research was only possible because of the queer activists in northwest China who opened their doors, hearts, and minds to me, graciously put up with my seemingly endless questions and ignorance, and helped me find my own place inside the circle. Their bravery, dedication, and integrity will always inspire me.

My study of the Chinese language was supported by a Foreign Language and Area Studies Fellowship from the Department of Education. My primary fieldwork in China was funded by a Fulbright Research Award from the Department of State, a Doctoral Dissertation Research Improvement Grant from the National Science Foundation Cultural Anthropology Program, a Doctoral Dissertation Research Fellowship from the Andrew W. Mellon Foundation, and other travel and research awards from the Graduate School of Arts and Sciences and the Department of Anthropology at Brandeis University. A very special thanks to Jonathan Akeley, Victoria Augustine, Julia Ji, Nathan Keltner, Janet Upton, and Deborah Winslow, and a shout-out to my fellow China Fulbrighters Nellie Chu, Rachel Core, Willa Dong, and Stephen Pan. The writing of my dissertation and this book were supported by a Doctoral Fellowship from the Chiang Ching-kuo Foundation for International Scholarly Exchange, a Ruth L. Kirschstein National Research Service Award from the National Institutes of Health, and a Faculty Rising Scholars Award from Muhlenberg College.

This project began more than twenty years ago when I was a student at the Li Po Chun United World College of Hong Kong. I am grateful for the caring and committed teachers at LPC, especially Jane Gallimore, Jason Jiang (whose insistence that homosexuality and Chinese culture are incompatible inspired me to prove him wrong), Michele Morvan, and Linda Olsen. My interests in China and politics were nurtured by the talented faculty at the University of Oxford and Harvard University, including Christopher Brooke, Arthur Kleinman, Rana Mitter, John Norvell, Elizabeth Perry, and James Watson. I will forever be indebted to my incredible Harvard Chinese language instructors Hsiu-hsien Chan (who gave me my Chinese name), Shengli Feng, Yu Feng, and Wenze Hu; the strong foundation they gave me in Chinese has afforded me so many amazing opportunities and experiences, many of which are described in the preceding pages.

This book is also a product of my academic and personal interactions with the students and faculty of the Department of Anthropology at Brandeis University. My fellow graduate students, including Rachana Agarwal, Casey Golomski, Anna Jaysane-Darr, Ieva Jusionyte, Elisabeth Moolenaar, and Mengqi Wang, have all been key sources of motivation and support over the years. My faculty mentors, especially Elizabeth Ferry, David Jacobson, Nina Kammerer, and Janet McIntosh, taught me so much in and out of the classroom. Thanks to Joan Kaufman for sharing her knowledge and contacts in China with me. I owe a special debt of gratitude to my doctoral committee, including Ellen Schattschneider, whose guidance and support over the years have benefited me greatly, and Robert Weller, for reading and offering feedback on this work. Most of all, I am indebted to my advisor, Sarah Lamb, whose keen intellect, warm heart, and incredibly generous spirit have continued to sustain, guide, and encourage me long after I departed Brandeis.

The conceptualization and writing of this book began while I was a visiting assistant professor in the Department of Anthropology at Bryn Mawr College and a postdoctoral research fellow at the Population Studies and Training Center at Brown University. My former Bryn Mawr colleagues, especially Susanna Fioratta, Shiamin Kwa, Maja Šešelj, Beth Uzwiak, and Susan White, were (and still are) invaluable sources of support and inspiration. The kindness and encouragement of my fellow postdocs and the faculty and staff at Brown, including Maria Abascal, Jo Fisher, Andrew Foster, Adriana Hyams, Michelle Jurkovich, David Kertzer, Jessaca Leinaweaver, Mao-Mei Liu, Katherine Mason, Kaitlin McCormick, Tyler Myroniuk, Perry Sherouse, Susan Short, and Susan Silveira, gave me a much-needed boost. Thanks also to the Association for Queer Anthropology, especially my Nominations Committee co-chair Justin Perez, for giving me a friendly home within the American Anthropological Association.

The faculty and students at Muhlenberg College have also contributed to this book in many ways. My comrades in the Department of Sociology and Anthropology, including Maura Finkelstein and Sahar Sadeghi, have all helped me grow personally and professionally. A special thanks to Ben Carter, Janine Chi, and Sue Curry Jansen for all their support, wisdom, and advice. Interdisciplinary conversations and collaborations with my colleagues in Asian studies and women's and gender studies, including Sharon Albert, Jacqueline Antonovich, Irene Chien, Nancy Collings, Steve Coutinho, Tineke D'Haeseleer, Yishen Lai, Cathy Marie Ouellette, Purvi Parikh, Ranajoy Ray-Chaudhuri, Kate Richmond, Kammie Takahashi, and Lufei Teng, have also succored and inspired me. Students in my 2021 Queer China seminar generously read and offered critical feedback on an early draft of the manuscript. I am also grateful for the many dedicated staff members at Muhlenberg, especially Fulvia Alderiso, Lori Flatto, Tom Janis, and Tracy Velekei.

My deepest thanks to my editor at Rutgers University Press, Kimberly Guinta, for believing in this project from the beginning, and to my two anonymous reviewers, whose perceptive comments greatly improved the manuscript. Thanks also to Catherine Denning, Cheryl Hirsch, Arielle Lewis, Carah Naseem, and to everyone at Rutgers and Westchester Publishing Services who helped bring this book into the world. Parts of chapter 5 appeared previously as an article in *Medical Anthropology Quarterly*; I thank the journal for allowing me to reprint this material here.

I also thank my friends and family for all their love and support, including my grandparents, David and Phyllis Perry, who encouraged and supported me in my academic endeavors; my parents, Janet and Randy Miller, who enabled and encouraged me to pursue my dreams; my sisters, Julia Miller and Clare Yegge, for their love and solidarity; and Don Devereaux and Kelly Pollard, whose weekly Zoom Catan sessions provided a welcome escape from writing. Last but certainly not least, I thank Yan Kung, my husband and best friend, who graciously put up with my many long absences during fieldwork, and without whose endless love, patience, and understanding I would be lost. I dedicate this book to you.

NOTES

CHAPTER 1 INTRODUCTION

1. To protect the identities of my informants, all names used in this book are pseudonyms unless otherwise noted. Many Chinese nicknames begin with *xiao*, which means "little" or "young," and is a term of endearment. A list of people's names and their meanings can be found at the end of the book.

2. Although very few people in northwest China use the term "queer" (*ku'er*) to refer to themselves or their communities, like many other queer anthropologists and sociologists (Boellstorff 2007a; Brainer 2019; Dave 2012; Engebretsen 2014; Stout 2014), I use the term to index a variety of nonnormative genders and sexualities.

3. I take inspiration here from Charles Taylor's (1995) argument about "cultural" versus "acultural" theories of modernity. .

4. See Bullough and Ruan 1993; Chiang 2010; Chou 2000; Dikötter 1995; Hinsch 1990; H. Huang 2011; Kang 2009; J. Liu and Ding 2005; Martin 2015; Ruan 1991; Ruan and Bullough 1992; Ruan and Tsai 1987; Samshasha 1984; Sang 1999, 2003; Sommer 1997, 2000, 2002; Song 2004; Szonyi 1998; Van Gulik 1961; Vitiello 1992, 1996, 2000, 2011; C. Wu 2004; J. Wu 2003.

5. Other notable early works on homosexuality in China include Zhang Beichuan's 1994 book *Same-Sex Love* and Fang Gang's 1995 work *Homosexuality in China*. For more recent Chinese-language monographs on queer China see Fu 2012; Tong 2005, 2007; Q. Wang 2011; Wei 2009, 2012; Wei and Cai 2012.

6. See Bao 2020; Brainier 2019; Chiang 2010; Engebretsen and Schroeder 2015; T. He 2009; P. Ho 1995; Kong 2011, 2012; Y. Li 2006; Nip 2004; Rofel 2013; Tang 2011; A. Wong 2002, 2005; A. Wong and Q. Zhang 2001; Zheng 2015.

7. For Beijing, see Bao 2018; Engebretsen 2009, 2014; Geyer 2002; X. He 2002, 2009, 2013; L. Ho 2010; Rofel 1999, 2007, 2010; Schroeder 2012; Zhou 2022. For Shanghai, see Bao 2012, 2018; Kam 2013; Sun, Farrer, and Choi 2006. For Guangzhou, see Bao 2018; Kong 2011.

8. For studies of queer China outside Beijing, Shanghai, and Guangzhou, see Fu 2012; Hu 2011; Miège 2009; Wei 2007; Wei and Cai 2012.

9. For studies on lesbian women, see Engebretsen 2009; 2014; Kam 2013; Nip 2004; Tang 2011. For studies on gay men, see Kong 2011; Miège 2009; Rofel 1999, 2007, 2010; Wei 2007; Zheng 2015; Zhou 2022. Studies on lesbian women and gay men include Brainer 2019; L. Ho 2010; Schroeder 2012.

10. Despite increasing visibility and tolerance in recent decades, the official state position on homosexuality can be summed up as the "three no's" (*san bu*): no approval, no disapproval, and no promotion (Engebretsen 2014, 16–17; see also Zheng 2015, 47–74).

11. See Fan 2021; Miller 2016a, 2016b; Wei 2015; Zheng 2015.

12. See also Sun, Farrer, and Choi 2006, 4–5; Wei 2015, 194–195.

13. See also Strathern 1988. For recent anthropological discussions of relational versus individualistic modes of personhood see Ikeuchi 2017; Lamb 2017; Sahlins 2011.

14. See also Brownell and Wasserstrom 2002; Farquhar 2002; Farrer 2002; Hershatter 1996; Jeffreys 2006; Pun 2003; Sigley 2006.

15. See Brook and Frolic 1997; Calhoun 1994; Chan 2005; D. Davis 1995; Flower and Leonard 1996; Frolic 1997; B. He 1993; Weller 1999; S. Wilson 2012.

16. See Kong 2011 for such a definition.

17. See Kao 2021 and W. Liu and C. Zhang 2022 for a similar argument. For a nuanced analysis of homonormativity and homonationalism in Chinese cultural contexts, see Ye 2021, 2022.

18. Xi'an is also home to a large community of Hui people, an officially recognized Islamic ethnic and religious minority group; see Gillette 2000.

19. As I detail in chapter 3, the longevity of male same-sex relationships in northwest China is often understood as being limited to a much shorter period of time, from a few months to one or two years.

CHAPTER 2   THE VIEW FROM INSIDE THE CIRCLE

1. I use the term "traditional" here to refer to long-established Chinese cultural beliefs and practices, such as "the patriarchal family organization of traditional China" or "traditional Chinese medicine." As Sarah Lamb (2009, 31) observes, tradition "is not something that is fixed and outside history and contemporary human agency, but rather something that is being actively constructed, interpreted, and used in the present." People in contemporary northwest China often use the word "traditional" (*chuantong*) to index practices and beliefs they regard as conventional or customary or as defining what they think it means to be "Chinese."

2. Built in 1965 in an imposing Stalinist architectural style, the Telecommunications Building is an eight-story structure in downtown Xi'an with a tall clock tower that broadcasts the time by playing "The East is Red," a patriotic song popular during the Cultural Revolution.

3. Although UNITE is a queer women's NGO, it did have some members who identified as men; likewise, although Tong'ai was a queer men's group it occasionally had female volunteers.

4. Other terms include "crowd" (*qun*) or "group" (*renqun*) as well as words that could be translated as "community" like *qunti, shequn,* or *shequ.* Although these words are often used interchangeably, many of my informants described queer people in China as lacking several essential features of a community, including a necessary degree of cohesiveness, structure, or purpose.

5. The notion of the circle also differs from Dennis Altman's (1996) influential idea of a monolithic, Westernized "global gay" identity, in that it imagines a kind of sameness based on sexuality without necessarily assuming that all queer identities across the world are the same or that they are the result of a unidirectional flow of sexual identities from the global North to the global South (see also Rofel 2007, 89–91; A. Wong and Q. Zhang 2001, 251–252).

6. For a similar description of the history of Shanghai's first queer spaces, see Bao 2018, 42–43.

7. Northwest China's gay and lesbian movement will be discussed in greater detail in chapters 4 and 5.

8. Interestingly, Tiantian Zheng (2015, 75) reports o as symbolizing the vagina among queer men in northeast China, rather than the anus.

9. *MAN* is a slang term for "masculine" or "manly" derived from the English word "man" and is used to describe both 1s and Ts.

10. Zhiming stated that the original word from the Japanese was shou (守) but that shou (受) is now more commonly used among gay men in northwest China.

11. C, or less commonly CC, is another slang term popular among queer men in northwest China derived from the English word "sissy," which is pronounced "see see" or "CC."

12. The literal meaning of mu is "mother" or "female," but inside the circle it is used to describe an effeminate gay man. The antonym of the slang term "pure top" is *da mu ling*, which can be translated as "big-old bottom."

13. While tongxinglian and tongzhi can refer to both men and women, the term huo is only used to refer to queer men. Members of queer men's NGOs also use the epidemiological term "men who have sex with men" (*nannan xing xingweizhe*), or MSM, synonymously with gay, tongzhi, and tongxinglian. Although intended to emphasize sexual behavior rather than identity, MSM has nonetheless become a term of identification for male same-sex attracted people and communities in postsocialist China and around the world (Boellstorff 2011; Khanna 2011).

14. Rofel argues that queer has become more popular in Taiwan, "Where it does not evoke the history of abjection that it does in the West" and is used "to refer to a broad range of transgressive possibilities" (2007, 103). The only people in northwest China who I heard use the term queer during fieldwork were a few UNITE volunteers in their twenties. This is perhaps because UNITE had greater ties to cosmopolitan queer activist networks, such as those in Beijing, than Tong'ai did. For a discussion of debates over queer theory in China, see Bao 2018, 29–30, 79–80, 85–87; Kam 2013, 107–108.

15. Zhiqiu Benson Zhou (2022, 285) reports similar findings among queer men in Beijing, although Zhou also writes that in Beijing the term tongzhi is associated with older and lower-class queer men, which I did not find to be the case in northwest China.

16. The Chinese term for male sex workers is "money boy" (MB). Money boys are generally young men, who often come from rural areas to work in the gay male sex trade in big cities; they do not necessarily identify (and are not necessarily identified by others) as gay; see Kong 2012; Rofel 2010.

17. For a detailed discussion of gay kinship in northwest China, see chapter 3.

18. Elsa Fan (2021, 134) reports hearing similar complaints "about the libertine sexual activities of their staff and volunteers" from MSM NGO leaders around the PRC. Although Fan suggests such complaints might stem from internalized homophobia, I believe this was not the case with Yuanzi, who seemed genuinely concerned with the health and well-being of his volunteers.

19. My thanks to an anonymous reviewer who pointed out this connection to me.

20. Lesbians in northwest China use a similar term, meizi or "little sister," to describe women they find attractive, using phrases like "she is my little sister" (ta shi wo de meizi) and "looking for a little sister" (zhao meizi).

21. Adding to this menagerie, Zhou (2022, 293) describes how queer men in Beijing and in some online spaces sometimes call each other "hens" (ji) or "slutty hens" (sao ji), parodic slang terms that poke fun at queer male promiscuity and gender nonconformity.

22. Once again, lesbians in northwest China also have similar sayings. The phrases "T-T love" (TT lian) and "P-P love" (PP lian) are used to describe affections between two T women or two P women. Such relationships are often seen as less normative than T-P relationships.

CHAPTER 3   "FALLING LEAVES RETURN TO THEIR ROOTS"

1. Although such developments are often described as resulting from China's postsocialist transition, these ideas are not necessarily new. For example, in 1947 Fei Xiaotong wrote, "I often think that the Chinese would sacrifice their families for their own self-interests" (1992, 69).

2. For more on the social pressures facing lesbian women in postsocialist China see Engebretsen 2009, 2017; Kam 2013; Lo 2020.

3. My findings in northwest China parallel those reported in the rest of the country. According to a nationwide 2016 survey of almost 17,000 queer people, "only 3% of gay and bisexual men and 6% of lesbian and bisexual women are totally out" to their families, and "34% of gay and bisexual men and 12% of lesbian and bisexual women surveyed were never out to anyone" (S. Huang and Brouwer 2018, 101).

4. Engebretsen (2009) describes how lesbian women in Beijing strategically negotiate intimate relationships and conventional marriage expectations. Writing about Taiwan, Amy Brainer (2019) shows how, before the 1980s, not discussing sexuality was one way that parents indicated their tacit approval of their queer children. While Brainer argues that queer children and parents in Taiwan after the 1970s increasingly emphasized disclosure and discussion of sexuality, I did not find that such a shift has occurred in northwest China.

5. For a discussion of the challenges faced by the wives of queer men in China, see X. Li et al. 2016; Rofel 2013, 160–161; Zheng 2015, 186–189; J. Zhu 2018.

6. Lesbian women in Beijing use similar language to describe the marriage problem (Engebretsen 2009, 8).

7. Kong (2011, 103, 167) reports similar findings in Hong Kong and Guangzhou.

8. The only similar example I could find in the literature is Andrew Wong and Qing Zhang's description of the "symbolic kinship" (2001, 69) terms used by columnists and readers of *G&L Magazine*, a Taiwanese publication.

9. Although I heard of similar lesbian families in northwest China, I was not able to study them in depth; for a discussion of lesbian kinship in Shanghai, see Kam 2013, 35–36.

10. Although they were relatively less formal, elaborated, and institutionalized, gay families in northwest China also resembled the kinship practices of the hijra in India described by Gayatri Reddy (2005), including both the master-disciple relationship and the bonds between mother-daughter and sister-sister.

11. The mother-daughter relationship in gay families in northwest China was often a mentor-mentee relationship, whereas Weston reports that by the 1980s gay mentoring was on the decline in San Francisco (1991, 121).

CHAPTER 4   "LIVING IN THE GRAY ZONE"

1. As Zhang Beichuan is a public figure, I use his actual name instead of a pseudonym.

2. For an analysis of how performance-based HIV prevention projects funded by global health initiatives like the Gates Foundation and Global Fund have affected grassroots gay NGOs and activism in northwest China, see chapter 5.

3. VCT involves giving a blood sample, completing a questionnaire regarding sexual knowledge and behavior, and both pre- and post-test counseling. Blood samples collected by Tong'ai that tested positive for HIV were forwarded to the China CDC for confirmation. Other STDs were treated by Xiao Pu, a physician and Tong'ai's third full-time staff member, either in the main office or at a satellite clinic located at the back of a local hospital. As greater numbers of MSM tested positive for HIV over the years, Tong'ai started offering more services to people living with HIV/AIDS (PLWA) including managing patients' medications and conducting periodic blood tests to monitor their CD4 levels.

4. For more about China's official drinking and banquet culture, see Mason 2013.

5. My thanks to an anonymous reviewer for pointing out this connection.

6. One ironic effect of the national birth control policy was a surplus of expiring condoms and personal lubricant packets that were regularly donated to queer NGOs by the state.

7. See also Hildebrandt 2011b; Miller 2016b.

8. For a description of this event, see chapter 6.

9. For a discussion of rainbow flags in northwest China, see chapter 6.

CHAPTER 5   "DYING FOR MONEY"

1. Portions of chapter 5 appeared previously in *Medical Anthropology Quarterly* as "Dying for Money: The Effects of Global Health Initiatives on NGOs Working with Gay Men and HIV/AIDS in Northwest China," vol. 30, no. 3 (Miller 2016a).

2. Because Wan Yanhai is a public figure, I use his actual name here instead of a pseudonym.

3. This strategy recalls how the Gates Foundation and the Global Fund paid NGOs for every blood sample they collected. Director Li told me that she halted the practice in March 2011 at the request of the Gates Foundation, perhaps due to criticisms of "spending money to buy blood" (*hua qian mai xue*).

4. Jennifer Cohn et al. describe outside groups like Yi De and RHI, which many in the queer community believed were only doing HIV/AIDS testing and treatment to capture global health initiative funds, as "briefcase NGOs" or "opportunistic organizations whose missions shift according to funding priorities and who do not have significant background or experience in the community" (2011, 696).

5. The tendency to downplay or ignore issues related to queer sexuality is not limited to the Chinese government but is also evident in U.S. federal funding for social science research. When my research abstract was published on a federal funding agency's website, I was shocked to discover that all mention of queer NGOs and even HIV/AIDS had been erased or replaced by abstract phrases like "men's groups" and "a global health crisis." I was later told by the program director that federal grants for social science research had come under congressional scrutiny and that the changes were made in order to avoid "unnecessary controversy."

6. This also resembles "philanthrocapitalism," which Vincanne Adams describes as a process whereby "life and labor are brought under conditions in which both public and private sector humanitarian relief efforts are beholden to market measures of success" and "grassroots volunteer groups are forced to scramble and compete for resources from wealthy donors by showing that they too can earn profits on the work of helping others" (2012, 208).

7. In 2007 the HIV infection rate among MSM tested by Tong'ai was around 4 percent; by 2010 the infection rate had almost doubled.

8. Elsa Fan (2021, 43) reports similar findings, suggesting that the burdensome bureaucratic and accountability measures that donor agencies imposed on organizations providing public health services to MSM could have caused rather than prevented problems of fraud.

CHAPTER 6   FROM RAINBOW FLAGS TO MR GAY WORLD

1. In recent years, the online availability of rainbow flags in the PRC has increased, making them easier to buy inside the country.

2. Although these newer iterations of the rainbow flag have become widespread in the United States, I have not yet seen them used by queer activists in mainland China.

3. This use of specific colors to denote sexual preferences resembles how some gay men in the United States use differently colored handkerchiefs to identify themselves to each other, a practice that originated in the mid-nineteenth century (Stryker and Van Buskirk 1996, 18). For more on the queer sex/gender system in northwest China, see chapter 2.

4. For critiques of Chou's argument, see H. Huang 2011; P. Liu 2010; J. Liu and Ding 2005.

5. See Bao 2018, 81–83 for a similar argument.

6. See also Hildebrandt 2012; Miller 2016a, 2016b; Wei 2015; Zheng 2015.

7. Such dangers are very real; in 2015 several feminist and queer activists, including Douzi from UNITE, were arrested before a planned public demonstration in Beijing on International Women's Day and charged with "picking quarrels and creating a disturbance" (Jacobs 2015).

8. Engebretsen (2015, 95) similarly describes "a strategic queer politics of contingency" used by queer Chinese activists that "appropriates tacit articulations of Pride politics and rights discourses . . . instead of giving primary to overt political confrontation directed at the government." These kinds of semivisible, contingent, and "nomadic" (Rofel 2013, 158) queer political strategies are not unique to contemporary urban China; for example, Ashley Currier (2012) also discusses the various "visibility strategies" deployed by queer Namibian and South African activists and organizations.

9. This idiom originates from an exchange between the Confucian philosopher Mencius (372–289 BCE) and King Xuan of the State of Qi (1046–221 BCE), in which Mencius admonishes Xuan for not sharing the joy of music with his people. It includes a play on words: in Chinese, the words "music" (le) and "happiness" (yue) are represented by the same character 乐.

10. Liu Xiaobo's empty chair at the 2010 Nobel Peace Prize ceremony recalls a similar empty chair at the screening of Chinese director Zhang Yuan's film *East Palace, West Palace* at the 1997 Cannes International Film Festival. Angered by the inclusion of the film, the first from mainland China with an explicitly queer theme, the Chinese government confiscated Zhang's passport to prevent him from traveling to Cannes and pressured the festival organizers to pull the film, which they refused to do. Instead, "by placing an empty chair on the stage to symbolize [Zhang's] absence, they simultaneously made both him and his absence present to the audience" (Berry 1998, 84).

REFERENCES

Abu-Lughod, Lila. 1991. "Writing Against Culture." In *Recapturing Anthropology: Working in the Present*, edited by Richard G. Fox, 137–162. Santa Fe, NM: School of American Research Press.

Adams, Vincanne. 2012. "The Other Road to Serfdom: Recovery by Market and the Affect Economy in New Orleans." *Public Culture* 24: 185–216.

Altman, Dennis. 1995. "Political Sexualities: Meanings and Identities in the Time of AIDS." In *Conceiving Sexuality: Approaches to Sex Research in a Postmodern World*, edited by Richard G. Parker and John H. Gagnon, 97–106. New York: Routledge.

———. 1996. "Rupture or Continuity? The Internationalization of Gay Identities." *Social Text* 48: 77–94.

Anderson, Benedict R. O'G. (1983) 1991. *Imagined Communities: Reflections on the Origin and Spread of Nationalism*. New York: Verso.

Anderson, Steven. 1993. "The Rainbow Flag." *Gaze Magazine* 191: 25.

Baker, Paul. 2002. *Polari—The Lost Language of Gay Men*. New York: Routledge.

Bao, Hongwei. 2012. "Queering/Querying Cosmopolitanism: Queer Spaces in Shanghai." *Culture Unbounded* 4: 97–102.

———. 2018. *Queer Comrades: Gay Identity and Tongzhi Activism in Postsocialist China*. Copenhagen: NIAS Press.

———. 2020. *Queer China: Lesbian and Gay Literature and Visual Culture under Postsocialism*. New York: Routledge.

Berry, Chris. 1998. "*East Palace, West Palace*: Staging Gay Life in China." *Jump Cut* 42: 84–89.

Biehl, João, and Adriana Petryna. 2013. "Critical Global Health." In *When People Come First: Critical Studies in Global Health*, edited by João Biehl and Adriana Petryna, 1–20. Princeton, NJ: Princeton University Press.

Blackwood, Evelyn. 2002. "Reading Sexualities across Cultures: Anthropology and Theories of Sexuality." In *Out in Theory: The Emergence of Lesbian and Gay Anthropology*, edited by Ellen Lewin and William L. Leap, 69–92. Urbana: University of Illinois Press.

Boellstorff, Tom. 2005. *The Gay Archipelago: Sexuality and Nation in Indonesia*. Princeton, NJ: Princeton University Press.

———. 2007a. "Queer Studies in the House of Anthropology." *Annual Review of Anthropology* 36: 17–35.

———. 2007b. "When Marriage Falls: Queer Coincidences in Straight Time." *GLQ: A Journal of Lesbian and Gay Studies* 13, no. 2–3: 227–248.

———. 2011. "But Do Not Identify as Gay: A Proleptic Genealogy of the MSM Category." *Cultural Anthropology* 26: 287–312.

Brainer, Amy. 2019. *Queer Kinship and Family Change in Taiwan*. New Brunswick, NJ: Rutgers University Press.

Brook, Timothy, and B. Michael Frolic. 1997. "The Ambiguous Challenge of Civil Society." In *Civil Society in China*, edited by Timothy Brook and B. Michael Frolic, 3–16. New York: M. E. Sharpe.

Brownell, Susan, and Jeffery N. Wasserstrom. 2002. "Introduction." In *Chinese Femininities, Chinese Masculinities: A Reader*, edited by Susan Brownell and Jeffrey N. Wasserstrom, 1–46. Berkeley: University of California Press.

Bullough, Vern L., and Fang Fu Ruan. 1993. "Same-Sex Love in Contemporary China." In *The Third Pink Book: A Global View of Lesbian and Gay Liberation and Oppression*, edited by Aart Hendriks, Rob Tielman, and Evert van der Veen, 46–53. Buffalo, NY: Prometheus Books.

Calhoun, Craig. 1994. *Neither Gods Nor Emperors: Students and the Struggle for Democracy in China*. Berkeley: University of California Press.

Chan, Kin-man. 2005. "The Development of NGOs under a Post-Totalitarian Regime: The Case of China." In *Civil Life, Globalization, and Political Change in Asia: Organizing Between Family and State*, edited by Robert P. Weller, 20–41. London: Routledge.

Chen Yifei. 2015. "Seeking a Lesbian Wife: Pressured Chinese Gays Turn to Online Dating for 'Cooperative Marriage.'" *South China Morning Post*, January 22, 2015. https://www.scmp.com /news/china/article/1688997/id-have-lesbian-wife-pressured-chinese-gays-turn-dating -apps-cooperative.

Chiang, Howard. 2010. "Epistemic Modernity and the Emergence of Homosexuality in China." *Gender & History* 22, no. 3: 629–657.

Chou Wah-shan. 2000. *Tongzhi: Politics of Same-Sex Eroticism in Chinese Societies*. New York: Haworth Press.

Chua, Lynette J., and Timothy Hildebrandt. 2014. "From Health Crisis to Rights Advocacy? HIV/AIDS and Gay Activism in China and Singapore." *Voluntas* 25: 1583–1605.

Cohn, Jennifer, Asia Russell, Brook Baker, Alice Kayongo, Esther Wanjiku, and Paul Davis. 2011. "Using Global Health Initiatives to Strengthen Health Systems: A Civil Society Perspective." *Global Public Health* 6: 687–702.

Cole, Jennifer, and Lynn Thomas, eds. 2009. *Love in Africa*. Chicago: University of Chicago Press.

Conner, Randy P., David Sparks, and Mariya Sparks. 1997. *Cassell's Encyclopedia of Queer Myth, Symbol, and Spirit*. London: Cassell.

Cruz-Malavé, Arnaldo, and Martin Manalansan. 2002. "Introduction: Dissident Sexualities/ Alternative Globalisms." In *Queer Globalizations: Citizenship and the Afterlife of Colonialism*, edited by Arnaldo Cruz-Malavé and Martin Manalansan, 1–10. New York: New York University Press.

Cui Zi'en dir. 2009. *Zhi tongzhi* [Queer China, "comrade" China]. 60 min. Cuizi DV Studio. China.

Cumming-Bruce, Nick. 2017. "China's Rights Crackdown Is Called 'Most Severe' since Tiananmen Square." *New York Times*, September 5, 2017. https://www.nytimes.com/2017/09/05 /world/asia/china-human-rights-united-nations.html.

Currier, Ashley. 2012. *Out in Africa: LGBT Organizing in Namibia and South Africa*. Minneapolis: University of Minnesota Press.

Dave, Naisargi N. 2012. *Queer Activism in India: A Story in the Anthropology of Ethics*. Durham, NC: Duke University Press.

Davis, Deborah S. 1995. "Introduction: Urban China." In *Urban Spaces in Contemporary China: The Potential for Autonomy and Community in Post-Mao China*, edited by Deborah S. Davis, Richard Kraus, Barry Naughton, and Elizabeth J. Perry, 1–19. Cambridge, UK: Cambridge University Press.

———. 2000. "Introduction: A Revolution in Consumption." In *The Consumer Revolution in Urban China*, edited by Deborah S. Davis, 1–24. Berkeley: University of California Press.

———. 2005. "Urban Consumer Culture." *China Quarterly* 183: 692–709.

———. 2014. "Privatization of Marriage in Post-Socialist China." *Modern China* 40, no. 6: 551–577.

Davis, Deborah S., and Sara L. Friedman. 2014. "Introduction." In *Wives, Husbands, and Lovers: Marriage and Sexuality in Hong Kong, Taiwan, and Urban China*, edited by Deborah S. Davis and Sara L. Friedman, 1–38. Stanford, CA: Stanford University Press.

Davis, Rebecca. 2021. "LGBTQ Social Media Groups at Most Major Chinese Universities Shuttered Overnight." *Variety*, July 6, 2021. https://variety.com/2021/politics/news/china -censors-lgbtq-campus-group-1235012809/.

Dean, Kenneth. 1997. "Ritual and Space: Civil Society or Popular Religion?" In *Civil Society in China*, edited by Timothy Brook and B. Michael Frolic, 172–192. New York: M. E. Sharpe.

Des Forges, Roger V. 1997. "States, Societies, and Civil Societies in Chinese History." In *Civil Society in China*, edited by Timothy Brook and B. Michael Frolic, 68–95. New York: M. E. Sharpe.

·Dikötter, Frank. 1995. *Sex, Culture, and Modernity in China: Medical Science and the Construction of Sexual Identities in the Early Republican Period*. Honolulu: University of Hawai'i Press.

Donham, Donald L. 1998. "Freeing South Africa: The 'Modernization' of Male-Male Sexuality in Soweto." *Cultural Anthropology* 13, no. 1: 3–21.

Duggan, Lisa. 2002. "The New Homonormativity: The Sexual Politics of Neoliberalism." In *Materializing Democracy: Toward a Revitalized Cultural Politics*, edited by Russ Castronovo and Dana D. Nelson, 175–194. Durham, NC: Duke University Press.

Economist, The. 2019. "Testing Times." 430, no. 9125: 36.

Edelman, Lee. 2004. *No Future: Queer Theory and the Death Drive*. Durham, NC: Duke University Press.

Ellis-Petersen, Hannah. 2016. "China Bans Depictions of Gay People on Television." *The Guardian*, March 4, 2016. https://www.theguardian.com/tv-and-radio/2016/mar/04/china-bans -gay-people-television-clampdown-xi-jinping-censorship.

Eng, David L., Judith Halberstam, and José Esteban Muñoz. 2005. "Introduction: What's Queer about Queer Studies Now?" *Social Text* 23/3–4, no. 84–85: 1–17.

Engebretsen, Elisabeth L. 2009. "Intimate Practices, Conjugal Ideals: Affective Ties and Relationship Strategies among Lala (Lesbian) Women in Contemporary Beijing." *Sexuality Research & Social Policy* 6, no. 3: 3–14.

———. 2014. *Queer Women in Urban China: An Ethnography*. New York: Routledge.

———. 2015. "Of Pride and Visibility: The Contingent Politics of Queer Grassroots Activism in China." In *Queer/Tongzhi China: New Perspectives on Research, Activism and Media Cultures*, edited by Elisabeth L. Engebretsen and William F. Schroeder, 89–110. Copenhagen: NIAS Press.

———. 2017. "Under Pressure: Lesbian-Gay Contract Marriages and Their Patriarchal Bargains." In *Transforming Patriarchy: Chinese Families in the Twenty-First Century*, edited by Gonçalo D. Santos and Stevan Herrell, 163–181. Seattle: University of Washington Press.

Engebretsen, Elisabeth L., and William F. Schroeder, eds. 2015. *Queer/Tongzhi China: New Perspectives on Research, Activism and Media Cultures*. Copenhagen: NIAS Press.

Evans, Harriet. 2020. *Beijing from Below: Stories of Marginal Lives in the Capital's Center*. Durham, NC: Duke University Press.

Fan, Elsa L. 2014. "HIV Testing as Prevention among MSM in China: The Business of Scaling-Up." *Global Public Health* 9: 85–97.

———. 2021. *Commodities of Care: The Business of HIV Testing in China*. Minneapolis: University of Minnesota Press.

Fang, Hanquan, and J. H. Heng. 1983. "Social Changes and Changing Address Norms in China." *Language and Society* 12: 495–507.

Fang Gang. 1995. *Tongxinglian zai Zhongguo* [Homosexuality in China]. Jilin, China: Jilin Renmin Chubanshe.

Farmer, Paul. 1992. *AIDS and Accusation: Haiti and the Geography of Blame*. Berkeley: University of California Press.

Farquhar, Judith. 2002. *Appetites: Food and Sex in Post-Socialist China*. Durham, NC: Duke University Press.

Farrer, James. 2002. *Opening Up: Youth Sex Culture and Market Reform in Shanghai*. Chicago: University of Chicago Press.

———. 2014. "Love, Sex, and Commitment: Delinking Premarital Intimacy from Marriage in Urban China." In *Wives, Husbands, and Lovers: Marriage and Sexuality in Hong Kong, Taiwan, and Urban China*, edited by Deborah S. Davis and Sara L. Friedman, 62–96. Stanford, CA: Stanford University Press.

Farrer, James, and Sun Zhongxin. 2003. "Extramarital Love in Shanghai." *The China Journal* 50: 1–36.

Fei Xiaotong. (1948) 1992. *From the Soil: The Foundations of Chinese Society*. Translated by Gary G. Hamilton and Wang Zheng. Berkeley: University of California Press.

Feng, Liangui, Xianbin Ding, Rongrong Lu, Jie Liu, Aileen Sy, Lin Ouyang, Chuanbo Pan, Huirong Yi, Honghong Liu, Jing Xu, and Jinkou Zhao. 2009. "High HIV Prevalence Detected in 2006 and 2007 among Men Who Have Sex with Men in China's Largest Principality: An Alarming Epidemic in Chongqing, China." *Journal of Acquired Immune Deficiency Syndromes* 52, no. 1: 79–85.

Ferguson, James. 1999. *Expectations of Modernity: Myths and Meanings of Urban Life on the Zambian Copperbelt*. Berkeley: University of California Press.

Ferrigan, James J. III. 1989. "The Evolution and Adoption of the Rainbow Flag in San Francisco." *The Flag Bulletin* 28, no. 130: 116–122.

Flower, John, and Pamela Leonard. 1996. "Community Values and State Cooptation: Civil Society in the Sichuan Countryside." In *Civil Society: Challenging Western Models*, edited by Chris Hann and Elizabeth Dunn, 199–221. New York: Routledge.

Frolic, B. Michael. 1997. "State-Led Civil Society." In *Civil Society in China*, edited by Timothy Brook and B. Michael Frolic, 46–67. New York: M. E. Sharpe.

Fu Xiaoxing. 2012. *Kongjian wenhua biaoyan: Dongbei A Shi nantongxinglian qunti de renleixue guancha* [Space culture performance: Anthropological observations on male homosexual community in City A in Dongbei]. Beijing, China: Guangming Ribao Chubanshe.

Geyer, Robert. 2002. "In Love and Gay." In *Popular China: Unofficial Culture in a Globalizing Society*, edited by Eugene Perry Link, Richard Madsen, and Paul Pickowicz, 251–274. Lanham, MD: Rowman and Littlefield.

Giddens, Anthony. 1992. *The Transformation of Intimacy: Sexuality, Love, and Eroticism in Modern Societies*. Stanford, CA: Stanford University Press.

Gil, Vincent E. 1992. "The Cut Sleeve Revisited: A Brief Ethnographic Interview with a Male Homosexual in Mainland China." *Journal of Sex Research* 29, no. 4: 569–577.

Gillette, Maris Boyd. 2000. *Between Mecca and Beijing: Modernization and Consumption among Urban Chinese Muslims*. Stanford, CA: Stanford University Press.

Global Fund. 2012. "China—Grant Portfolio." Accessed February 13, 2013. http://portfolio .theglobalfund.org/en/Country/Index/CHN.

Green, Alex V. 2021. "The Pride Flag Has a Representation Problem." *The Atlantic*, June 23, 2021. https://www.theatlantic.com/culture/archive/2021/06/pride-flag-has-representation -problem/619273/.

Habermas, Jürgen. 1989. *The Structural Transformation of the Public Sphere: An Inquiry into a Category of Bourgeois Society*, translated by Thomas Burger. Cambridge, MA: MIT Press.

Haggerty, George E. 2000. "Rainbow Flag." In *Gay Histories and Cultures: An Encyclopedia*, edited by George E. Haggerty, 733–734. New York: Garland Publishing.

Hanefeld, Johanna. 2010. "The Impact of Global Health Initiatives at National and Sub-national Levels—A Policy Analysis of Their Role in Implementation Processes of Antiretroviral (ART) Roll-Out in Zambia and South Africa." *AIDS Care* 22: 93–102.

———. 2014. "The Global Fund to Fight AIDS, Tuberculosis and Malaria: 10 Years On." *Clinical Medicine* 14: 54–57.

Hann, Chris. 1996. "Introduction: Political Society and Civil Anthropology." In *Civil Society: Challenging Western Models*, edited by Chris Hann and Elizabeth Dunn, 1–26. New York: Routledge.

Harbaugh, Rick. 1998. Chinese Characters: A Genealogy and Dictionary. New Haven, CT: Yale University Press.

He, Terri. 2009. "Online Tongzhi? Subcultural Practices in the Gay and Lesbian Community of Spiteful Tots." In *Internationalizing Internet Studies: Beyond Anglophone Paradigms*, edited by Gerard Goggin and Mark McLelland, 302–315. New York: Routledge.

He, Xiaopei. 2002. "Chinese Tongzhi Women Organizing in the 1990s." *Inter-Asia Cultural Studies* 3, no. 3: 479–491.

———. 2009. "My Fake Wedding: Stirring Up the Tongzhi Movement in China." *Development* 51, no. 1: 101–104.

———. 2013. "Building a Movement for Sexual Rights and Pleasure." In *Women, Sexuality, and the Political Power of Pleasure*, edited by Susie Jolly, Andrea Cornwall, and Kate Hawkins, 93–110. New York: Zed Books.

He Baogang. 1993. "The Making of a Nascent Civil Society in China." In *Civil Society in Asia*, edited by David C. Schak and Wayne Hudson, 114–139. Aldershot, UK: Ashgate.

Heckert, Carina. 2018. *Fault Lines of Care: Gender, HIV, and Global Health in Bolivia*. New Brunswick, NJ: Rutgers University Press.

Hernández, Javier C., and Zoe Mou. 2018. "Chinese Social Media Site Reverses Gay Content Ban after Uproar." *New York Times*, April 16, 2018. https://www.nytimes.com/2018/04/16/world/asia/china-weibo-gay.html.

Hershatter, Gail. 1996. "Sexing Modern China." In *Remapping China: Fissures in Historical Terrain*, edited by Gail Hershatter, Emily Honig, Jonathan N. Lipman, and Randall Stross, 77–93. Stanford, CA: Stanford University Press.

Herzog, Gerhard, trans. n.d. "The Heart Sutra in English." Accessed March 2, 2013. http://buddhism.lib.ntu.edu.tw/BDLM/sutra/en_pdf/heart_sutra_english.pdf.

Hildebrandt, Timothy. 2011a. "The Political Economy of Social Organization Registration in China." *China Quarterly* 208: 970–989.

———. 2011b. "Same-Sex Marriage in China? The Strategic Promulgation of a Progressive Policy and Its Impact on LGBT Activism." *Review of International Studies* 27: 1313–1333.

———. 2012. "Development and Division: The Effect of Transnational Linkages and Local Politics on LGBT Activism in China." *Journal of Contemporary China* 21, no. 77: 845–862.

Hinsch, Brett. 1990. *Passions of the Cut Sleeve: The Male Homosexual Tradition in China*. Berkeley: University of California Press.

Ho, Loretta Wing Wah. 2010. *Gay and Lesbian Subculture in Urban China*. New York: Routledge.

Ho, Petula Sik-Ying. 1995. "Male Homosexual Identity in Hong Kong: A Social Construction." *Journal of Homosexuality* 29, no. 1: 71–88.

Huang, Hans Tao-Ming. 2011. *Queer Politics and Sexual Modernity in Taiwan*. Hong Kong: Hong Kong University Press.

Huang, Shuzhen. 2018. "Beyond the Sex–Love–Marriage Alignment: *Xinghun* among Queer People in Mainland China." In *Queer Families and Relationships after Marriage Equality*, edited by Michael W. Yarbrough, Angela Jones, and Joseph Nicholas DeFilippis, 136–149. New York: Routledge.

Huang, Shuzhen, and Daniel C. Brouwer. 2018. "Coming Out, Coming Home, Coming With: Models of Queer Sexuality in Contemporary China." *Journal or International and Intercultural Communication* 11, no. 2: 97–116.

Humphreys, Laud. (1970) 1975. *Tearoom Trade: Impersonal Sex in Public Places*. New York: Aldine.

Hu Qunqiong. 2011. "*Rentong de zhengzha: Xi'an Y Jiuba tongxinglian qunti yanjiu*" [Identity struggles: Gay community research in Xi'an's Y Bar]. Master's thesis, Department of Ethnology, Shaanxi Normal University.

Hyde, Sandra Teresa. 2007. *Eating Spring Rice: The Cultural Politics of AIDS in Southwest China.* Berkeley: University of California Press.

Ikels, Charlotte. 1996. *The Return of the God of Wealth: The Transition to a Market Economy in Urban China.* Stanford, CA: Stanford University Press.

———. 2004. "Introduction." In *Filial Piety: Practice and Discourse in Contemporary East Asia*, edited by Charlotte Ikels, 1–15. Stanford, CA: Stanford University Press.

Ikeuchi, Suma. 2017. "Accompanied Self: Debating Pentecostal Individual and Japanese Relational Selves in Transnational Japan." *Ethos* 45, no. 1: 3–23.

Inda, Jonathan X., and Renato Rosaldo. 2002. "Introduction: A World in Motion." In *The Anthropology of Globalization*, edited by Jonathan Xavier Inda and Renato Rosaldo, 1–34. Malden, MA: Blackwell Publishing.

Jacobs, Andrew. 2009. "H.I.V. Tests Turn Blood into Cash in China." *New York Times*, December 2, 2009. http://www.nytimes.com/2009/12/03/health/policy/03china.html.

———. 2010. "Chinese Gay Pageant Is Shut Down." *New York Times*, January 15, 2010. https://www.nytimes.com/2010/01/16/world/asia/16beijing.html.

———. 2015. "Taking Feminist Battle to China's Streets, and Landing in Jail." *New York Times*, April 5, 2015. https://www.nytimes.com/2015/04/06/world/asia/chinese-womens-rights-activists-fall-afoul-of-officials.html.

Jankowiak, William R. 1993. *Sex, Death, and Hierarchy in a Chinese City: An Anthropological Account.* New York: Columbia University Press.

Jankowiak, William R., and Edward F. Fischer. 1992. "A Cross-Cultural Perspective on Romantic Love." *Ethnology* 31, no. 2: 149–155.

Jeffreys, Elaine. 2006. "Introduction: Talking Sex and Sexuality in China." In *Sex and Sexuality in China*, edited by Elaine Jeffreys, 1–20. New York: Routledge.

Jia Ping. 2012. "*Qianqiu Jijin de bian: Zhongguo aizibing feizhengfu zuzhi mianlin de tiaozhan ji qi yingdui*" [Change of the Global Fund: Challenges to China's AIDS NGOs and their response]. *Zhongguo Quanqiu Jijin Guancha* 18: 2–5.

Kam, Lucetta Yip Lo. 2013. *Shanghai Lalas: Female Tongzhi Communities and Politics in Urban China.* Hong Kong: Hong Kong University Press.

Kang, Wenqing. 2009. *Obsession: Male Same-Sex Relations in China, 1900–1950.* Hong Kong: Hong Kong University Press.

Kao, Ying-Chao. Forthcoming. "The Coloniality of Queer Theory: The Effects of 'Homonormativity' on Transnational Taiwan's Path to Equality." *Sexualities*.

Kapilashrami, Anuj, and Barbara McPake. 2013. "Transforming Governance or Reinforcing Hierarchies and Competition: Examining the Public and Hidden Transcripts of the Global Fund and HIV in India." *Health Policy and Planning* 28: 626–635.

Kapilashrami, Anuj, and Oonagh O'Brien. 2012. "The Global Fund and the Re-Configuration and Re-Emergence of 'Civil Society': Widening or Closing the Democratic Deficit?" *Global Public Health* 7: 437–451.

Kaufman, Joan. 2009. "The Role of NGOs in China's AIDS Crisis: Challenges and Possibilities." In *State and Society Responses to Social Welfare Needs in China: Serving the People*, edited by Jonathan Schwartz and Shawn Shieh, 156–173. New York: Routledge.

———. 2011. "Turning Points in China's Fight against AIDS since 1985." In *Governance of Life in Chinese Moral Experience: The Quest for an Adequate Life*, edited by Everett Zhang, Arthur Kleinman, and Tu Weiming, 163–181. New York: Routledge.

———. 2012. "China's Evolving AIDS Policy: The Influence of Global Norms and Transnational Non-Governmental Organizations." *Contemporary Politics* 18, no. 2: 225–238.

Kaufman, Joan, Arthur Kleinman, and Tony Saich. 2006. "Introduction: Social Policy and HIV/AIDS in China." In *AIDS and Social Policy in China*, edited by Joan Kaufman, Arthur Kleinman, and Tony Saich, 3–14. Cambridge, MA: HIV/AIDS Public Policy Project.

Keimig, Rose K. 2021. *Growing Old in a New China: Transitions in Elder Care*. New Brunswick, NJ: Rutgers University Press.

Khanna, Akshay. 2009. "Taming of the Shrewd Meyeli Chhele: A Political Economy of Development's Sexual Subject." *Development* 52: 43–51.

———. 2011. "*Meyeli Chhele* Becomes MSM: Transformations of Idioms of Sexualness into Epidemiological Forms in India." In *Men and Development: Politicizing Masculinities*, edited by Andrea Cornwall, Jerker Edström, and Alan Greig, 47–57. London: Zed Books.

Kleinman, Arthur, Yunxiang Yan, Jing Jun, Sing Lee, Everett Zhang, Pan Tianshu, Wu Fei, and Guo Jinhua. 2011. "Introduction." In *Deep China: The Moral Life of the Person; What Anthropology and Psychiatry Tell Us about China Today*, edited by Arthur Kleinman et al., 1–35. Berkeley: University of California Press.

Kong, Travis S. K. 2011. *Chinese Male Homosexualities: Memba, Tongzhi, and Golden Boy*. New York: Routledge.

———. 2012. "Reinventing the Self under Socialism: The Case of Migrant Male Sex Workers ('Money Boys') in China." *Critical Asian Studies* 44, no. 3: 283–309.

Kurtz, Donald L. 1996. "Hegemony and Anthropology: Gramsci, Exegeses, Reinterpretations." *Critique of Anthropology* 16, no. 2: 103–135.

LaFraniere, Sharon. 2011. "AIDS Funds Frozen for China in Grant Dispute." *New York Times*, May 20, 2011. http://www.nytimes.com/2011/05/21/world/asia/21china.html.

Lamb, Sarah. 2000. *White Saris and Sweet Mangoes: Aging, Gender, and Body in North India*. Berkeley: University of California Press.

———. 2009. *Aging and the Indian Diaspora: Cosmopolitan Families in India and Abroad*. Bloomington: Indiana University Press.

———. 2017. "Being Single in India: Gendered Identities, Class Mobilities, and Personhoods in Flux." *Ethos* 46, no. 1: 49–69.

Levin, Dan. 2014. "Chinese Court Sides with Gay Man in 'Conversion' Suit." *New York Times*, December 19, 2014. https://www.nytimes.com/2014/12/20/world/asia/chinese-court -sides-with-gay-man-against-clinic-that-tried-to-convert-him.html.

Lewin, Ellen. 2016. "Who's Queer? What's Queer? Queer Anthropology through the Lens of Ethnography." *Cultural Anthropology* 31, no. 4: 598–606.

Lewin, Ellen, and William L. Leap. 2002. "Introduction." In *Out in Theory: The Emergence of Lesbian and Gay Anthropology*, edited by Ellen Lewin and William L. Leap, 1–15. Urbana: University of Illinois Press.

Li, Xianhong, Beichuan Zhang, Yang Li, Anna Liza Malazarte Antonio, Yunliang Chen, and Ann Bartley Williams. 2016. "Mental Health and Suicidal Ideation among Chinese Women Who Have Sex with Men Who Have Sex with Men (MSM)." *Women & Health* 56, no. 8: 940–956.

Lin Qi. 2010. "The Dating Game by Jiangsu TV." *China Daily*, April 24, 2010. https://www .chinadaily.com.cn/china/2010-04/24/content_9770152.htm.

Liu, Petrus. 2010. "Why Does Queer Theory Need China?" *Positions* 18, no. 2: 291–320.

———. 2015. *Queer Marxism in Two Chinas*. Durham, NC: Duke University Press.

Liu, Wen, and Charlie Yi Zhang. 2022. "Homonationalism as a Site of Contestation and Transformation: On Queer Subjectivities and Homotransnationalism across Sinophone Societies." In *Homonationalism, Femonationalism and Ablenationalism: Critical Pedagogies Contextualized*, edited by Angeliki Sifaki, C. L. Quinan, and Katarina Lončarević, 31–47. New York: Routledge.

Liu Jen-peng and Ding Naifei. 2005. "Reticent Poetics, Queer Politics." *Inter-Asia Cultural Studies* 6, no. 1: 30–55.

Livingston, Jennie, dir. (1990) 2005. *Paris Is Burning*. Burbank: Miramax Home Entertainment. DVD.

Li Yinhe. 2006. "Regulating Male Same-Sex Relationships in the People's Republic of China." In *Sex and Sexuality in China*, edited by Elaine Jeffreys, 82–101. New York: Routledge.

Li Yinhe and Wang Xiaobo. 1992. *Tamen de shijie: Zhongguo nan tongxinglian qunluo toushi* [Their world: Looking into the male homosexual community in China]. Taiyuan, China: Shanxi Renmin Chubanshe.

Lo, Iris Po Yee. 2020. "Family Formation among Lalas (Lesbians) in Urban China: Strategies for Forming Families and Navigating Relationships with Families of Origin." *Journal of Sociology* 56, no. 4: 629–645.

Ma, Xiaoyan, Qiyun Zhang, Xiong He, Weidong Sun, Hai Yue, Sanny Chen, H. Fisher Raymond, Yang Li, Min Xu, Hui Du, and Willi McFarland. 2007. "Trends in Prevalence of HIV, Syphilis, Hepatitis C, Hepatitis B, and Sexual Risk Behavior among Men Who Have Sex with Men: Results of 3 Consecutive Respondent-Driven Sampling Surveys in Beijing, 2004 through 2007." *Journal of Acquired Immune Deficiency Syndromes* 45, no. 5: 581–587.

Malinowski, Bronislaw. (1922) 1984. *Argonauts of the Western Pacific*. London: George Routledge and Sons.

Marriott, McKim. 1976. "Hindu Transactions: Diversity without Dualism." In *Transaction and Meaning: Directions in the Anthropology of Exchange and Symbolic Behavior*, edited by Bruce Kapferer, 109–42. Philadelphia: Institute for the Study of Human Issues.

Martin, Fran. 2015. "Transnational Queer Sinophone Cultures." In *Routledge Handbook of Sexuality Studies in East Asia*, edited by Mark McLelland and Vera Mackie, 35–48. New York: Routledge.

Marvin, Carolyn, and David W. Ingle. 1999. *Blood Sacrifice and Nation: Totem Rituals and the American Flag*. Cambridge, UK: Cambridge University Press.

Marx, Karl. (1844) 1978a. "Economic and Philosophic Manuscripts of 1844." In *The Marx-Engels Reader*, edited by Robert Tucker, 66–125. New York: W. W. Norton & Co.

———. (1867) 1978b. "The German Ideology: Part I." In *The Marx-Engels Reader*, edited by Robert Tucker, 146–200. New York: W. W. Norton & Co.

Mason, Katherine A. 2013. "To Your Health! Toasting, Intoxication and Gendered Critique among Banqueting Women." *The China Journal* 69: 108–133.

McDonald, Scott, and Karl Ritter. 2010. "Chinese Dissident Liu Wins Nobel Peace Prize." *The Boston Globe*, October 8, 2010. http://archive.boston.com/news/world/asia/articles/2010/10/08/china_denounces_award_of_nobel_prize_to_dissident/.

Miège, Pierre. 2009. "In My Opinion, Most Tongzhi Are Dutiful Sons!" *China Perspectives* 1: 40–53.

Miller, Casey J. 2016a. "Dying for Money: The Effects of Global Health Initiatives on NGOs Working with Gay Men and HIV/AIDS in Northwest China." *Medical Anthropology Quarterly* 30, no. 3: 414–430.

———. 2016b. "We Can Only Be Healthy if We Love Ourselves: Queer AIDS NGOs, Kinship, and Alternative Families of Care in China." *AIDS Care* 28, sup. 4: 51–60.

Mudde, Cas. 2003. "Civil Society in Post-Communist Europe: Lessons from the Dark Side." In *Uncivil Society? Contentious Politics in Post-Communist Europe*, edited by Petr Kopecký and Cas Mudde, 152–165. New York: Routledge.

National Bureau of Statistics of China. 2020. "China Statistical Yearbook." http://www.stats.gov.cn/tjsj/ndsj/2020/indexeh.htm. Accessed September 2, 2022.

New York Times. 2011. "China: Health Fund Will again Finance Programs." August 24, 2011. https://www.nytimes.com/2011/08/24/world/asia/24briefs-Chinahealth.html.

Nip, Joyce Y. M. 2004. "The Queer Sisters and Its Electronic Bulletin Board: A Study of the Internet for Social Movement Mobilization." *Information, Communication & Society* 7, no. 1: 23–49.

Ong, Aihwa. 1999. "Introduction: Flexible Citizenship: The Cultural Logics of Transnationality." In *The Cultural Logics of Transnationality*, edited by Aihwa Ong, 1–26. Berkeley: University of California Press.

Ong, Aihwa, and Li Zhang. 2008. "Introduction: Privatizing China: Powers of the Self, Socialism from Afar." In *Privatizing China: Socialism from Afar*, edited by Aihwa Ong and Li Zhang, 1–19. Ithaca, NY: Cornell University Press.

Ortner, Sherry B. 2016. "Dark Anthropology and Its Others: Theory since the Eighties." *HAU: Journal of Ethnographic Theory* 6, no. 1: 47–73.

Padilla, Mark B., Jennifer S. Hirsch, Miguel Muños-Laboy, Robert E. Sember, and Richard G. Parker, eds. 2007. *Love and Globalization: Transformations of Intimacy in the Contemporary World*. Nashville, TN: Vanderbilt University Press.

Parker, Richard G. 1999. *Beneath the Equator: Cultures of Desire, Male Homosexuality, and Emerging Gay Communities in Brazil*. New York: Routledge.

Patton, Cindy. 1990. *Inventing AIDS*. New York: Routledge.

Perry, David. 1989. "The Betsy Ross of the Rainbow Banner: How Gilbert Baker's 'Fabulous' Flag Became the International Gay Symbol." *The Advocate* 527: 42–43.

Pfeiffer, James. 2013. "The Struggle for a Public Sector: PEPFAR in Mozambique." In *When People Come First: Critical Studies in Global Health*, edited by João Biehl and Adriana Petryna, 166–181. Princeton, NJ: Princeton University Press.

Phillips, Adam. 1994. *On Flirtation*. Cambridge, MA: Harvard University Press.

Pimentel, Ellen E. 2000. "Just How Do I Love Thee? Marital Relations in Urban China." *Journal of Marriage and the Family* 62: 32–47.

Pun Ngai. 2003. "Subsumption or Consumption? The Phantom of Consumer Revolution in 'Globalizing' China." *Cultural Anthropology* 18, no. 4: 469–492.

Reddy, Gayatri. 2005. *With Respect to Sex: Negotiating Hijra Identity in South India*. Chicago: University of Chicago Press.

Rich, Adrienne. 1980. "Compulsory Heterosexuality and Lesbian Existence." *Signs* 5, no. 4: 631–660.

Rofel, Lisa. 1999. "Qualities of Desire: Imagining Gay Identities in China." *GLQ: A Journal of Lesbian and Gay Studies* 5, no. 4: 61–86.

———. 2007. *Desiring China: Experiments in Neoliberalism, Sexuality, and Public Culture*. Durham, NC: Duke University Press.

———. 2010. "The Traffic in Money Boys." *Positions* 18, no. 2: 425–458.

———. 2013. "Grassroots Activism: Non-Normative Sexual Politics in Post-Socialist China." In *Unequal China: The Political Economy and Cultural Politics of Inequality*, edited by Wanning Sun and Yingjie Guo, 154–167. London: Routledge.

Rosaldo, Renato. 2000. "Of Headhunters and Soldiers: Separating Cultural and Ethical Relativism." *Issues in Ethics* 11, no. 1: 2–6.

Ruan, Fang Fu. 1991. *Sex in China: Studies in the Sexology of Chinese Culture*. New York: Plenum Press.

Ruan, Fang Fu, and Vern L. Bullough. 1992. "Lesbianism in China." *Archives of Sexual Behavior* 21: 217–226.

Ruan, Fang-fu, and Yung-mei Tsai. 1987. "Male Homosexuality in Traditional Chinese Literature." *Journal of Homosexuality* 14, no. 3–4: 21–34.

Rubin, Gayle. 1975. "The Traffic of Women: Notes on the 'Political Economy' of Sex." In *Toward an Anthropology of Women*, edited by Rayna R. Reiter, 157–210. New York: Monthly Review Press.

Sahlins, Marshall. 2011. "What Kinship Is (Part One)." *Journal of the Royal Anthropological Institute* 17: 2–19.

Samshasha. 1984. *Zhongguo tongxinglian shilu* [History of homosexuality in China]. Hong Kong: Rosa Winkel Press.

Sang, Tze-lan Deborah. 1999. "Translating Homosexuality: The Discourse of Tongxing'ai in Republican China." In *Tokens of Exchange: The Problem of Translation in Global Circulations*, edited by Lydia H. Liu, 276–304. Durham, NC: Duke University Press.

———. 2003. *The Emerging Lesbian: Female Same-Sex Desire in Modern China*. Chicago: Chicago University Press.

Scheper-Hughes, Nancy. 1992. *Death without Weeping: The Violence of Everyday Life in Brazil*. Berkeley: University of California Press.

Schneider, David. (1964) 1980. *American Kinship: A Cultural Account*. Chicago: University of Chicago Press.

Schroeder, William F. 2012. "Beyond Resistance: Gay and Lala Recreation in Beijing." In *Understanding Global Sexualities: New Frontiers*, edited by Peter Aggleton, Paul Boyce, Henrietta L Moore, and Richard Parker, 108–123. New York: Routledge.

Scott, James C. 1990. *Domination and the Arts of Resistance: Hidden Transcripts*. New Haven, CT: Yale University Press.

Scotton, Carol Myers, and Zhu Wanjin. 1983. "*Tóngzhì* in China: Language Change and Its Conversational Consequences." *Language in Society* 12: 477–94.

Shanafelt, Robert. 2009. "The Nature of Flag Power: How Flags Entail Dominance, Subordination, and Social Solidarity." *Politics and the Life Sciences* 27, no. 2: 13–27.

Shan Juan. 2011. "Fight Will Go on Despite Grant Cut." *China Daily*, November 1, 2011. http://www.chinadaily.com.cn/china/2011–11/01/content_14011836.htm.

Shieh, Shawn, and Jonathan Schwartz. 2009. "State and Society Responses to China's Social Welfare Needs: An Introduction to the Debate." In *State and Society Responses to Social Welfare Needs in China: Serving the People*, edited by Jonathan Schwartz and Shawn Shieh, 3–21. New York: Routledge.

Shostak, Marjorie. (1981) 2000. *Nisa: The Life and Words of a !Kung Woman*. Cambridge, MA: Harvard University Press.

Sigley, Gary. 2006. "Sex, Politics, and the Policing of Virtue in the People's Republic of China." In *Sex and Sexuality in China*, edited by Elaine Jeffreys, 43–61. New York: Routledge.

Snow, Edgar. 1938. *Red Star over China*. New York: Random House.

Sommer, Matthew H. 1997. "The Penetrated Male in Late Imperial China: Judicial Constructions and Social Stigma." *Modern China* 23, no. 2: 140–180.

———. 2000. *Sex, Law, and Society in Late Imperial China*. Stanford, CA: Stanford University Press.

———. 2002. "Dangerous Males, Vulnerable Males, and Polluted Males: The Regulation of Masculinity in Qing Dynasty Law." In *Chinese Femininities/Chinese Masculinities: A Reader*, edited by Susan Brownell and Jeffrey N. Wasserstrom, 67–88. Berkeley: University of California Press.

Song Geng. 2004. *The Fragile Scholar: Power and Masculinity in Chinese Culture*. Hong Kong: Hong Kong University Press.

Spicer, Neil, Julia Aleshkina, Regien Biesma, Ruairi Brugha, Carlos Caceres, Baltazar Chilundo, Ketevan Chkhatarashvili, Andrew Harmer, Pierre Miege, Gulgun Murzalieva, Phillimon Ndubani, Natia Rukhadze, Tetyana Semigina, Aisling Walsh, Gill Walt, and Xiulan Zhang. 2010. "National and Subnational HIV/AIDS Coordination: Are Global Health Initiatives Closing the Gap between Intent and Practice?" *Globalization and Health* 6: 1–16.

State Council AIDS Working Committee Office and UN Theme Group on AIDS. 2008. "UNGASS Country Progress Report—PR China." Accessed December 21, 2009. http://data.unaids.org/pub/Report/2008/china_2008_country_progress_report_en.pdf.

Stout, Noelle M. 2014. *After Love: Queer Intimacy and Erotic Economies in Post-Soviet Cuba*. Durham, NC: Duke University Press.

Strathern, Marilyn. 1988. *The Gender of the Gift: Problems with Women and Problems with Society in Melanesia*. Berkeley: University of California Press.

Stryker, Susan, and Jim Van Buskirk. 1996. *Gay by the Bay: A History of Queer Culture in the San Francisco Bay Area*. San Francisco: Chronicle Books.

Sun Zhongxin, James Farrer, and Kyung-hee Choi. 2006. "Sexual Identity among Men Who Have Sex with Men in Shanghai." *China Perspectives* 64: 1–13.

Szonyi, Michael. 1998. "The Cult of Hu Tianbao and the Eighteenth-Century Discourse of Homosexuality." *Late Imperial China* 19, no. 1: 1–25.

Tang, Denise Tse-Shang. 2011. *Conditional Spaces: Hong Kong Lesbian Desires and Everyday Life*. Hong Kong: Hong Kong University Press.

Taylor, Charles. 1995. "Two Theories of Modernity." *Hastings Center Report* 25, no. 2: 24–33.

Tong Ge. 2005. *Zhongguoren de nannan xingxingwei: Xing yu ziwo rentong zhuangtai diaocha* [Men who have sex with men in China: A survey on sexuality and self-identity]. Beijing, China: Beijing Jiande Zixun Zhongxin.

———. 2007. *Zhongguo nannan xingjiaoyi zhuangtai diaocha* [Study on male sex workers in China]. Beijing, China: Beijing Jiande Zixun Zhongxin.

Tsing, Anna Lowenhaupt. 2000. "The Global Situation." *Cultural Anthropology* 15, no. 3: 327–360.

———. 2004. *Friction: An Ethnography of Global Connection*. Princeton, NJ: Princeton University Press.

United Nations. 2019. "World Population Prospects 2019." Accessed June 4, 2021. https://population.un.org/wpp/.

———. 2020. "World Social Report: Inequality in a Rapidly Changing World." Accessed June 4, 2021. https://www.un.org/development/desa/dspd/wp-content/uploads/sites/22/2020/01/World-Social-Report-2020-FullReport.pdf.

van Gulik, R. H. 1961. *Sexual Life in Ancient China, A Preliminary Survey of Chinese Sex and Society from ca. 1500 B.C. till 1644*. Leiden, Netherlands: E. J. Brill.

Vezeris, Steve. 1995. "History of the Rainbow Flag." In *Out in All Directions: The Almanac of Gay and Lesbian America*, edited by Lynn Witt, Sherry Thomas, and Eric Marcus, 435. New York: Warner Books.

Vitiello, Giovanni. 1992. "The Dragon's Whim: Ming and Qing Homoerotic Tales from 'The Cut Sleeve.'" *T'oung Pao* 78, no. 4–5: 341–372.

———. 1996. "The Fantastic Journey of an Ugly Boy: Homosexuality and Salvation in Late Ming Pornography." *Positions* 4, no. 2: 291–320.

———. 2000. "Exemplary Sodomites: Chivalry and Love in Late Ming Culture." *Nan Nü* 2, no. 2: 207–258.

———. 2011. *The Libertine's Friend: Homosexuality and Masculinity in Late Imperial China*. Chicago: University of Chicago Press.

Wang, Amber. 2019. "#LoveWon: Taiwan Legalises Same-Sex Marriage in Landmark First for Asia." *Hong Kong Free Press*, May 17, 2019. https://hongkongfp.com/2019/05/17/breaking-taiwan-legalises-sex-marriage-landmark-first-asia/.

Wang, Lu, Ning Wang, Liyan Wang, Dongmin Li, Manhong Jia, Xing Gao, Shuquan Qu, Qianqian Qin, Yanhe Wang, and Kumi Smith. 2009. "The 2007 Estimates for People at Risk for and Living with HIV in China: Progress and Challenges." *Journal of Acquired Immune Deficiency Syndromes* 50, no. 4: 414–418.

Wang, Stephanie Yingyi. 2019. "When Tongzhi Marry: Experiments of Cooperative Marriage between Lalas and Gay Men in Urban China." *Feminist Studies* 45, no. 1: 13–35.

Wang Qingfeng. 2011. "*Shengcun xianzhuang, huayu yanbian he yizhi di shengyin: Jiushi niandai yilai di tongxinglian yanjiu*" [Living status, discourse evolution and heterogeneous voices: Homosexuality research from the 1990s in China]. *Qingnian Yanjiu*, no. 5: 83–93.

Wang Shaoguang. 1991. "*Guanyu 'shimin shehui' de ji dian sikao*" [Some reflections on "civil society"]. *Ershiyi Shiji* 8: 102–114.

Wardlow, Holly, and Jennifer S. Hirsch. 2006. "Introduction." In *Modern Loves: The Anthropology of Romantic Courtship and Companionate Marriage*, edited by Holly Wardlow and Jennifer S. Hirsch, 1–31. Ann Arbor: University of Michigan Press.

Wasserstrom, Jeffrey N., and Liu Xinyong. 1995. "Student Associations and Mass Movements." In *Urban Spaces in Contemporary China: The Potential for Autonomy and Community in Post-Mao China*, edited by Deborah S. Davis, Richard Kraus, Barry Naughton, and Elizabeth J. Perry, 362–393. Cambridge, UK: Cambridge University Press.

Weber, Max. (1956) 1968a. *Economy and Society: An Outline of Interpretive Sociology*, vol. 3, edited by Guenther Roth and Claus Wittich. New York: Bedminster Press.

———. 1968b. *Max Weber on Charisma and Institution Building; Selected Papers*, edited by S. N. Eisenstadt. Chicago: University of Chicago Press.

Wei, Wei. 2007. "'Wandering Men' No Longer Wander Around: The Production and Transformation of Local Homosexual Identities in Contemporary Chengdu, China." *Inter-Asia Cultural Studies* 8, no. 4: 572–588.

———. 2009. "*Xiaofeizhuyi he 'tongzhi' kongjian: Dushi shenghuo di linglei yuwangditu*" [Consumerism and "tongzhi" space: An alternative map of desires in urban life]. *Shehui* 4, no. 29: 79–106.

———. 2012. *Gongkai: Dangdai Chengdu "tongzhi" kongjian de xingcheng he bianqian* [Going public: The production and transformation of "queer" space in contemporary Chengdu]. Shanghai, China: Shanghai Sanlian Shudian Chubanshe.

———. 2015. "Queer Organizing and HIV/AIDS Activism: An Ethnographic Study of a Local Tongzhi Organization in Chengdu." In *Queer/Tongzhi China: New Perspectives on Research, Activism and Media Cultures*, edited by Elisabeth L. Engebretsen and William F. Schroeder, 192–216. Copenhagen: NIAS Press.

Wei, Wei, and Cai Siqing. 2012. "*Tansuo xin di guanxi he shenghuo moshi: Guanyu Chengdu nan tongxinglian banlu guanxi he shengho shijian di yanjiu*" [Exploring a new relationship model and lifestyle: A study of partnership and family practice among gay couples in Chengdu]. *Shehui* 6, no. 32: 57–84.

Weller, Robert P. 1999. *Alternate Civilities: Democracy and Culture in China and Taiwan*. Boulder, CO: Westview Press.

———. 2005. "Introduction: Civil Institutions and the State." In *Civil Life, Globalization, and Political Change in Asia: Organizing Between Family and State*, edited by Robert P. Weller, 1–19. New York: Routledge.

Weston, Kath. 1991. *Families We Choose: Lesbians, Gays, Kinship*. New York: Columbia University Press.

———. 1993. "Lesbian/Gay Studies in the House of Anthropology." *Annual Review of Anthropology* 22: 339–367.

Whyte, Susan Reynolds, Michael A. Whyte, Lotte Meinert, and Jenipher Twebaze. 2013. "Therapeutic Clientship: Belonging in Uganda's Projectified Landscape of AIDS Care." In *When People Come First: Critical Studies in Global Health*, edited by João Biehl and Adriana Petryna, 140–165. Princeton, NJ: Princeton University Press.

Wiegman, Robyn, and Elizabeth A. Wilson. 2015. "Introduction: Antinormativity's Queer Conventions." *Differences* 26, no. 1: 1–25.

Williams, Raymond. 1961. *The Long Revolution*. Harmondsworth, UK: Penguin.

———. (1976) 1983. *Keywords: A Vocabulary of Culture and Society*. New York: Oxford University Press.

Wilson, Scott. 2012. "Introduction." *Journal of Contemporary China* 21, no. 76: 551–567.

Wolf, Margery. 1972. *Women and the Family in Rural Taiwan*. Stanford, CA: Stanford University Press.

Wong, Andrew. 2002. "The Semantic Derogation of Tongzhi: A Synchronic Perspective." In *Language and Sexuality: Contesting Meaning in Theory and Practice*, edited by Katherine

Campbell-Kibler, Robert J. Podesva, Sarah Roberts, and Andrew Wong, 161–174. Stanford, CA: Center for the Study of Language and Information.

———. 2005. "The Reappropriation of *Tongzhi*." *Language in Society* 34: 763–793.

Wong, Andrew, and Qing Zhang. 2001. "The Linguistic Construction of the Tóngzhì Community." *Journal of Linguistic Anthropology* 10, no. 2: 248–278.

Wong, Edward. 2010. "Chinese Contestant Enters Worldwide Gay Pageant." *New York Times*, February 12, 2010. https://www.nytimes.com/2010/02/13/world/asia/13pageant.html.

———. 2011. "China TV Grows Racy, and Gets a Chaperon." *New York Times*, December 31, 2011. http://www.nytimes.com/2012/01/01/world/asia/censors-pull-reins-as-china-tv-chasing -profit-gets-racy.html.

———. 2015. "China Releases 5 Women's Rights Activists Detained for Weeks." *New York Times*, April 13, 2015. https://www.nytimes.com/2015/04/14/world/asia/china-releases-3 -of-5-detained-womens-rights-activists.html.

Wong, Frank Y., Z. Jennifer Huang, Weibing Wang, Na He, Jamie Marzzurco, Stephanie Frangos, Michelle E. Buchholz, Darwin Young, and Brian D. Smith. 2009. "STIs and HIV among Men Having Sex with Men in China: A Ticking Time Bomb?" *AIDS Education and Prevention* 21, no. 5: 430–446.

Wong, Gillian. 2010. "Beijing Police Raid Gay Hangout." *Huffington Post*, September 28, 2010. http://www.huffingtonpost.com/2010/09/28/beijing-police-raid-gay-s_n_741613.html.

World Health Organization. 1986. *Weekly Epidemiological Record* 61, no. 29: 221–228.

Wright, Timothy. 2005. "Gay Organizations, NGOs, and the Globalization of Sexual Identity: The Case of Bolivia." In *Same-Sex Cultures and Sexualities: An Anthropological Reader*, edited by Jennifer Robertson, 279–294. London: Blackwell.

Wu, Jing. 2003. "From '*Long Yang*' and '*Dui Shi*' to Tongzhi: Homosexuality in China." *Journal of Gay & Lesbian Psychotherapy* 7, no. 1–2: 117–143.

Wu Cuncun. 2004. *Homoerotic Sensibilities in Late Imperial China*. New York: Routledge Curzon.

Yan, Yunxiang. 2003. *Private Life under Socialism: Love, Intimacy, and Family Change in a Chinese Village, 1949–1999*. Stanford, CA: Stanford University Press.

———. 2009. *The Individualization of Chinese Society*. Oxford, UK: Berg.

———. 2011. "The Changing Moral Landscape." In *Deep China: The Moral Life of the Person; What Anthropology and Psychiatry Tell Us about China Today*, edited by Arthur Kleinman, Yunxiang Yan, Jing Jun, Sing Lee, Everett Zhang, Pan Tianshu, Wu Fei, and Guo Jinhua, 36–77. Berkeley: University of California Press.

———. 2016. "Intergenerational Intimacy and Descending Familism in Rural North China." *American Anthropologist* 118, no. 2: 244–257.

———. 2017. "Doing Personhood in Chinese Culture: The Desiring Individual, Moralist Self and Relational Person." *The Cambridge Journal of Anthropology* 35, no. 2: 1–17.

Yan, Yunxiang, and Wei Wei. 2021. "Rainbow Parents and the Familial Model of Tongzhi (LGBT) Activism in Contemporary China." *Chinese Sociological Review* 53, no. 5: 451–72.

Ye, Shana. 2021. "'Paris' and 'Scar': Queer Social Reproduction, Homonormative Division of Labour and HIV/AIDS Economy in Postsocialist China." *Gender, Place & Culture* 28, no. 12: 1778–1798.

———. Forthcoming. "*Word of Honor* and Brand Homonationalism with 'Chinese Characteristics': The *Dangai* Industry, Queer Masculinity and the 'Opacity' of the State." *Feminist Media Studies*.

Zhang, Everett Yuehong. 2011. "China's Sexual Revolution." In *Deep China: The Moral Life of the Person; What Anthropology and Psychiatry Tell Us about China Today*, edited by Arthur Kleinman, Yunxiang Yan, Jing Jun, Sing Lee, Everett Zhang, Pan Tianshu, Wu Fei, and Guo Jinhua, 106–151. Berkeley: University of California Press.

Zhang, Hong. 2009. "The New Realities of Aging in Contemporary China: Coping with the Decline in Family Care." In *The Cultural Context of Aging: Worldwide Perspectives*, edited by Jay Sokolovsky, 196–215. Westport, CT: Praeger.

Zhang, Yunqiu. 1997. "From State Corporatism to Social Representation: Local Trade Unions in the Reform Years." In *Civil Society in China*, edited by Timothy Brook and B. Michael Frolic, 124–148. New York: M. E. Sharpe.

Zhang Beichuan. 1994. *Tongxing'ai* [Same-sex love]. Jinan, China: Shandong Kexue Jishu Chubanshe.

Zhang Beichuan and Joan Kaufman. 2005. "The Rights of People with Same Sex Sexual Behavior: Recent Progress and Continuing Challenges in China." In *Sexuality, Gender and Rights: Exploring Theory and Practice in South and Southeast Asia*, edited by Geeta Misra and Radhika Chandiramani, 113–130. New Delhi: Sage Publications.

Zheng, Tiantian. 2015. *Tongzhi Living: Men Attracted to Men in Postsocialist China*. Minneapolis: University of Minnesota Press.

Zhou, Zhiqiu Benson. 2022. "Besides *Tongzhi*: Tactics for Constructing and Communicating Sexual Identities in China." *Journal of Linguistic Anthropology* 32, no. 2: 282–300.

Zhu, Jingshu. 2018. "'Unqueer' Kinship? Critical Reflections on 'Marriage Fraud' in Mainland China." *Sexualities* 21, no. 7: 1075–1091.

Zola, Irving Kenneth. 1972. "Medicine as an Institution of Social Control." *The Sociological Review* 20, no. 4: 487–504.

INDEX

Note: Page numbers in *italics* refer to figures and tables.

ABOUT THE AUTHOR

CASEY JAMES MILLER is an assistant professor of anthropology at Muhlenberg College in Allentown, Pennsylvania. His research on queer anthropology, the anthropology of gender and sexuality, and contemporary Chinese culture and society has been supported by fellowships and awards from the Fulbright Program, the National Institutes of Health, and the National Science Foundation.